WOMEN'S WRITING OF THE ROMANTIC PERIOD 1789–1836: AN ANTHOLOGY

For my mother
(1900–1966)

WOMEN'S WRITING OF THE ROMANTIC PERIOD 1789–1836: AN ANTHOLOGY

Edited by

Harriet Devine Jump

EDINBURGH UNIVERSITY PRESS

Edinburgh University Press
22 George Square, Edinburgh

Typeset in Bulmer
by Pioneer Associates, Perthshire, and
printed and bound in Great Britain

A CIP record for this book is available from the
British Library

ISBN 0 7486 0806 0 (hbk)
ISBN 0 7486 0915 6 (pbk)

CONTENTS

Introduction   xi

Acknowledgements   xix

Chronology   xxi

1789   1   Charlotte Smith: *Written in the Churchyard at*
                Middleton in Sussex   1
            2   Eleanor Butler: from *Diaries*   1
            3   Elizabeth Hands: *A Poem, On the Supposition of an*
                Advertisement appearing in a Morning Paper, of the
                Publication of a Volume of Poems, by a Servant-Maid   3
            4   Hester Lynch Piozzi: from *Observations and*
                Reflections made in the Course of a Journey through
                France, Italy and Germany [*Italy*]   5
            5   Anna Seward: *Sonnet: To France on her Present*
                Exertions   6

1790   6   Mary Wollstonecraft: from *A Vindication of the*
                Rights of Men   7
            7   Eleanor Butler: from *Diaries*   9
            8   Catharine Macaulay: from *Letters on Education*   10
            9   Helen Maria Williams: from *Letters Written in*
                France, in the Summer of 1790   14

1791   10   Anna Barbauld: from *Epistle to William Wilberforce,*
                Esq. On the Rejection of the Bill for Abolishing the
                Slave Trade   16

1792   11   Mary Wollstonecraft: from *Vindication of the Rights*
                of Woman   18
           12   Clara Reeve: from *Plans of Education*   22

v

1793 13 Hannah More: from *Village Politics: A Dialogue between Jack Anvil, the Blacksmith, and Tom Hod, the Mason* 25

14 Charlotte Smith: from *The Emigrants (Book II)* 28

15 Laetitia Hawkins: from *Letters on the Female Mind* 30

16 Mary Hays: from *Letters and Essays* 33

1794 17 Hester Lynch Piozzi: from *British Synonymy* 34

1795 18 Maria Edgeworth: from *Letters for Literary Ladies* 36

19 Ann Yearsley: *Anarchy* 39

20 Ann Yearsley: from *Dedicated to Louis XVI* 40

1796 21 Mary Wollstonecraft: from *Letters Written during a Short Residence in Sweden, Norway and Denmark* 42

22 Mary Robinson: from *Sappho and Phaon* 46

1797 23 Mary Wollstonecraft: *On Poetry, and Our Relish for the Beauties of Nature* 48

1798 24 Dorothy Wordsworth: from *Journals* 52

25 [Mary Hays]: from *An Appeal to the Men of Great Britain in Behalf of Women* 55

26 Matilda Betham: *We Wish not the Mechanic Arts to Scan* 58

27 Priscilla Wakefield: from *Reflections on the Present Condition of the Female Sex* 59

28 Joanna Baillie: from *Introductory Discourse: Plays on the Passions* 61

29 Mary Wollstonecraft: from *Hints* 64

1799 30 Anna Seward: *To the Poppy* 65

31 Mary Ann Radcliffe: from *The Female Advocate* 65

32 'Anne Frances Randall' [Mary Robinson]: from *A Letter to the Women of England, on the Injustice of Mental Subordination* 67

33 Hannah More: from *Strictures on the Modern System of Female Education* 68

34 Mary Alcock: *The Body-Politic* 71

1800 35 Dorothy Wordsworth: from *Grasmere Journal* 73

36 Jane West: from *Letters to a Young Lady* 75

1801 37 Elizabeth Hamilton: from *Letters on the Elementary Principles of Education*   77
        38 Mary Robinson: from *Memoirs*   79

1802 39 Amelia Opie: *The Dying Daughter to her Mother*   81

1803 40 Dorothy Wordsworth: from *A Tour Made in Scotland*   84

1805 41 Mary Tighe: from *Psyche; or The Legend of Love*   87

1806 42 Mary Robinson: *Stanzas to a Friend who wished to have my Portrait*   89

1807 43 Anne Grant: from *Letters from the Mountains*   91
        44 Elizabeth Inchbald: from *On Novel Writing*   94
        45 Charlotte Smith: from *Beachy Head*   96

1808 46 Felicia Hemans: from *England and Spain; or, Valour and Patriotism*   97

1809 47 Sydney Owenson, Lady Morgan: from *Patriotic Sketches of Ireland*   99

1810 48 Lucy Aikin: from *Epistles on the Character and Conditions of Women*   100
        49 Anna Barbauld: from *On the Origin and Progress of Novel Writing*   102

1811 50 Elizabeth Hamilton: from *Observations on the Power of Imagination*   104
        51 Mary Tighe: *Written at Scarborough, August, 1799*   108

1812 52 Anna Barbauld: from *Eighteen Hundred and Eleven: A Poem*   109

1814 53 Dorothy Wordsworth: from *A Narrative Concerning George and Sarah Green*   111
        54 Isabella Lickbarrow: *Introductory Address: To the Muse*   114
        55 Claire Clairmont: from *Journals*   115

1815   56   Mary Ann Lamb: *On Needlework*   117

1816   57   Mary Shelley: from *History of a Six Weeks' Tour*   122
            58   Jane Taylor: from *Prejudice*   124

1817   59   Anne Lister: from *Diaries*   126

1818   60   Elizabeth Hamilton: from *Journals*   127
            61   Anne Lister: from *Diaries*   129

1819   62   Anne Lister: from *Diaries*   129
            63   Eleanor Butler: from *Diaries*   129

1820   64   Anne Lister: from *Diaries*   130

1821   65   Anne Lister: from *Diaries*   131
            66   Mary Hays: from *Caroline, Wife of George IV*   131
            67   Sydney Owenson, Lady Morgan: from *Italy*   135

1822   68   Harriet Martineau: *On Female Education*   137

1823   69   Felicia Hemans: *The Voice of Spring*   144

1824   70   Mary Shelley: *On Ghosts*   147

1825   71   Harriette Wilson: from *Memoirs*   153
            72   Maria Jane Jewsbury: from *Woman's Love*   155

1826   73   Anna Barbauld: from *On Female Studies*   158
            74   Ann Radcliffe: from *On the Supernatural in Poetry*   160

1827   75   Claire Clairmont: from *Journals*   163

1828   76   Felicia Hemans: *Properzia Rossi*   164

1829   77   Laetitia Landon: from *A History of the Lyre*   168
            78   Sydney Owenson, Lady Morgan: from *Mathematical
                  Ladies*   168
            79   Felicia Hemans: *Woman and Fame*   170
            80   Anna Jameson: from *Heroines of Modern Poetry*   171

81   Caroline Lamb: *Thou Woulds't Not Do What I Have
     Done*   173
82   Caroline Lamb: *Lines to Harriette Wilson*   173

1830   83   Sydney Owenson, Lady Morgan: from *Anglomania*   174

1831   84   Maria Jane Jewsbury: *Review of Joanna Baillie, 'The
                Nature and Dignity of Christ'*   176
           85   Maria Jane Jewsbury: from *Review of Shelley, 'The
                Wandering Jew'*   178

1832   86   Frances Trollope: from *Domestic Manners of the
                Americans*   181

1833   87   Sarah Flower Adams: from *A National Gallery*   184

1834   88   Marguerite, Countess of Blessington: from
                Conversations with Byron   187
           89   Mary Leman Grimstone: *Acephala*   190

1835   90   Laetitia Landon: from *On the Character of
                Mrs Heman's Writings*   196
           91   Laetitia Landon: *The Factory*   199

1836   92   Caroline Bowles: from *The Birthday*   202

     Notes   204

     Biographical notes   219

     Bibliography   234

     Index of authors   239

     Index of themes   240

INTRODUCTION

Survey with me, what ne'er our fathers saw,
A female band despising NATURE's law,
As 'proud defiance' flashes from their arms,
And vengeance smothers all their softer charms.
(Richard Polwhele, *The Unsexed Females*, 1798)

At the beginning of the eighteenth century, women writers in all genres were few and far between. By the 1790s, they had advanced so much, at least in the genres thought proper for them, fiction and poetry, that the *Monthly Review* was celebrating 'the age of ingenious and learned ladies' (n.s. xxvii p. 441). As Richard Polwhele's nervous attack indicates, however, women writers in the Revolutionary decade were no longer satisfied by their confinement to the literary discourses which were conventionally assigned to them. While they continued to excel in what the *Monthly Review* called the 'more elegant branches of literature' (*ibid*), they were also venturing into territory traditionally allotted to men: public and political themes, learned and philosophical treatises, essays on aesthetics and the sublime.

There were two distinct waves of women's writing in the era we call Romantic. The first ten years of the period were particularly rich in a confident diversity and range of genres, styles and themes, many of them highly polemical and politicized. This peak was followed by a hiatus, largely attributable to the anti-feminist backlash of which Polwhele's poem is a representative text. Women did not stop writing – indeed, the flow of novels remained steady throughout the period – but they became more cautious about breaking the bounds of decorum. By the 1820s, a second wave was gathering momentum. At its head were Felicia Hemans and Laetitia Landon, two of the most successful and widely-read poets of the nineteenth century. In addition, women again began to excel as reviewers, essayists and theorists in such diverse fields as education, social reform, political commentary and literary criticism.

Given this proliferation of female-authored texts, it is a curious and depressing fact that when the Romantic canon was formed, in the 1960s, largely owing to the efforts of a group of male American critics, it consisted entirely of male writers.[1] When, in the 1980s, women writers began to be included most courses on Romanticism in most universities included at best the work of three or four female authors: Mary Wollstonecraft, Dorothy Wordsworth, Jane Austen and Mary Shelley.

The 1990s have witnessed a change of climate, in which gender studies and interest in all forms of feminist literary criticism has never been higher. Not surprisingly, this development has affected the study and teaching of even the most conventional, historically-based courses, among them Romanticism. A number of important critical works have begun to re-examine and re-evaluate the literary productions of women writers of this period.[2] But there is still a crucial lack of availability of texts. At the time of writing, no anthology has yet appeared which does justice to the range and diversity of material written and published by women during this important literary era. While it is true that the most recent 'Romantic period' anthologies have begun to include some women's texts, the proportions are still so radically out of balance that it is difficult to defend them against a charge of tokenism. And, while two collections of Romantic women poets have recently been published, there remains a real need for a broader perspective and fuller coverage of writing by women across the genres.

It could, of course, be argued that the production of a single-sex anthology only compounds the problems which already exist. The danger is that such a text creates a cabinet of curiosities, interesting to look at but quite separate from the main concerns and issues of Romanticism. In an ideal world, perhaps, a truly balanced collection of texts would include an approximately equal amount of work of high quality by both female and male authors. But the scales have been so heavily weighted in the other direction, and the conditions in which most of us read, study and teach are still so far from ideal, that a powerful counter-measure is needed. This anthology attempts to redress the balance by demonstrating for the first time how much, how widely, how diversely and how effectively female-authored discourse was being produced between 1789 and 1836. The volume will give students access to many texts which are central to long-standing critical debates concerning the relation between gender, women's writing, and the Romantic canon. I hope it will help to do two important and necessary things: create a demand for more and fuller editions of women's texts, and change the way we view what we call Romanticism.

Given the long history of critical and scholarly disagreement over what exactly constitutes Romanticism, it is hardly surprising that any dates assigned to the Romantic period are bound to appear arbitrary. Until recently most popularly supposed to have begun with the publication of Blake's *Songs of Innocence* (1789) and to have ended with the death of Coleridge (1834), the time-span has shown an alarming tendency of late to expand in both directions.[3] Rather than attempt to tread a safe path through the minefield of definitions – which seem, in any case, to be so radically problematised in the case of female authors as to become almost, though by no means entirely, irrelevant – I have chosen to eschew aesthetic criteria altogether and to take my dates from external (non-literary, historical) events. Thus, the period covered by the present volume begins with the year of the French Revolution, and ends just before the accession of Queen Victoria. This arrangement does, at least, have the virtue of allowing questions to be raised concerning the relationship of gender, writing, and political change.

The political allegiances of female-authored texts during the period were complex. In the 1790s, a strong strand of radicalism permeates much of the writing produced by women. Many of the important women writers of this early part of the period emerged from radical or dissenting backgrounds. Several were active in the anti-slavery movement of the late 1780s and early 1790s, and many were sympathetic to the French Revolution, at least in its early stages. Indeed, the events taking place across the Channel were largely responsible for the production of a work which not only was of primary importance in itself but also set in motion a debate that would resonate throughout the remainder of the period. This was, of course, Mary Wollstonecraft's *Vindication of the Rights of Woman* (1792), a highly politicised text in which women's oppression was explicitly linked with that of other marginalised groups. Wollstonecraft's 'Revolutionary feminism'[4] initially found many supporters among other female writers. By the mid-1790s, however, the excesses of the Terror led to a conservative, anti-Revolutionary backlash which affected all but the most radical thinkers. In addition, Wollstonecraft's reputation suffered a massive blow after her death in 1797, when her widower William Godwin published his *Memoirs of the Author of a Vindication of the Rights of Woman* (1798). His well-meaning revelations of her attempts to live by her own radical feminist principles included the fact that she had lived with a lover and given birth to an illegitimate child. This was seized upon by the conservative 'anti-jacobin' press as proof that feminist radicalism was directly associated with sexual transgression, and had the effect of destroying not only Wollstonecraft's reputation but also the possibility of other women writers' continued adherence to Revolutionary feminism. The small number of radical feminist texts that did appear after her death were either published anonymously, like Mary Hays, *Appeal to the Men of Great Britain* (1798) and Mary Ann Radcliffe, *The Female Advocate* (1799), or, as in the case of Mary Robinson's *A Letter to the Women of England* (1799), under a pseudonym ('Anne Frances Randall').

As the eighteenth century came to a close, Revolutionary feminism effectively ceased to exist. Women did not stop writing, but they became increasingly wary about public, professional authorship, especially in traditionally masculine genres such as journalism and philosophical and political writing. The sole female voice of political protest in the later part of the era belongs to Sydney Owenson, Lady Morgan, whose strong Irish nationalist views and willingness to expose the worst excesses of British foreign policy (made from the safety of residence outside Britain) brought her many attacks from Tory reviewers. Acceptably 'feminine' discourses such as educational writing showed a new caution, and took care to repudiate what Hannah More called 'the disgusting and unnatural character' of feminist polemicism in favour of a safer construction of woman associated with the domestic and familial sphere. Another 'safe' non-fiction prose discourse was travel writing, a genre which was both popular and saleable. It also had the virtue of being one of the few ways in which women writers could acceptably write autobiography: the only female authors apart from travel writers who wrote publicly about their own lives and experiences were so-called 'fallen' women such as the courtesan Harriette Wilson and Byron's discarded mistress Lady Caroline Lamb. History, mainly of a domestic kind, was also permissible, and some interesting and useful re-evaluations of woman's place in history were published in the acceptable form of biography or memoirs: Mary Hays' *Memoirs of Queens* (1821), for example.

If the first half of the Romantic period was dominated, in the political sphere, by revolutions, popular protest, and war, the second half was predominantly concerned with reform. On the national, parliamentary front, this encompassed, among other things, the abolition of the slave trade in 1807 and of the East India Company's monopoly in 1815, the legalisation of trade unions in 1825, the Catholic Emancipation Act in 1829, and the Great Reform Bill of 1832. Excluded by law from active participation in politics either as electors or as elected, women writers were silent, in public at least, on these issues. However, in an age where philanthropy became an increasing preoccupation for middle-class women, other, more domestic, measures were open to female authors for comment and discussion. The Factory Act of 1833 in particular, which was perceived as being lamentably defective in its curtailment of child labour, elicited important verse commentary from several women poets.[5]

By the last part of the Romantic period, another change had taken place. Owing in great part to the proliferation of annuals and periodicals, women writers were again turning to journalism both as an (often essential) means of livelihood and as an outlet for the dissemination of ideas. The 1830s, in particular, found an increasing number of female reviewers and essayists, including Maria Jane Jewsbury, Mary Shelley, Harriet Martineau, Sarah Flower Adams and Mary Leman Grimstone. Mostly writing anonymously (Jewsbury in the *Athenaeum*, Martineau, Adams and Grimstone in the *Monthly Repository*), this impressively intellectual and clear-headed group of prose writers began once again to address issues related to women in society as well as participating in the (re-)masculinised discourse of literary criticism.

The change from the 1790s' confident engagement in social, political and feminist polemics to the post-Revolutionary construction of 'domestic woman' is nowhere more evident than in women's poetry. At the beginning of the revolutionary decade, women as diverse as Ann Yearsley, Charlotte Smith, Mary Alcock and Anna Seward were writing and publishing poems of frequently radical commentary on political events. By the early 1800s, this subject matter is no longer to be found, although social protest persists in the poetry of, for example, Amelia Opie. Anna Barbauld, one of the most powerfully intellectual women writers of the early part of the period, ventured into political commentary as late as 1812 with her *Eighteen Hundred and Eleven: A Poem*, but the hostile response which greeted her attack on Britain's commercial and imperialist tendencies effectively silenced her as a poet from then on. The second wave of women poets, including Hemans and Landon, built their success on the ways in which their poetry idealised domesticity (one of Hemans' early volumes was called *The Domestic Affections*) as central to a wide range of social and political concerns. 'Domestic woman', hearth and home are seen as essential safeguards of national identity, and strongholds against the encroachments of social and political conflict. But at the same time, there is in much of this late-Romantic women's poetry a prevailing sense of the ultimate unsatisfactoriness of woman's lot and of the price, for a woman writer, of engagement in the public sphere.

It is, perhaps, ironic, in a period which takes its very name and existence largely from a group of poets who were responsible for the cult of nature, the transcendental self, and the sublime, that so little of any such concerns may be found in the writing of female poets. Arguably, the only fully 'Romantic' woman's writing of the period is not poetry but the late prose

of Mary Wollstonecraft, whose essay *On Poetry* anticipates in many
respects later, male-authored, Romantic prose manifestos. At the risk of
over-simplification, I suppose the reason is that women in this era lacked
the leisure and above all the confidence needed to deal in transcendental
absolutes. The sublime, the aesthetic category invoked implicitly in 'male'
Romanticism, had been decidedly and influentially gendered masculine by
Burke in his *On the Sublime and Beautiful* as early as 1756, leaving the
softer, weaker, gentler category of the beautiful to be assigned to the female.
The poet's inspiration – whether named as the Muse or as Nature – was,
on the other hand, invariably gendered as female, a radically disabling
trope for women poets. Finally, Wordsworth's Preface to *Lyrical Ballads*
(1800), by describing the poet as 'a man speaking to men', added further
pressing reasons why, at a period when gender issues were crucially at stake,
women poets were unwilling to venture into such obviously masculinist
discourse.[6]

It has recently been suggested that women writers of the Romantic era
typically show 'an investment in quotidian tones and details, and a por-
trayal of alienated sensibility'.[7] Readers who are interested in such issues
will find the 'quotidian' demonstrated in, for example, the journals of
Eleanor Butler and Dorothy Wordsworth, and the poetry of Jane Taylor.
Charlotte Smith must remain the archetypal poet of 'alienated sensibility',
although Ann Yearsley and Anna Seward provide variations on the theme.

Little has been written on the subject of the depiction of sexuality in the
period. The social pressures in operation ensured that even private writings were silent on this important area: much discussion has been devoted
to the status of the relationship between Eleanor Butler and her 'beloved'
Sarah Ponsonby (the Ladies of Llangollen), for example. A lively exception
is the diary of Anne Lister, although it is notable that her revelations of her
lesbian feelings and activities were written in code. Even the courtesan
memoirs of Harriette Wilson, while they are predicated on the existence of
extensive illicit sexual activity, do not describe it in any detail. Women
writers who wished to depict sexual desire did so by retreating to the classical past: a powerful and passionate sensuality is present in Mary
Robinson's *Sappho and Phaon* sonnet sequence, and in Mary Tighe's
Psyche, for example.

I must end with an anthologiser's commonplace apology. Those who
are familiar with women's writing of the period will doubtless feel that
there are regrettable omissions here, but it is, of course, impossible to
please everyone. I have tried simultaneously to provide lively, interesting,
readable materials and to give a true sense of the range of female-authored
texts of the period. In the final analysis, I have included works which I have

enjoyed reading myself, and which seem to me to be useful for teaching purposes. I hope others will agree with me.

Editorial Matters

Most anthologies are arranged either thematically or by chronological date of birth of the author. This volume is arranged by date of publication of the text. Why is this? A thematic arrangement seemed to me too reductive, although an index of themes has been included for those who would like to follow ideas through the period. Author-based grouping has also been rejected, though again, readers who are interested in the authors will find short biographical entries on each at the back of the volume. In the present arrangement, I hope to show more clearly both the way in which these texts fit into the context of the period as a whole (a chronological table of the whole period, including historical events and significant male-authored publications, is also included) and the ways in which the texts react and respond to each other. Writing does not exist in a vacuum: it comes into being as a result of a complex interplay of historical, social, and cultural pressures which will, I hope, be revealed more adequately by this arrangement than by the usual and more conventional one.

This being said, however, some editorial decisions have been taken that have resulted in a picture by no means wholly representative. Two of the most important genres in which women were writing, fiction and drama, have been excluded altogether. This is partly owing to pressures of space, but also, and equally important, I have felt that while it is possible to make excerpts from non-fiction prose without doing it too much damage, the same cannot be said of either novels or plays. This has led to a slightly skewed perspective, and readers should be aware of the fact that some of the most important female writers of the era are either missing altogether (Fanny Burney, Jane Austen, Mary Brunton, Susan Ferrier) or represented only by what might be regarded as the more marginal elements of their total output (Maria Edgeworth, Elizabeth Inchbald, Joanna Baillie, Mary Shelley). Although poetry is now available elsewhere, I have included a limited amount in the interest of as wide a representation of the period as possible.

Although most of the texts included here did find their way into the public domain, I have been aware of the need to do justice to those writers who, for whatever reason, avoided publication for some or all of their literary productions. This unpublished material is represented by journal entries. Letters have been excluded, largely on the grounds of lack of space.

An attempt has been made to strike a balance between the desire to give as wide a range of material as possible and the wish not to confine the contents solely to short extracts taken from larger works. Bearing in mind the strictures of Hannah More, who wrote of the proliferation of anthologies for women composed of 'elegant extracts' that:

> A few fine passages from the poets (passages perhaps which derived their chief beauty from their position and connection) are huddled together by some extract maker, whose brief and disconnected patches of broken and discordant materials neither fill the mind nor form the taste . . .[8]

a number of essays, as well as poems, have been given in their entirety.

In general, the copy-texts of the works included are those of the first published editions. Obvious printers' errors have been silently corrected, and proper names have been adjusted (Wollstonecraft and Shakespeare seem particularly prone to mis-spelling). Texts have in general been modernised as far as spelling is concerned, and initial capitalisation of nouns has been removed except in the case of personifications.

Notes at the back of the volume give the source for each text. Brief contextual background and explanatory notes have been added where necessary. Notes provided by the authors themselves were often copious, and have not always been given in full.

Notes

1. For a useful discussion of formation of the Romantic canon see Linkin (1991).
2. Among the most important recent works are Clarke (1990), Feldman and Kelley (1995), Kelly (1993), Mellor (1988, 1993).
3. Jerome McGann (1993) has fixed on the publication of the Della Cruscan *Florence Miscellany* (1785) as a beginning date, although he ends perhaps rather earlier than some with the publication of Tennyson's first volume in 1832. The same dates are favoured by Jennifer Breen (1992). Anthony Ashfield (1995) plunges even further back into the eighteenth century, beginning in 1770, and ends with the juvenilia of Elizabeth Barrett and the Brontes in 1838, while Duncan Wu (1994) includes some material from the 1840s and even one extract from the 1870s.
4. The term is taken from Kelly (1992).
5. In addition to the Landon poem included here, Caroline Bowles and Caroline Norton also published long protest poems on child labour in the factories.
6. An important early discussion of these matters is that of Homans (1980). More recently, see for example Curran (1988), Mellor (1993), Ross (1989).
7. See Curran (1988), p. 303.
8. More (1799), vol. 1, p. 61.

ACKNOWLEDGEMENTS

Extracts from M. K. and D. Stocking (eds), *The Journals of Claire Clairmont* (1968) by permission of Harvard University Press. Extracts from E. De Selincourt (ed.), *The Journals of Dorothy Wordsworth* (2 vols, 1941) by permission of Macmillan. Extracts from E. De Selincourt (ed.), *Dorothy Wordsworth: A Narrative Concerning George and Sarah Green* (1936) by permission of Oxford University Press. Extracts from E. Mavor (ed.), *A Year with the Ladies of Llangollen* (1968) by permission of Penguin Books.

CHRONOLOGY

1789   French Revolution; slave-trade resolutions introduced by
       Wilberforce
       William Blake, *Songs of Innocence* and *Book of Thel*; W. L. Bowles,
       Sonnets; Charlotte Smith, *Ethelinda*
1790   Edmund Burke, *Reflections*; Helen Maria Williams, *Julia*; Ann
       Radcliffe, *A Sicilian Romance*
1791   Wilberforce's abolition motion rejected
       Elizabeth Inchbald, *A Simple Story*; Thomas Paine, *Rights of Man*
       (Part I); Ann Radcliffe, *Romance of the Forest*
1792   French Republic declared
       Birth of Shelley
       Paine, *Rights of Man* (Part II)
1793   Execution of Louis XVI (Jan) and Marie Antoinette (Oct); war
       with France (Feb); Reign of Terror begins (June)
       William Godwin, *Political Justice*; Blake, *Marriage of Heaven and
       Hell*, *America*, *Visions of the Daughters of Albion*; William
       Wordsworth, *Evening Walk* and *Descriptive Sketches*
1794   Execution of Robespierre (July)
       Blake, *Songs of Experience*, *Book of Urizen*, *Europe*; Radcliffe,
       Mysteries of Udolpho; Godwin, *Caleb Williams*
1795   Births of Keats and Carlyle
1796   Threatened French invasion
       Death of Burns
       Mary Hays, *Memoirs of Emma Courtney*; Fanny Burney, *Camilla*;
       S. T. Coleridge, *Poems on Various Subjects*
1797   Death of Burke
       Napoleon invades Austria and Venice
       Radcliffe, *The Italian*
1798   Nelson defeats French fleet in Battle of the Nile
       Thomas Malthus, *Essay on the Principles of Population*;
       Wordsworth and Coleridge, *Lyrical Ballads*; Godwin, *Memoirs of
       the Author of a Vindication of the Rights of Woman*

1799   Trade unions suppressed: Napoleon appointed First Consul in
        France
        Hays, *Victim of Prejudice*
1800   Napoleon defeats Austria at Battle of Marengo
        Death of Cowper
        Wordsworth and Coleridge, *Lyrical Ballads*, 2nd edn, with
        Preface; Maria Edgeworth, *Castle Rackrent*
1801   Union with Ireland; first British census
        Edgeworth, *Belinda*
1802   Peace with France; Napoleon becomes Consul; first factory legis-
        lation
        Edinburgh Review founded; Coleridge, *Poems*
1803   War with France; General Enclosure Act
1804   Napoleon becomes Emperor; Spain declares war on Britain
        Blake, *Jerusalem*; Amelia Opie, *Adeline Mowbray*
1805   French and Spanish defeated at Battle of Trafalgar; death of
        Nelson
        Walter Scott, *Lay of the Last Minstrel*
1806   British blockade of French Empire; dissolution of Holy Roman
        Empire
        Lady Morgan, *The Wild Irish Girl*
1807   Napoleon attacks Russia; abolition of slave trade in British Empire
        Wordsworth, *Poems in Two Volumes*; Lord Byron, *Hours of
        Idleness*; Charles and Mary Lamb, *Tales from Shakespeare*
1808   Napoleon invades Spain; Peninsular War begins
        Scott, *Marmion*
1809   Napoleon captures Vienna, imprisons the Pope
        Birth of Tennyson
        Hannah More, *Coelebs in Search of a Wife*
1810   Birth of Elizabeth Gaskell
        Wordsworth, *Guide to the Lakes*
1811   Luddite riots; Prince of Wales becomes Regent
        Jane Austen, *Sense and Sensibility*; Mary Brunton, *Self Control*
1812   Napoleon invades Russia (June); retreats from Moscow
        (Oct–Dec); Wellington defeats French at Salamanca, occupies
        Madrid; US declares war against Britain
        Births of Dickens and Browning
        Byron, *Childe Harold* 1 & 2
1813   East India Company monopoly abolished; Wellington drives
        French from Spain
        Southey becomes Poet Laureate

Byron, *The Bride of Abydos*, *The Corsair*, *The Giaour*; P. B. Shelley, *Queen Mab*; Austen, *Pride and Prejudice*

1814   Napoleon abdicates, is exiled to Elba; peace between US and Britain
       Wordsworth, *Excursion*; Austen, *Mansfield Park*; Scott, *Waverley*; Edgeworth, *Patronage*; Brunton, *Discipline*; Burney, *The Wanderer*

1815   Napoleon escapes Elba, is defeated at Battle of Waterloo; peace in Europe
       Austen, *Emma*; Wordsworth, *Poems*

1816   Birth of Charlotte Bronte
       Coleridge, *Christabel and Other Poems*; Byron, *Childe Harold 3*; Shelley, *Alastor*

1817   John Keats, *Poems*; Coleridge, *Biographia Literaria* and *Sibylline Leaves*

1818   Birth of Emily Bronte
       Death of Austen (*Persuasion*, *Northanger Abbey* published posthumously)
       Mary Shelley, *Frankenstein*; Byron, *Childe Harold 4*; Keats, *Endymion*; Susan Ferrier, *Marriage*

1819   Peterloo massacre
       Births of George Eliot and Queen Victoria
       Shelley, *Mask of Anarchy*; Byron, *Don Juan* 1 & 2

1820   Death of George III, accession of George IV
       Birth of Anne Bronte
       Shelley, *Prometheus Unbound*; Keats, *Lamia, Isabella, Eve of St Agnes*

1821   Start of 3-year famine in Ireland
       Death of Keats
       Thomas De Quincey, *Confessions of an English Opium Eater*; William Hazlitt, *Table Talk*; Shelley, *Adonais, Epipsychidion*

1822   Death of Shelley

1823   Charles Lamb, *Essays of Elia*

1824   Death of Byron

1825   Trade unions legalised; first railway opens in England
       Hazlitt, *Spirit of the Age*

1826

1827   Death of Blake

1828   Coleridge, *Poetical Works* (3 vols); Hazlitt, *Life of Napoleon*

1829   Catholic Emancipation

1830   Death of George IV, accession of William IV; independence of Greece; start of British cholera epidemic; first long-distance railway

opens (Manchester–Liverpool)
Death of Hazlitt
Alfred Tennyson, *Poems, Chiefly Lyrical*
1831   Rural riots against mechanised agriculture
1832   Great Reform Bill
Death of Scott
1833   Factory Act limits child labour
Thomas Carlyle, *Sartor Resartus*; Charles Lamb, *Essays of Elia*
(2nd series); Tennyson, *Poems*; Robert Browning, *Pauline*
1834   Slavery abolished in British Empire
Deaths of Coleridge and Charles Lamb
1835   Municipal Reform Act
1836   Death of Godwin
1837   Death of William IV; accession of Victoria

1789

1. Charlotte Smith
Written in the Churchyard at Middleton in Sussex

Pressed by the moon, mute arbitress of tides,
    While the loud equinox its power combines,
    The sea no more its sweeping surge confines
But o'er the shrinking land sublimely rides.
The wild blast, rising from the western cave,
    Drives the huge billows from their heaving bed,
    Tears from their grassy tombs the village dead,
And breaks the silent sabbath of the grave!
With shells and sea-weed mingled, on the shore
    Lo! their bones whiten in the frequent wave;
    But vain to them the winds and waters rave;
They hear the warring elements no more:
While I am doomed – by life's long storm oppressed,
To gaze with envy on their gloomy rest.

—

2. Eleanor Butler
from *Diaries*

Thursday January 1st
The Dee is frozen all over. Shanette, the reputed witch of the village, brought
us for new year's gift a large parcel of apples tied up in a neat white napkin.
I met her as she was coming in with her gift. She insisted on kissing my
hand. A compliment I could well have excused, but could not avoid for
fear of giving her pain. I think my hand feels chill and numbed since . . .

* * * *

Sunday January 4th

Snow deep. A few sheep wandering about the field in great distress. One of them apparently consumptive and coughing up its poor lungs. Made my heart ache. I wish they could take money, or that I could relieve them in their own simple way.

* * * *

Tuesday January 20th

Freezing hard. Windy. Cold, but very comfortable in the dressing room – an excellent fire. Shutters closed. Curtain let down. Candles lighted – our pens and ink. Spent the evening very pleasantly reading *Tristram Shandy* aloud – adjourned to the library. Worked – laughed. From home since the first of January 1789. Not once thank Heaven.

Wednesday January 21st

The chimney sweep came at last. A child on horseback, but tho' a child in years an ancient in understanding. A day of delicious retirement.

* * * *

Saturday April 4th

Mutton from Oswestry of a great size and vast price . . . My beloved and I walked many times on the Esplanade. Clear evening, but sharp and cold beyond expression. A comfortable well clad old woman rode up the field with a pipe of tobacco in her mouth, the puffs from which softened the keenness of the air and must make her journey over the mountains delectable.

* * * *

Saturday September 5th

Carpets and cheese from Kendal, not in the least resembling the pattern we bespoke which was a modest blue tinged with black – these have every fiery tawdry colour in worsted, green and blue – red and purple and yellow – huge roses and tulips and poppies sprawling about – the cheese which we particularly ordered might be the best (Berkeley hundred) proves no better than a common Gloucester. *Mem*: never again to deal with Mr Kendal for any article whatsoever.

* * * *

Saturday November 21st

Our poor Landlord came to ask us how the broth we ordered for his wife was to be made. His tears – his regret for her illness – his recapitulation of her goodness, and the happy life they had led together these fifty years affected us and called forth our tears. Reading. Writing. Saw the burial of a little girl coming thro' the field. Enquired the reason of its being attended by such a multitude of children. The person of whom we enquired said it was the custom here when a child died that all its companions and play-mates of the same age attended the funeral and bore the coffin to the grave.

❊ ❊ ❊ ❊

Friday December 25th

A tall thin old man came to the door and sung a Christmas carol in a melo-dious, solemn voice. Listened to it with pleasure. Three dinner. Roast beef, mince pies.

―

3. Elizabeth Hands

A Poem, On the Supposition of an Advertisement appearing
in a Morning Paper, of the Publication of a Volume of Poems,
by a Servant-Maid

> The tea-kettle bubbled, the tea things were set,
> The candles were lighted, the ladies were met;
> The how d'ye's were over, and entering bustle,
> The company seated, and silks ceased to rustle:
> The great Mrs. Consequence opened her fan,
> And thus the discourse in an instant began
> (All affected reserve and formality scorning):
> 'I suppose you all saw in the paper this morning
> A volume of *Poems* advertised – 'tis said
> They're produced by the pen of a poor servant-maid.'
> 'A servant write verses!' says Madam Du Bloom:
> 'Pray what is the subject – a mop, or a broom?'
> 'He, he, he,' says Miss Flounce: 'I suppose we shall see
> An Ode on a Dishclout – what else can it be?'
> Says Miss Coquettilla, 'Why, ladies, so tart?
> Perhaps Tom the footman has fired her heart;

And she'll tell us how charming he looks in new clothes,
And how nimble his hand moves in brushing the shoes;
Or how, the last time that he went to May Fair,
He bought her some sweethearts of gingerbread ware.'
'For my part I think,' says old Lady Marr-joy,
'A servant might find herself other employ:
Was she mine I'd employ her as long as 'twas light,
And send her to bed without candle at night.'
'Why so?', says Miss Rhymer, displeased: 'I protest
'Tis pity a genius should be so depressed!'
'What ideas can such low-bred creatures conceive?'
Says Mrs Notworthy, and laughed in her sleeve.
Says old Mrs Prudella, 'If servants can tell
How to write to their mothers, to say they are well,
And read on a Sunday *The Duty of Man*,
Which is more I believe than one half of them can;
I think 'tis more properer they should rest there,
Than be reaching at things so much out of their sphere.'
Says old Mrs Candour, 'I've now got a maid
That's the plague of my life – a young gossiping jade;
There's no end of the people that after her come,
And whenever I'm out, she is never at home;
I'd rather ten times she would sit down and write,
Than gossip all over the town every night.'
'Some whimsical trollop most like', says Miss Prim,
'Has been scribbling of nonsense, just out of a whim,
And, conscious it neither is witty or pretty
Conceals her true name, and ascribes it to Betty.'
'I once had a servant myself,' says Miss Pines,
'That wrote on a wedding some very good lines.'
Says Mrs Domestic, 'And when they were done,
I can't see for my part what use they were *on*;
Had she wrote a receipt, to've instructed you how
To warm a cold breast of veal, like a ragout,
Or to make cowslip wine, that would pass for Champagne,
It might have been useful, again and again.'
On the sofa was old Lady Pedigree placed;
She owned that for poetry she had no taste,
That the study of heraldry was more in fashion,
And boasted she knew all the crests in the nation.

Says Mrs Routella, 'Tom, take out the urn,
And stir up the fire, you see it don't burn.'
The tea things removed, and the tea-table gone,
The card-tables brought, and the cards laid thereon,
The ladies, ambitious for each others' crown,
Like courtiers contending for honours, sat down.

4. Hester Lynch Piozzi
from *Observations and Reflections made in the Course of a
Journey through France, Italy and Germany [Italy]*

Ladies of distinction bring with them when they marry, besides fortune, as many clothes as will last them seven years; for fashions do not change here as often as at London or Paris; yet is pin-money allowed, and an attention paid to the wife that no English-woman can form an idea of: in every family her duties are few; for, as I have observed, household management falls to the master's share of course, when all the servants are men almost, and those all paid by the week or day. Children are very seldom seen by those who visit great houses: if they *do* come down for five minutes after dinner, the parents are talked of as *doting* on them, and nothing can equal the pious and tender return made to fathers and mothers in this country, for even an apparently moderate share of fondness shown to them in a state of infancy. I saw an old Marchioness the other day, who had I believe been exquisitely beautiful, lying in bed in a spacious apartment, just like ours in the old palaces, with the tester touching the top almost: she had her three grown-up sons standing round her, with an affectionate desire of pleasing, and showing her whatever could soothe or amuse her – so it charmed me; and I was told, and observed indeed, that when they quitted her presence a half-kneeling bow, and a kind kiss of her still white hand, was the ceremony used. I knew myself brought thither only that she might be entertained by the sight of a foreigner – and was equally struck at her appearance – more so I should imagine than she could be at mine; when these dear men assisted in moving her pillows with emulative attention, and rejoiced with each other apart, that their mother looked so well today. Two or three servants out of livery brought us refreshments I remember; but her maid attended in the antechamber, and answered the bell at her bed's head, which was exceedingly magnificent in the old style of grandeur – crimson damask, if I recollect right, with family arms at the back; and she lay on nine or eleven pillows, laced with ribbon, and two large bows to each, very elegant and expensive in any country: – with all this, to prove that the Italians have little sensation of cold, here was no fire, but a suffocating brazier, which stood near the door that opened, and was kept open, into the maid's apartment.

A woman here in every stage of life has really a degree of attention shown her that is surprising: – if conjugal disputes arise in a family, so as to make them become what we call town-talk, the public voice is sure to run against the husband; if separation ensues, all possible countenance is given to the wife, while the gentleman is somewhat less willingly received; and all the stories of past disgusts are related to *his* prejudices: nor will the lady he wishes to serve look very kindly on a man who treats his own wife with unpoliteness. *Che cuore deve avere!* says she: What a heart he must have! *Io non mene fido sicuro:* I shall take care not to trust him sure.

---

5. Anna Seward
Sonnet: To France on her Present Exertions

Thou, that where Freedom's sacred fountains play,
    Which sprung effulgent, though with crimson stains,
    On transatlantic shores, and widening plains,
    Hast, in their living waters washed away
Those cankering spots, shed by tyrannic sway
    On thy long drooping lilies, English veins
    Swell with the tide of exultation gay,
    To see thee spurn thy deep-galling chains.
Few of Britannia's free-born sons forbear
    To bless thy cause; – cold is the heart that breathes
    No wish fraternal. – France, we bid thee share
The blessings twining with our civic wreaths,
    While Victory's trophies, permanent as fair,
    Crown the bright sword that Liberty unsheathes.

1790

6. Mary Wollstonecraft
from *A Vindication of the Rights of Men*

Reading your Reflections warily over, it has continually and forcibly struck me, that had you been a Frenchman, you would have been, in spite of your respect for rank and antiquity, a violent revolutionist; and deceived, as you now probably are, by the passions that cloud your reason, have termed your romantic enthusiasm an enlightened love of your country, a benevolent respect for the rights of men. Your imagination would have taken fire, and have found arguments, full as ingenious as those you now offer, to prove that the constitution, of which so few pillars remained, that constitution which time had almost obliterated, was not a model sufficiently noble to deserve close adherence. And, for the English constitution, you might not have had such a profound veneration as you have lately acquired; nay, it is not impossible that you might have entertained the same opinion of the English parliament, that you professed to have during the American war.

Another observation which, by frequently occurring, has grown almost into a conviction, is simply this, that had the English in general reprobated the French revolution, you would have stood forth alone, and been the avowed Goliath of liberty. But, not liking to see so many brothers near the throne of fame, you have turned the current of your passions, and consequently of your reasoning, another way. Had Dr Price's sermon not lighted some sparks very like envy in your bosom, I shrewdly suspect that he would have been treated with more candour; nor is it charitable to suppose that any thing but personal pique and hurt vanity could have dictated such bitter sarcasms and reiterated expressions of contempt as occur in your Reflections.

But without fixed principles even goodness of heart is no security from inconsistency, and mild affectionate sensibility only renders a man more ingeniously cruel, when the pangs of hurt vanity are mistaken for virtuous indignation, and the gall of bitterness for the milk of Christian charity.

Where is the dignity, the infallibility of sensibility, in the fair ladies, whom, if the voice of rumour is to be credited, the captive negroes curse in all the agony of bodily pain, for the unheard of tortures they invent? It is probable that some of them, after the sight of a flagellation, compose their ruffled spirits and exercise their tender feelings by the perusal of the last imported novel. – How true theses tears are to nature, I leave you to determine. But these ladies may have read your *Enquiry concerning the*

origin of our ideas of the Sublime and Beautiful, and, convinced by your
arguments, may have laboured to be pretty, by counterfeiting weakness.

You may have convinced them that *littleness* and *weakness* are the very
essence of beauty; and that the Supreme Being, in giving women beauty in
the most supereminent degree, seemed to command them, by the powerful
voice of nature, not to cultivate the moral virtues that might chance to
excite respect, and interfere with the pleasing sensations they were created
to inspire. Thus confining truth, fortitude, and humanity, within the rigid
pale of manly morals, they might justly argue, that to be loved, woman's
high end and great distinction! they should 'learn to lisp, to totter in their
walk, and nick-name God's creatures.' Never, they might repeat after you,
was any man, much less a woman, rendered amiable by the force of those
exalted qualities, fortitude, justice, wisdom, and truth; and thus fore-
warned of the sacrifice they must make to those austere, unnatural virtues,
they would be authorized to turn all their attention to their persons, systematically neglecting morals to secure beauty. – Some rational old woman
indeed might chance to stumble at this doctrine, and hint, that in avoiding
atheism you had not steered clear of the musselman's creed; but you could
readily exculpate yourself by turning the charge on Nature, who made our
idea of beauty independent of reason. Nor would it be unnecessary for you
to recollect, that if virtue has any other foundation than worldly utility, you
have clearly proved that one half of the human species, at least, have not
souls; and that Nature, by making women *little, smooth, delicate, fair*
creatures, never designed that they should exercise their reason to acquire
the virtues that produce opposite, if not contradictory, feelings. The affection they excite, to be uniform and perfect, should not be tinctured with
the respect which moral virtues inspire, lest pain should be blended
with pleasure, and admiration disturb the soft intimacy of love. This laxity
of morals in the female world is certainly more captivating to a libertine
imagination than the cold arguments of reason, that give no sex to virtue.
If beautiful weakness be interwoven in a woman's frame, if the chief business of her life be (as you insinuate) to inspire love, and Nature has made
an eternal distinction between the qualities that dignify a rational being
and this animal perfection, her duty and happiness in this life must clash
with any preparation for a more exalted state. So that Plato and Milton
were grossly mistaken in asserting that human love led to heavenly, and
was only an exaltation of the same affection; for the love of the Deity, which
is mixed with the most profound reverence, must be love of perfection,
and not compassion for weakness.

* * * *

But should experience prove that there is a beauty in virtue, a charm in order, which necessarily implies exertion, a depraved sensual taste may give way to a more manly one – and *melting* feelings to rational satisfactions. Both may be equally natural to man; the test is their moral difference, and that point reason alone can decide.

Such a glorious change can only be produced by liberty. Inequality of rank must ever impede the growth of virtue, by vitiating the mind that submits or domineers; that is ever employed to procure nourishment for the body, or amusement for the mind. And if this grand example may be set by an assembly of unlettered clowns, if they can produce a crisis that may involve Europe, and 'more than Europe', you must allow us to respect unsophisticated reason, and reverence the active exertions that were not relaxed by a fastidious respect for the beauty of rank, or a dread of the deformity produced by any *void* in the social structure.

---

7. Eleanor Butler
from *Diaries*

Sunday January 17th

There is no describing the blazing beauty of this morning. All the mountains a glorious purple and gold. Woods sparkling with gems. Smoke silently spinning in columns to heaven – chorus of birds hymning their thanksgiving in every thicket – tender transparent mist exhaling from the river and brooks – the hoar frost melting before the sun's brilliant rays and disclosing such verdure.

✳ ✳ ✳ ✳

Friday January 29th

Sent for Baillis – made him examine the chimney after that little boy who said he had and whom we paid for sweeping it. The odious brat had gone no further than the middle. Baillis with a long broom finished it.

✳ ✳ ✳ ✳

Monday February 4th

My head which has ached more or less these three weeks grew very bad. And my beloved ever anxious – ever tender made me take a mustard emetic, which effectually removed my complaint. How could it fail when administered by her. I grew perfectly well. And then my beloved and I sat by the excellent dressing room fire – got the backgammon table and played 'till twelve.

* * * *

Wednesday July 14th

The sky like a sea of blood. Never beheld anything like it but once before – that was the evening of the fire kindled by Lord George Gordon in London. I tremble for France.

* * * *

Tuesday November 23rd

Sent for the man of the hand – paid him – then sent him to the village for the man with the bear – the man brought it – a tame huge animal – female I suppose – by the master calling it Nancy. We fed it with bread and mutton. It drank small beer. It was exhibited in the field before our cottage.

———

8. Catharine Macaulay
from *Letters on Education*

The moderns, in the education of their children, have too much followed the stiff and prudish manners of ancient days, in the separating the male and female children of a family. This is well adapted to the absurd unsocial rigour of Grecian manners; but as it is not so agreeable to that mixture of the sexes in a more advanced age, which prevails in all European societies, it is not easy to be accounted for, but from the absurd notion, that the education of females should be of an opposite kind to that of males. How many nervous diseases have been contracted? How much feebleness of constitution has been acquired, by forming a false idea of female excellence, and endeavouring, by our art, to bring Nature to the ply of our imagination. Our sons are suffered to enjoy with freedom that time which is not devoted to study, and follow, unmolested, those strong impulses which Nature has wisely given for furtherance of her benevolent purposes: but if, before her native vivacity is entirely subdued by habit, little Miss is inclined to show her locomotive tricks in a manner not entirely agreeable to the trammels of custom, she is reproved with a sharpness which gives her a consciousness of having highly transgressed the laws of decorum; and what with the vigilance of those who are appointed to superintend her conduct, and the false bias they have imposed in her mind, every vigorous exertion is suppressed, the mind and body yield to the tyranny of error, and Nature is charged with all those imperfections which we alone owe to the blunders of art.

* * * *

There is another prejudice, Hortensia, which affects yet more deeply female happiness, and female importance; a prejudice, which ought ever to have been confined to the regions of the east . . . the state of slavery to which female nature in that part of the world has ever been subjected, and can only suit with the notion of a positive inferiority in the intellectual powers of the female mind. You will soon perceive, that the prejudice which I mean, is that degrading difference in the culture of the understanding, which has prevailed for several centuries in all European societies. Our ancestors, on the first revival of letters, dispensed with an equal hand the advantages of a classical education to all their offspring; but as pedantry was the fault of that age, a female student might not at that time be a very agreeable character. True philosophy in those ages was rarely an attendant on learning, even in the male sex; but it must be obvious to those who are not blinded by the mists of prejudice, that there is no cultivation which yields so promising a harvest as the cultivation of the understanding; and that a mind, irradiated by the clear light of wisdom, must be equal to every task which reason imposes on it. The social duties in the interesting characters of daughter, wife, and mother, will be but ill performed by ignorance and levity; and in the domestic converse of husband and wife, the alternative of an enlightened or unenlightened companion cannot be indifferent to any man of taste and true knowledge. Be no longer niggards, then, all ye parents, in bestowing on your offspring, every blessing which nature and fortune renders them capable of enjoying! Confine not the education of your daughters to what is regarded as the ornamental part of it, nor deny the graces to your sons. Suffer no prejudices to prevail on you to weaken Nature, in order to render her more beautiful; take measures for the virtue and harmony of your family, by uniting the young minds early in the soft bonds of friendship. Let your children be brought up together; let their sports and studies be the same; let them enjoy, in the constant presence of those who are set over them, all that freedom which innocence renders harmless, and in which Nature rejoices. By the uninterrupted intercourse which you will thus establish, both sexes will find, that friendship may be enjoyed between them without passion. The wisdom of your daughters will preserve them from the bane of coquetry, and even at the age of desire, objects of temptation will lose somewhat of their stimuli, by losing their novelty. Your sons will look for something more solid in women, than a mere outside; and be no longer the dupes of the meanest, the weakest, and the most profligate of their sex. They will become the constant benefactors of that part of their family who stand in need of their assistance; and in regard to all matters of domestic concern, the unjust distinction of primogeniture will be deprived of its sting.

* * * *

The great difference, that is observable in the characters of the sexes, Hortensia, as they display themselves in the scenes of social life, has given rise to much false speculation on the natural qualities of the female mind. . . .

It must be confessed, that the virtues of the males among the human species, though mixed and blended with a variety of vices and errors, have displayed a bolder and a more consistent picture of excellence than female nature has hitherto done. It is on these reasons that, when we compliment the appearance of a more than ordinary energy in the female mind, we call it masculine; and hence it is, that Pope has elegantly said *a perfect woman's but a softer man.* And if we take in the consideration, that there can be only one rule of moral excellence for beings made of the same materials, organized after the same manner, and subjected to similar laws of Nature, we must either agree with Mr Pope, or we must reverse the proposition, and say, that *a perfect man is a woman formed after a coarser mould.* The difference that actually does subsist between the sexes, is too flattering for men to be willingly imputed to accident; for what accident occasions, wisdom might correct; and it is better, says pride, to give up the advantages we might derive from the perfection of our fellow associates, than to own that Nature has been just in the equal distribution of her favours. These are the sentiments of men; but mark how readily they are yielded to by the women; not from humility I assure you, but merely to preserve with character those fond vanities on which they set their hearts. No; suffer them to idolize their persons, to throw away their life in the pursuit of trifles, and to indulge in the gratification of the meaner passions, and they will heartily join in the sentence of their degradation.

* * * *

But whatever might be the wise purpose of Providence in such a disposition of things, certain it is, that some degree of inferiority, in point of corporeal strength, seems always to have existed between the two sexes; and this advantage, in the barbarous age of mankind, was abused to such a degree, as to destroy all the natural rights of the female species, and reduce them to a state of abject slavery. What accidents have contributed in Europe to better their condition, would not be to my purpose to relate; for

I do not intend to give you a history of women; I mean only to trace the sources of their peculiar foibles and vices; and these I firmly believe to originate in situation and education only: for so little did a wise and just Providence intend to make the condition of slavery an unalterable law of female nature, that in the same proportion as the male sex have consulted the interest of their own happiness, they have relaxed in their tyranny over women; and such is their use in the system of mundane creatures, and such their natural influence over the male mind, that were these advantages properly exerted, they might carry every point of any importance to their honour and happiness. However, till that period arrives in which women will act wisely, we will amuse ourselves in talking of their follies.

The situation and education of women, Hortensia, is precisely that which must necessarily tend to corrupt and debilitate both the powers of mind and body. From a false notion of beauty and delicacy, their system of nerves is depraved before they come out of the nursery; and this kind of depravity has more influence over morals, than is commonly apprehended. But it would be well if such causes only acted towards the debasement of the sex; their moral education is, if possible, more absurd than their physical. The principles and nature of virtue, which is never properly explained to boys, is kept quite a mystery to girls. They are told, indeed, that they must abstain from those vices which are contrary to their personal happiness, or they will be regarded as criminals, both by God and man; but all the higher parts of rectitude, every thing that ennobles our being, and that renders us both innoxious and useful, is either not taught, or is taught in such a manner as to leave no proper impression on the mind. This is so obvious a truth, that the defects of female education have been ever a fruitful topic of declamation for the moralist; but not one of this class of writers have laid down any judicious rules for amendment. While we still retain the absurd notion of a sexual excellence, it will militate against the perfecting a plan of education for either sex. The judicious Addison animadverts on the absurdity of bringing up a young lady with no higher idea of the end of an education than to make her agreeable to a husband, and confining the necessary excellence for this happy acquisition to the mere graces of person.

Every parent and tutor may not express himself in the same manner as is marked out by Addison; yet certain it is, that the admiration of the other sex is held out as the highest honour they can attain; and whilst this is considered as their *summum bonum*, and the beauty of their persons as the chief *desideratum* of men, vanity, and its companion envy, must taint, in their characters, every native and every acquired excellence. Nor can you, Hortensia, deny, that these qualities, when united to ignorance, are fully equal to the engendering and riveting all those vices and foibles which are peculiar to the female sex; vices and foibles which have caused them to be considered, in ancient times, beneath cultivation, and in modern days subjected them to the censure and ridicule of writers of all descriptions, from the deep thinking philosopher to the man of *ton* and gallantry, who, by the bye, sometimes distinguishes himself by qualities which are not greatly superior to those he despises in women. Nor can I better illustrate the truth of this observation than by the following picture, to be found in the polite and gallant Chesterfield. 'Women', says his Lordship, 'are only children of a larger growth. They have an entertaining tattle, sometimes wit; but for solid reasoning, and good sense, I never in my life knew one that had it, or who acted or reasoned in consequence of it for four and twenty hours together. A man of sense only trifles with them, plays with them, humours and flatters them, as he does an engaging child; but he neither consults them, nor trusts them in serious matters.'

9. Helen Maria Williams
from *Letters Written in France, in the Summer of 1790*

Before I suffered my friends at Paris to conduct me though the usual routine of convents, convents, churches, and palaces, I requested to visit the Bastille; feeling a much stronger desire to contemplate the ruins of that building than the most perfect edifices of Paris. When we got into the carriage, our French servant called to the coachman, with an air of triumph, 'A la Bastille – mais nous n'y restons pas.' We drove under that porch which so many wretches have entered never to repass, and alighting from the carriage descended with difficulty into the dungeons, which were too low to admit of our standing upright, and so dark that we were obliged at noon-day to visit them with the light of a candle. We saw the hooks of those chains by which the prisoners were fastened round the neck, to the walls of their cells; many of which being below the level of the water, are in a constant state of humidity; and a noxious vapour issued from them, which more than once extinguished the candle, and was so insufferable that it required a strong spirit of curiosity to tempt one to enter. Good God! and to these regions of horror were human creatures dragged at the caprice of despotic power. What a melancholy consideration, that

> – Man! proud man,
> Dressed in a little, brief authority,

Plays such fantastic tricks before high heaven,
As make the angels weep. –

There appears to be a greater number of these dungeons than one could have imagined the hard heart of tyranny itself would contrive; for, since the destruction of the building, many subterraneous cells have been discovered underneath a piece of ground which was enclosed within the walls of the Bastille, but which seemed a bank of solid earth before the horrid secrets of this prison-house were disclosed. Some skeletons were found in these recesses, with irons still fastened on their decaying bones.

After having visited the Bastille, we may indeed be surprized, that a nation so enlightened as the French, submitted so long to the oppressions of their government; but we must cease to wonder that their indignant spirits at length shook off the galling yoke.

Those who have contemplated the dungeons of the Bastille, without rejoicing in the French revolution, may, for aught I know, be very respectable persons, and very agreeable companions in the hours of prosperity; but, if my heart were sinking with anguish, I should not fly to those persons for consolation. Sterne says, that a man is incapable of loving one woman as he ought, who has not a sort of an affection for the whole sex; and as little should I look for particular sympathy from those who have no feelings of general philanthropy. If the splendours of a despotic throne can only shine like the radiance of lightening, while all around is involved in gloom and horror, in the name of heaven let its baleful lustre be extinguished for ever.

❧ ❧ ❧ ❧

Every visitor brings me intelligence from France full of dismay and horror. I hear of nothing but crimes, assassinations, torture, and death. I am told that every day witnesses a conspiracy; that every town is the scene of a massacre; that every street is blackened with a gallows, and every highway deluged with blood. I hear these things, and repeat to myself, Is this the picture of France? Are these the images of universal joy, which called tears into my eyes, and made my heart throb with sympathy? – To me, the land which these mighty magicians have suddenly covered with darkness, where, waving their evil wand, they have reared the dismal scaffold, have clotted the knife of the assassin with gore, have called forth the shriek of despair, and the agony of torture; to me, this land of desolation appeared dressed in additional beauty beneath the genial smile of liberty. The woods seemed to cast a more refreshing shade, and the lawns to wear a brighter verdure, while the carols of freedom burst from the cottage of the peasant, and the voice of joy resounded on the hill, and in the valley.

Must I be told that my mind is perverted, that I am dead to all sensations of sympathy, because I do not weep with those who have lost a part of their superfluities, rather than rejoice that the oppressed are protected, that the wronged are redressed, that the captive is set at liberty, and that the poor have bread?

———

1791

10. Anna Barbauld
from *Epistle to William Wilberforce, Esq.*
On the Rejection of the Bill for Abolishing the Slave Trade

Cease, Wilberforce, to urge thy generous aim!
Thy country knows the sin, and stands the shame!
The preacher, poet, senator in vain
Has rattled in her sight the negro's chain;
With his deep groans assailed her startled ear,
And rent the veil that hid her constant tear;
Forced her averted eyes his stripes to scan,
Beneath the bloody scourge laid bare the man,
Claimed pity's tear, urged conscience' strong control,
And flashed conviction on her shrinking soul.
The muse too, soon awaked, with ready tongue
At mercy's shrine applausive paeans rung;
And freedom's eager sons in vain foretold
A new Astrean reign, an age of gold:
She knows and she persists – Still Afric bleeds,
Unchecked, the human traffic still proceeds;
She stamps her infamy to future time,
And on her hardened forehead seals the crime.

In vain, to thy white standard gathering round,
Wit, worth, and parts and eloquence are found:
In vain, to push to birth thy great design,
Contending chiefs, and hostile virtues join;
All, from conflicting ranks, of power possessed
To rouse, to melt, or to inform the breast.

Where seasoned tools of avarice prevail,
A nation's eloquence, combined, must fail:
Each flimsy sophistry by turns they try;
The plausive argument, the daring lie,
The artful gloss, that moral sense confounds,
The acknowledged thirst of gain that honour wounds:
Bane of ingenious minds! the unfeeling sneer,
Which sudden turns to stone the falling tear:
They search assiduous, with inverted skill,
For forms of wrong, and precedents of ill;
With impious mockery wrest the sacred page,
And glean up crimes from each remoter age:
Wrung nature's tortures, shuddering, while you tell,
From scoffing fiends bursts forth the laugh of hell;
In Britain's senate, misery's pangs give birth
To jests unseemly, and to horrid mirth –
Forbear! – thy virtues but provoke our doom,
And swell the account of vengeance yet to come;
For, not unmarked in Heaven's impartial plan,
Shall man, proud worm, condemn his fellow-man!

❋ ❋ ❋ ❋

Lo! where reclined, pale beauty courts the breeze,
Diffused on sofas of voluptuous ease;
With anxious awe her menial train around
Catch her faint whispers of half-uttered sound;
See her, in monstrous fellowship, unite
At once the Scythian and the Sybarite!
Blending repugnant vices, misallied,
Which frugal nature purposed to divide;
See her, with indolence to fierceness joined,
Of body delicate, infirm of mind,
With languid tones imperious mandates urge;
With arm recumbent wield the household scourge;
And with unruffled mien, and placid sounds,
Contriving torture, and inflicting wounds.

Nor, in their palmy walks and spicy groves,
The form benign of rural pleasure roves;
No milk-maid's song, or hum of village talk,
Soothes the lone poet in his evening walk:

No willing arm the flail unwearied plies,
Where the mixed sounds of cheerful labour rise;
No blooming maids and frolic swains are seen
To pay gay homage to their harvest queen:
No heart-expanding scenes their eyes must prove
Of thriving industry and faithful love:
But shrieks and yells disturb the balmy air,
Dull sullen looks of woe announce despair,
And angry eyes through dusky features glare.
Far from the sounding lash the muses fly,
And sensual riot drowns each finer joy.

* * * *

Friends of the friendless – Hail, ye generous band!
Whose efforts yet arrest Heaven's lifted hand,
Around whose steady brows, in union bright,
The civic wreath and Christian's palms unite:
Your merit stands, no greater and no less,
Without, or with, the varnish of success:
But seek no more to break a nation's fall,
For ye have saved yourselves – and that is all.
Succeeding times your struggles, and their fate,
With mingled shame and triumph shall relate;
While faithful history, in her various page,
Marking the features of this motley age,
To shed a glory, and to fix a stain,
Tells how you strove, and that you strove in vain.

1792

11. Mary Wollstonecraft

from *Vindication of the Rights of Woman*

After considering the historic page, and viewing the living world with
anxious solicitude, the most melancholy emotions of sorrowful indignation
have depressed my spirits, and I have sighed when obliged to confess, that
either nature has made a great difference between man and man, or that

the civilization which has hitherto taken place in the world has been very partial. I have turned over various books written on the subject of education, and patiently observed the conduct of parents and the management of schools; but what has been the result? – a profound conviction that the neglected education of my fellow-creatures is the grand source of the misery I deplore; and that women, in particular, are rendered weak and wretched by a variety of concurring causes, originating in one hasty conclusion. The conduct and manners of women, in fact, evidently prove that their minds are not in a healthy state; for, like the flowers which are planted in too rich a soil, strength and usefulness are sacrificed to beauty; and the flaunting leaves, after having pleased a fastidious eye, fade, disregarded on the stalk, long before the season when they ought to have arrived at maturity. – One cause of this barren blooming I attribute to a false system of education, gathered from the books written on the subject by men who, considering females rather as women than human creatures, have been more anxious to make them alluring mistresses than affectionate wives and rational mothers; and the understanding of the sex has been so bubbled by this specious homage, that the civilized women of the present century, with a few exceptions, are only anxious to inspire love, when they ought to cherish a nobler ambition, and by their abilities and virtues exact respect.

❋ ❋ ❋ ❋

The education of women has, of late, been more attended to than formerly; yet they are still reckoned a frivolous sex, and ridiculed or pitied by the writers who endeavour by satire or instruction to improve them. It is acknowledged that they spend many of the first years of their lives in acquiring a smattering of accomplishments; meanwhile strength of body and mind are sacrificed to libertine notions of beauty, to the desire of establishing themselves, – the only way women can rise in the world, – by marriage. And this desire making mere animals of them, when they marry they act as such children may be expected to act: – they dress; they paint, and nickname God's creatures. – Surely these weak beings are only fit for a seraglio! – Can they be expected to govern a family with judgement, or take care of the poor babes whom they bring into the world?

❋ ❋ ❋ ❋

The most perfect education, in my opinion, is such an exercise of the understanding as is best calculated to strengthen the body and form the heart. Or, in other words, to enable the individual to attain such habits of virtue as will render it independent. In fact, it is a farce to call any being virtuous whose virtues do not result from the exercise of its own reason

.... [W]omen ... have been drawn out of their sphere by false refinement, and not by an endeavour to acquire masculine qualities. Still the
regal homage which they receive is so intoxicating, that till the manners of
the time are changed, and formed on more reasonable principles, it may be
impossible to convince them that the illegitimate power, which they obtain,
by degrading themselves, is a curse, and that they must return to nature
and equality, if they wish to secure the placid satisfaction that unsophisticated affections impart. But for this epoch we must wait – wait, perhaps,
till kings and nobles, enlightened by reason, throw off their gaudy hereditary trappings: and if women do not then resign the arbitrary power of
beauty – they will prove that they have *less* mind than man.

* * * *

Many are the causes that, in the present corrupt state of society, contribute to enslave women by cramping their understandings and sharpening
their senses. One, perhaps, that silently does more mischief than all the
rest, is their disregard of order.

To do every thing in an orderly manner, is a most important precept,
which women, who, generally speaking, receive only a disorderly kind of
education, seldom attend to with that degree of exactness that men, who
from their infancy are broken into method, observe. This negligent kind of
guess-work, for what other epithet can be used to point out the random
exertions of a sort of instinctive common sense, never brought to the test
of reason? prevents their generalizing matters of fact – so they do today,
what they did yesterday, merely because they did it yesterday.

This contempt of the understanding in early life has more baneful
consequences than is commonly supposed; for the little knowledge which
women of strong minds attain is, from various circumstances, of a more
desultory kind than the knowledge of men, and it is acquired more by
sheer observations on real life, than from comparing what has been individually observed with the results of experience generalized by speculation.
Led by their dependent situation and domestic employments more into
society, what they learn is rather by snatches; and as learning is with them,
in general, only a secondary thing, they do not pursue any one branch
with that persevering ardour necessary to give vigour to the faculties and
clearness to the judgement. In the present state of society, a little learning
is required to support the character of a gentleman; and boys are obliged
to submit to a few years of discipline. But in the education of women, the
cultivation of the understanding is always subordinate to some corporeal
accomplishments; even while enervated by confinement and false notions

of modesty, the body is prevented from attaining that grace and beauty which relaxed half-formed limbs never exhibit. Besides, in youth their faculties are not brought forward by emulation; and having no serious scientific study, if they have natural sagacity it is turned too soon on life and manners. They dwell on effects, and modifications, without tracing them back to causes; and complicated rules to adjust behaviour are a weak substitute for simple principles.

* * * *

Women might certainly study the art of healing, and be physicians as well as nurses. . . . Business of various kinds, they might likewise pursue, if they were educated in a more orderly manner, which might save many from common and legal prostitution. Women would not then marry for a support, as men accept of places under a government, and neglect the implied duties; nor would an attempt to earn their own subsistence, a most laudable one! sink them almost to the level of those poor abandoned creatures who live by prostitution. For are not milliners and mantua-makers reckoned the next class? The few employments open to women, so far from being liberal, are menial; and when a superior education enables them to take charge of the education of children as governesses, they are not treated like the tutors of sons. . . . How many women thus waste life away the prey of discontent, who might have practised as physicians, regulated a farm, managed a shop, and stood erect, supported by their own industry.

* * * *

[D]ay schools, for particular ages, should be established by government, in which boys and girls might be educated together. The school for the younger children, from five to nine, should be absolutely free and open to all classes. . . . To prevent any of the distinctions of vanity, [the children] should be dressed alike, and all obliged to submit to the same discipline, or leave the school. The school-room ought to be surrounded by a large piece of ground, in which the children might be usefully exercised, for at this age they should not be confined to any sedentary employment for more than an hour at a time. But these relaxations might all be rendered a part of elementary education, for many things improve and amuse the senses, when introduced as a kind of show, to the principles of which, dryly laid down, children would turn a deaf ear. For instance, botany, mechanics, and astronomy. Reading, writing, arithmetic, natural history, and some simple experiments in natural philosophy, might fill up the day;

but these pursuits should never encroach on gymnastic plays in the open air. The elements of religion, history, the history of man, and politics, might also be taught by conversations, in the Socratic form.

After the age of nine, girls and boys, intended for domestic employments, or mechanical trades, ought to be removed to other schools, and receive instruction, in some measure appropriate to the destination of each individual, the two sexes being still together in the morning; but in the afternoon, the girls should attend a school, where plain-work, mantua-making, millinery, etc would be their employment.

The young people of superior abilities, or fortune, might now be taught, in another school, the dead and living languages, the elements of science, and continue the study of history and politics, on a more extensive scale, which would not exclude polite literature.

---

12. Clara Reeve
from *Plans of Education*

I have been assured, both by natives of the West Indies, and by those occasionally resident there, that the accounts given by the patrons of the negroes are in some instances false, and in most of the others highly exaggerated. That they are, in general, much happier than in their native country; that the grief and sullenness they show, when they are first carried over, is owing to an apprehension that they are saved only to be killed and eaten; and that, when this is cured, they soon recover their health and spirits; – that they are lazy beyond conception, and must be governed by strict discipline; that they are malicious and revengeful, and, if they had the power, would be cruel.

If their masters were cruel enough to inflict stripes and torments upon them, merely to gratify their humours, their interest would forbid it; but it is to be hoped, this can scarce ever happen. – Englishmen were never reckoned cruel, though there may have been some instances of it, as there have of the most exalted virtues in the Negro race: but these do not characterize a whole nation. It is degrading to our country and countrymen, to suppose them guilty of wanton cruelty to their slaves, and then to reason upon it, as if it were generally true. Could our enemies speak worse of us than our brethren have done?

If what the West Indians assert be true, that every Negro has a little spot of ground, and is allowed time to cultivate it; that from these the markets are supplied with vegetables; that from the produce of these, they are allowed to have merry meetings of their own race, with music, dancing, and other recreations; – that those who are careful and prudent frequently save money enough to purchase their freedom; if these things be true, and they have not yet been disproved, surely it would be better if the gentlemen engaged in the Negro cause would turn the current of their charity into another channel, and leave this matter as they found it.

* * * *

The defects in the present system of female education in this country, are generally acknowledged, by all who have considered and remarked upon it; they are, indeed, too apparent in the manners of English women of the present times. – They have formerly been celebrated for the modesty of their dress and deportment, for the purity and even sanctity of their manners. It is believed that there are still a great number of individuals, who deserve and support the national character; but it is indisputable, that the manners of our country women in general have sustained a great and alarming alteration in the course of the present century.

The decrease of marriages, the increase of divorces, the frequency of separations, bear melancholy testimony to the truth of these assertions. The great number of public victims of pride, vanity, and dissipation, are too apparent and frequent, to leave any doubt remaining of this general declension of manners.

Among those respectable women who support the national character, there are many who lament this alarming alteration; who are solicitous to stop the torrent of vice and folly, to investigate the causes of it, and to seek out a remedy.

They think this must be found in a better system of education, by which the rising generation may be preserved from the contagion of bad example, and be enabled to restore the national character of virtue, modesty, and discretion.

It is certain, that the principal causes of this declension of manners, are, first, a bad method of education; and, secondly, a series of bad examples after this education is completed. Leaving the latter article to the investigation of abler hands, we shall pursue the first, as the object of our present enquiry.

It is the general method of people of condition to give their children, from the state of infancy, to the care of nurses, and servants of a low class; to persons generally ignorant and mercenary, frequently unprincipled. These preceptors prevent the seeds of virtue from germinating, and cultivate in the young and flexible heart the weeds of pride, self-consequence, fraud, and artifice, and every bad propensity.

Those parents can never be too highly honoured, who themselves superintend the education of their children; for though they only fulfil their duties, yet, considering the great numbers who neglect them, they are entitled to praise and respect; there is no kind of education equal to that of a wise and virtuous mother; but this character is every day less common among us.

* * * *

When we consider the great increase of boarding schools, we ought not to be surprised at the increase of evils arising from them. In every town, village, or even hamlet, there are persons to be found who take upon them the great and important charge of female education: and over their doors are seen in letters of gold,

A Boarding School for Young Ladies

Adventurers of all kinds have found resources in this profession: needy foreigners, without friends or characters; broken traders; ladies of doubtful virtue; ladies' waiting maids; nay, even low and menial servants, have succeeded in raising a boarding school. What must we think of the negligence and credulity of such parents as intrust their most precious treasures, their children, the sacred deposits of heaven and their country, to the care of unknown – perhaps, ignorant, – perhaps, unprincipled people?

We do not mean to include all boarding schools under this description; we know there are some, which answer every purpose of virtuous and ingenious education, such as we encourage and recommend; but we insist, that far the greater number, are either useless, or pernicious, especially to the lower classes of people: and even among those of the better kinds, the attention is chiefly paid to external accomplishments, and the social virtues are neglected, or slightly attended to.

How often do we see the young girls come from these schools, full of pride, vanity, and self-consequence! – ignorant of the duties and virtues of a domestic life, insolent to their inferiors, proud and saucy to their equals, impertinent to their parents; without that sweet modesty and delicacy of mind and manners, which are the surest guards of female virtue, and the best omens of their future characters as wives, mothers, and mistresses of families; and which nothing can compensate for the want of.

* * * *

We have observed from the increase in boarding schools, and from the general style of education among the middling and lower ranks of people, every degree educating their children in a way above their present circumstances, and future expectations; that a great number of young women come into the world without fortunes suitable to their educations, and afterwards, by the death or misconduct of their friends, are exposed to all the dangers of a friendless situation. – Their parents are, perhaps, justly punished for their vanity and ambition; but, surely, the unfortunate sufferers are the objects of our tenderest pity; and if they fall into errors of conduct, we should reflect, that their faults are not originally their own. How often are they seduced by designing men! or become the victims of their own credulity and innocence, How are they shunned and insulted by those who never experienced their trials. The retrospect is painful; – and it is increased by the consideration of the number of victims thus sacrificed. – Among these, we find the daughters of indigent clergymen, of officers in the army and navy, of placemen of all kinds, and, in short, of all whose incomes depend on their lives, and who generally leave their children unprovided for.

1793

13. Hannah More

from *Village Politics: A Dialogue between Jack Anvil, the Blacksmith, and Tom Hod, the Mason*

Jack   What's the matter, Tom? Why dost look so dismal?

Tom   Dismal indeed! Well enough I may.

Jack   What! is the old mare dead? or work scarce?

Tom   No, no, work's plenty enough, if a man had but the heart to go to it.

Jack   What book art reading? Why dost look so like a hang dog?

Tom   (*looking on his book*) Cause enough. Why I find here that I'm very unhappy, and very miserable; which I should never have known if I had not had the good luck to meet with this book. O, 'tis a precious book!

Jack   A good sign, tho', that you can't find out you're unhappy without looking into a book for it. What is the matter?

Tom   Matter? Why, I want liberty.

Jack Liberty! What, has anyone fetched up a warrant for thee? Come, man, cheer up, I'll be bound for thee. – Thou art an honest fellow in the main, tho' thou dost tipple and prate a little too much at the Rose and Crown.

Tom No, no, I want a new constitution.

Jack Indeed! Why, I thought thou hadst been a desperate healthy fellow. Send for the doctor then.

Tom I'm not sick; I want Liberty and Equality, and the Rights of Man.

Jack O now I understand thee. What, thou art a leveller and a republican, I warrant!

Tom I'm a friend to the people. I want a reform.

Jack Then the shortest way is to mend thyself.

Tom But I want a *general reform*.

Jack Then let every one mend one.

Tom Pooh! I want freedom and happiness, the same as they have got in France.

Jack What, Tom, we imitate them? We follow the French! Why they only begun all this mischief at first in order to be just what *we* are already! Why I'd sooner go to the Negers to get learning, or to the Turks to get religion, than to the French for freedom and happiness.

Tom What do you mean by that? ar'n't the French free?

Jack Free, Tom! aye, free with a witness. They are all so free, that there's nobody safe. They make free to rob whom they will, and kill whom they will. If they don't like a man's looks, they make free to hang him without judge or jury, and the next lamp-post does for the gallows; so then they call themselves free, because you see they have no king to take them up and hang them for it.

Tom Ah, but Jack, didn't their King formerly hang people for nothing too? and, besides, weren't they all Papists before the Revolution?

Jack Why, true enough, they had but a poor sort of religion; but bad is better than none, Tom. And so was the government bad enough too; for they could clap an innocent man into prison, and keep him there too as long as they would, and never say, with your leave, or by your leave, Gentlemen of the Jury. But what's all that to us?

Tom To us! Why, don't our governors put many of our poor folks in prison against our will? What are all the gaols for? Down with the gaols, I say; all men should be free.

Jack Hark'ee, Tom, a few rogues in prison keep the rest in order, and then honest men go about their business, afraid of nobody; that's the way to be free. And let me tell thee, Tom, thou and I are tried by our peers as much as a lord is. Why the *King* can't send me to prison if I do no harm, and if I do, there's reason good why I should go there. I may go to law with Sir John, at the great castle yonder; and he no more dares lift his finger against me than if I were his equal. A lord is hanged for a hanging matter, as thou or I should be; and if it will be of any comfort to thee, I myself remember a Peer of the Realm being hanged for killing his man, just the same as the man would have been for killing *him*.

Tom   Well, that is some comfort, to be sure. – But have you read the *Rights of Man*?

Jack   No, not I: I had rather by half read the *Whole Duty of Man*. I have but little time for reading, and such as I should therefore only read a bit of the best.

❀ ❀ ❀ ❀

Tom   But I say all men are equal. Why should one be above another?

Jack   If that's thy talk, Tom, thou dost quarrel with Providence, and not with government. For the woman is below her husband, and the children are below their mother, and the servant is below his master.

❀ ❀ ❀ ❀

Tom   What, then, dost thou take French *liberty* to be?

Jack   To murder more men in one night than ever their poor king did in his whole life.

Tom   And what dost thou take a *Democrat* to be?

Jack   One who likes to be governed by a thousand tyrants, and yet can't bear a king.

Tom   What is *Equality*?

Jack   For every man to pull down every one that is above him, till they're all as low as the lowest.

Tom   What is *the new Rights of Man*?

Jack   Battle, murder, and sudden death.

Tom   What is it to be an *enlightened people*?

Jack   To put out the light of the gospel, confound right and wrong, and grope about in pitch darkness.

Tom   What is *Philosophy*, that Tim Standish talks so much about?

Jack   To believe there's neither God, nor devil, nor heaven, nor hell.

❀ ❀ ❀ ❀

Tom	And yet Tim says he never shall be happy until all these fine things are brought over to England.
Jack	What! into this Christian country, Tom? Why, dost know they have no *Sabbath*? Their mob parliament meets on a Sunday to do their wicked work, as naturally as we do to go to church. They have renounced God's word and God's day, and they don't even date in the year of our Lord. Why, dost turn pale man? And the rogues are always making such a noise, Tom, in the midst of their parliament house, that their speaker rings a bell, like our penny-postman, because he can't keep them in order.
Tom	And dost thou think our Rights of Man will lead to all this wickedness?
Jack	As sure as eggs are eggs.
Tom	I begin to think we're better off as we are.

❋ ❋ ❋ ❋

Jack	Thou art an honest fellow, Tom.
Tom	This is the Rose and Crown night, and Tim Standish is now at his mischief; but we'll go and put an end to that fellow's work.
Jack	Come along.
Tom	No; first I'll stay and burn my book, and then I'll go and make a bonfire and –
Jack	Hold, Tom. There is but one thing worse than a bitter enemy, and that is an imprudent friend. If thou woulds't show thy love to thy king and country, let's have no drinking, no riot, no bonfires; but put in practice this text, which our parson preached on last Sunday, 'Study to be quiet, work with your own hands, and mind your own business.'
Tom	And so I will, Jack – Come on.

—

14. Charlotte Smith
from *The Emigrants* (Book II)

Long wintry months are past; the moon that now
Lights her pale crescent even at noon, has made
Four times her revolution, since with step,
Mournful and slow, along the wave-worn cliff,
Pensive I took my solitary way,
Lost in despondence, while contemplating

Not my own wayward destiny alone,
(Hard as it is, and difficult to bear!)
But in beholding the unhappy lot
Of the lorn exiles; who, amid the storms
Of wild disastrous anarchy, are thrown,
Like shipwrecked sufferers, on England's coast,
To see, perhaps, no more their native land,
Where desolation riots: They, like me,
From fairer hopes and happier prospects driven,
Shrink from the future, and regret the past.
But on this upland scene, while April comes,
With fragrant airs, to fan my throbbing breast,
Fain would I snatch an interval from care,
That weighs my wearied spirit down to earth;
Courting, once more, the influence of hope
(For 'hope' still waits upon the flowery prime)
As here I mark spring's humid hand unfold
The early leaves that fear capricious winds,
While, even on sheltered banks, the timid flowers
Give, half reluctantly, their warmer hues
To mingle with the primroses' pale stars.
No shade the leafless copses yet afford,
Nor hide the mossy labours of the thrush,
That, startled, darts across the narrow path;
But quickly reassured, resumes his task,
Or adds his louder notes to those that rise
From yonder tufted brake; where the white buds
Of the first thorn are mingled with the leaves
Of that which blossoms on the brow of May.
          Ah! 'twill not be: – So many years have passed,
Since, on my native hills, I learned to gaze
On these delightful landscapes; and those years
Have taught me so much sorrow, that my soul
Feels not the joy reviving Nature brings;
But, in dark retrospect, dejected dwells
On human follies, and on human woes. –
What is the promise of the infant year,
The lively verdure, or the bursting blooms,
To those, who shrink from horrors such as war
Spreads o'er the affrighted world? With swimming eye,
Back on the past they throw their mournful looks,

And see the temple, which they fondly hoped
Reason would raise to Liberty, destroyed
By ruffian hands; while, on the ruined mass,
Flushed with hot blood, the fiend of Discord sits
In savage triumph; mocking every plea
Of Policy and Justice, as she shows
The headless corse of one, whose only crime
Was being born a monarch – Mercy turns,
From spectacle so dire, her swollen eyes;
And Liberty, with calm, unruffled brow
Magnanimous, as conscious of her strength
In Reason's panoply, scorns to disdain
Her righteous cause with carnage, and resigns
To Fraud and Anarchy the infuriate crowd.

———

15. Laetitia Hawkins
from *Letters on the Female Mind*

It cannot, I think, be truly asserted, that the intellectual powers know no difference of sex. Nature certainly intended a distinction; but it is a distinction that is far from degrading us. Instances, without doubt, may be adduced, where talents truly masculine, and of superior masculine excellence, have been bestowed on the softer sex; but they are so rare, that the union is not to be looked for. In general, and almost universally, the feminine intellect has less strength but more acuteness; consequently, in our exercise of it, we show less perseverance and more vivacity. We are not formed for those deep investigations that tend to bring to light reluctant truth; but once she has appeared . . . then it is within the female province to give her spirit and decoration, which the less flexible and less volatile male mind would fail in attempting.

That we were not designed for the exertion of intense thought, may be fairly inferred from the effect it produces on the countenance and features. The contracted brow, the prolated visage, the motionless eye-ball, and the fixed attitude, though they may give force and dignity to the strong lines of the male countenance, can give nothing to soft features that is not unpleasant . . . the new character is unsuitable and unmanageable, not only useless but oppressive.

In contemplating this subject, I have always imagined this difference to subsist between the minds of the different sexes. Male genius fetches its treasures from the depths of science, and the accumulated wisdom of ages: the female finds hers in the lighter regions of fancy and the passing knowledge of the day. There are, unquestionably, approximations between them that render it sometimes difficult to ascertain the precise point at which they diverge, as in all other works of the creation links are found which form, by regular gradations, the various dissimilarities of being into one regular progression; but still the generic and specific distinction exists, though to our obtuse faculties scarcely perceptible but when magnified by some degrees of distance.

In this age of liberality and refinement in female education, (for which no one is more thankful than myself) whatever is ingenious, shrewd, elegant, and sportive; whatever requires pathos and the energy of plaintive eloquence, may be looked for from our young women; and their invention renders the field assigned them a source of inexhaustible production, in which, while confining their attention, they do not weaken their powers, they need fear no rival; but if they prefer the mine to the flowery face of nature, if they will dig for casual diamonds instead of weaving fragrant garlands, let them not be disappointed if they fail, or angry if the trespass is retorted more to their harm.

While I confine the powers of women to lighter subjects of exertion, I would not be understood as insinuating, that they are incapable of any thing serious: I mean only that they misapply them, when, descending below the level of necessity, they fancy they find pleasure in what they are not fitted to comprehend. Dividing subjects of thought into abstruse, serious, and light, I consider only the former and the latter as peculiarly appropriated by either sex; the centre is common to both: it is the key-note uniting the two chords, equally useful and necessary to both.

The peculiar properties of the female mind I should therefore reckon acuteness of perception, vivacity of imagination, and a concatenation of invention that disdains all limit. The corporeal part of our composition here lends its aid, and while it produces, perhaps, only pains to the body, adds every possible intellectual charm to the mind: our irritable nerves are our torments and our grace; what we conceive quickly and clearly, we feel exquisitely; natural eloquence gives to these feelings the power of conveying themselves to others, and gratified with the incontrovertible testimony of our power, we are apt to suppose it of a species very different from what it really is: we take it for strength, when it is only the property of penetration; we fancy we wield a pike, when it is but a needle; and we suppose the world subdued by our arguments, when it has yielded only to our persuasions.

If this desultory sketch is believed to comprehend nearly the whole brief catalogue of female powers, where shall we look for subjects fitted to their exertions? Let not the advocate of female excellence be alarmed; the field is ample, and little is excluded from its boundary; every shrub, every flower of literature is contained within it; forest trees only are excluded: and surely no woman, who has ever contemplated the oak, will complain that she is not permitted to bear it away from its native soil.

I know no useful, and I am sure there is no ornamental science or study, that is not within the reach of a feminine capacity. Whatever the most assiduous daughter, the most active wife, or most anxious mother, even when, alas! left sole parent, can need to direct her, and enable her to discharge the duties of her station gracefully, modern education permits and includes . . . a mother may, with great comfort and credit, teach her infant son not only to read and write her own language, but she may very much lighten the most laborious part of a school education, that of learning the accidence of Latin grammar, before any idea can be obtained of what grammar is. This has been done by many ladies totally ignorant of any language but their own; how much greater then would be the advantage were they able to explain what they impose only as a charge on the memory!

Arithmetic, geography, natural philosophy, natural history, civil history, biography may be added, with the utmost propriety, to the attainment of all the languages a female education points to; and when relieved by a taste for and a perfection in music, an adroitness and delicacy in the exercise of the imitative arts, we pronounce the mind, where they have fixed their abode, an accomplished one; and if they meet a bodily form, on which the less important but more showy cares of the dancing-master have been happily bestowed, the world pronounces, and pronounces truly, that this is an accomplished woman.

✳ ✳ ✳ ✳

Admitting, then, that there are some few things locked up from female research, it remains to discover what those are. Whatever our personal strength is unequal to, will, I suppose, be granted me, as improper for our sex to engage in. To navigate a ship, or to build a church, have not yet been the objects of our emulation. The practice of physic in its extent, the toil of pleading at the bar, and the vigils of other occupations, have not yet held forth allurements sufficient to attract us. Divinity has an aspect less attractive than almost any other study, when operating on a lively imagination, and I trust no ladies will think me injurious to their rights, if I dismiss it from the catalogue of their studies.

16. Mary Hays
from *Letters and Essays*

Of all bondage, mental bondage is surely the most fatal; the absurd despotism which has hitherto, with more than gothic barbarity, enslaved the female mind, the enervating and degrading system of manners by which the understandings of women have been chained down to frivolity and trifles, have increased the general tide of effeminacy and corruption. To conform to the perpetual fluctuation of fashion . . . requires almost their whole time and attention, and leaves little leisure for intellectual improvement. . . . It has been alleged, that this constant variation of mode is serviceable to commerce, and promotes a brisk circulation of money; or with more propriety it might be said a quick succession of bankruptcies: but however this may be, it is I conceive making too expensive an offering at the golden shrine of Plutus to sacrifice all the dignified and rational pursuits of life. A few distinguished individuals, feeling the powers of their own minds (for what can curb the celestial energy of genius?) are endeavouring to dispel the magical illusions of custom, and restore degraded woman to the glory of rationality, and to a fitness for immortality. The rights of woman, and the name of Wollstonecraft, will go down to posterity with reverence, when the pointless sarcasms of witlings are forgotten. I am aware that some men of real good sense and candour, have supposed that the idea of there being no sexual character, is carried in this admirable work a little too far. Let them reflect for a moment on the extremes which the opposite opinion has produced; and say from whence arises the most formidable danger? Is there any cause to apprehend that we may subject our feelings too much to the guidance of reason? Or that we shall conduct the business of our families with too much order and equity: to the wise and good only, I now appeal! would you not dare to give up any of the allurements of the mistress (if indeed any need to be given up worth the preserving) to the refined pleasure of living with a rational and equal companion? In such an intercourse, when enlivened by love, if happiness resides on earth, surely it is to be found! where the advantages are reciprocal, for each reflects back with interest, the light they receive. Similarity of mind and principle is the only true basis of harmony. Great superiority of either side causes a narrow jealousy, or a painful constraint; there is nothing so irksome as to converse with people who cannot understand you. . . .

Let those who love influence seek it by surer methods; bolts and bars may confine for a time the feeble body, but can never enchain the noble, the free-born mind; the only true grounds of power are reason and affection, vows of obedience are lighter than vanity, but the sensible heart rejoices to anticipate the wishes of the object of its tenderness. Ye simple men! so tenacious of your prerogative, insinuate yourselves gently into our affections and understandings, respect in us the majesty of rationality, upon which you so justly value yourselves, and ye will have no cause to complain that like wayward children, spoilt by equally misjudged caresses and correction, we in fact tyrannise over you by our caprices, while you are deluded with mock ensigns of power. And even while this is not the case, and the brute prevails over the weak infant, or the heart-broken slave, say! what are the mighty advantages you reap from your dear-bought victory? Sullen acquiescence, gloomy resignation, fretful impatience, or degrading servility; all the virtues of the woman (for virtue is not the child of constraint) sunk in the poor spiritless contemptible slave. . . .

Lovers of truth! be not partial in your researches. Men of sense and science! remember, by degrading our understandings, you incapacitate us for knowing your value, and make coxcombs take place of you in our esteem. The ignorant and the vulgar prove their cunning by levelling principles; but you! how impolitic to throw a veil over our eyes, that we may not distinguish the radiance that surrounds you!

—

1794

17. Hester Lynch Piozzi
from *British Synonymy*

TO ABANDON, FORSAKE, RELINQUISH, GIVE UP, DESERT, QUIT, LEAVE.
Of these seven verbs then, so variously derived, though at first sight apparently synonymous, conversing does certainly better shew the peculiar appropriation, than books, however learned; for whilst through them by study all due information may certainly be obtained, familiar talk tells us in half an hour. – That a man FORSAKES his mistress, ABANDONS all hope of regaining her lost esteem, RELINQUISHES his pretensions in favour of another; GIVES UP a place of trust he held under the government,

DESERTS his party, LEAVES his parents in affliction, and QUITS the king-dom forever.

Other instances will quickly prove to a foreigner that 'tis a well-received colloquial phrase to say, You LEAVE London for the country. Telling us you QUIT it seems to convey a notion of your going suddenly to the Continent. – That any one DESERTS it can scarcely be said with propriety, unless at a time of pestilence or tumults of a dangerous nature, when we observe that the capital is DESERTED: although by an overstrained com-pliment a lady may possibly hear such a word from a man who pretends affectedly to consider her desertion of the metropolis as half criminal. That you GIVE UP London looks as if you meant in future to reside upon your own estate in the country, I think; while to RELINQUISH a town life seems as if something was required to make the sentence complete – as we RELINQUISH the joys of society for the tranquil sweets of solitude – and the like. To FORSAKE London would be a foppish expression; and to say we were going to ABANDON it, as if it could scarcely subsist without us, would set people a'laughing. The participles from these verbs evince the various acceptations of their principles. – That fellow is GIVEN UP to every vice, is an expression popular and common; but when we speak of him as ABANDONED of all virtue, or FORSAKEN of all good, the phrase approaches to solemnity, and is at least expressive of the man's total ruin even in this transitory world.

He is now nearly GIVEN UP by society, say people in common con-versation, when telling rakish stories of a man whose conduct has merited the neglect of his virtuous companions; but soon as they describe a human creature DESERTED of every friend, and LEFT on a desolate island, ABANDONED to sorrow and remorse; new sensations are excited, commiseration takes its turn, nor can the most rigid refuse pity in such a state of distress.

❋ ❋ ❋ ❋

FANCY, IMAGINATION

These elegant and airy substantives are not, as one might at first suspect, wholly synonymous. A well-instructed foreigner will soon discern, that though in poetry there seems little distinction, yet when they both come to be talked of in a conversation circle we do say, that Milton has displayed a boundless IMAGINATION in his poem of Paradise Lost – transporting us as it were into the very depths of eternity, while he describes the journey of Satan and the games of the fallen angels, but that Pope's Rape of the Lock is a work of exquisite FANCY, almost emulative of Shakespeare's creative powers – not servilely imitating him. An intelligent stranger will observe too, that although we give sex very arbitrarily to personified qualities – yet he will commonly find FANCY feminine, IMAGINATION masculine, I scarce know why.

———

1795

18. Maria Edgeworth
from *Letters for Literary Ladies*

[Letter from a Gentleman to his Friend upon the Birth of a Daughter]
Women of literature are much more numerous of late than they were a few years ago. They make a class in society, they fill the public eye, and have acquired a degree of consequence and an appropriate character. The esteem of private friends, and the admiration of the public for their talents, are circumstances highly flattering to their vanity; and as such will allow them to be substantial pleasures. I am also ready to acknowledge that a taste for literature adds much to the happiness of life, and that women may enjoy to a certain degree this happiness, as well as men. But with literary women this silent happiness seems at best but a subordinate consideration; it is not by the treasures they possess, but by those which they have an opportunity of displaying, that they estimate their wealth. To obtain public applause, they are betrayed too often into a miserable ostentation of their learning. . . .

The pleasure of being admired for wit or erudition, I cannot exactly measure in a female mind; but state it to be as delightful as you can imagine it to be, there are evils attendant upon it, which, in the estimation of a prudent father, may overbalance the good. The intoxicating effect of wit upon the brain has been well remarked by a poet, who was a friend to the fair sex; and too many ridiculous, and too many disgusting examples confirm the truth of the observation. The deference that is paid to genius, sometimes makes the fair sex forget, that genius will be respected only when united with discretion. Those who have acquired fame, fancy that they can afford to sacrifice reputation. I will suppose, however, that their heads shall be strong enough to bear inebriating admiration, and that their conduct shall be essentially irreproachable; yet they will show in their manners and conversation that contempt of inferior minds, and that neglect of common forms and customs, which will provoke the indignation of fools, and which cannot escape the censure of the wise. Even whilst we are secure of their innocence, we dislike that daring spirit in the female sex, which delights to oppose the common opinions of society, and from apparent trifles we draw unfavourable omens, which experience too often confirms. You ask me why I should suppose that wits are more liable to be spoiled by admiration than beauties, who have usually a larger share of it, and who are not more exempt from vanity? Those who are vain of trifling accomplishments, of rank, of riches, or of beauty, depend upon the world for their immediate gratification. They are sensible of their dependence; they listen with deference to the maxims, and attend with anxiety the opinions of those, from whom they expect their reward and their daily amusements. In their subjection consists their safety, whilst women, who neither feel dependent for amusement nor for self-approbation upon company and public places, are apt to consider this subjection as humiliating, if not insupportable: perceiving their own superiority, they despise, and even set at defiance, the opinions of their acquaintance of inferior abilities: contempt, where it cannot be openly retorted, produces aversion, not the less to be dreaded because constrained to silence: envy, considered as the involuntary tribute extorted by merit, is flattering to pride: and I know that many women delight to excite envy, even whilst they affect to fear its consequences. But they who imprudently provoke it, are little aware of the torments they prepare for themselves.

. . . Men of literature, if we may trust to the bitter expressions of anguish in their writings, and in their private letters, feel acutely all the stings of envy. Women, who have more susceptibility of temper, and less strength of mind, and who, from the delicate nature of their reputation, are more exposed to attack, are also less able to endure it. Malignant critics, when they cannot attack an author's peace in his writings, frequently scrutinize his private life; and every personal anecdote is published without regard to truth or propriety. How will the delicacy of the female character endure this treatment? how will her friends bear to see her pursued even in domestic retirement, if she should be wise enough to make that retirement her choice? how will they like to see premature memoirs, and spurious collections of familiar letters published by needy booksellers or designing enemies? Yet to all these things men of letters are subject; and such must literary ladies expect, if they attain to any degree of eminence. – Judging, then, from the experience of our sex, I may pronounce envy to be one of the evils which women of uncommon genius have to dread.

. . . Your daughter, perhaps, shall be above scandal. She shall despise the idle whisper, and the common tattle of her sex; her soul shall be raised above the ignorant and the frivolous; she shall have a relish for higher conversation, and a taste for higher society. But, where is she to find this society? how is she to obtain this society? You make her incapable of friendship with her own sex. Where is she to look for friends, for companions, for equals? Amongst men? Amongst what class of men? Not amongst men of business, or men of gallantry, but amongst men of literature.

... [L]earned men have usually chosen for their wives, or for their companions, women who were rather below than above the standard of mediocrity: this seems to me natural and reasonable. Such men, probably, feel their own incapacity for the daily business of life, their ignorance of the world, and neglect of domestic affairs. They do not want wives who have precisely their own defects; they rather desire to find such as shall, by the opposite habits and virtues, supply their deficiencies. I do not see why two books should marry, any more than two estates.

* * * *

[Answer to the Preceding Letter]
Do not, my dear Sir, call me *a champion for the rights of women*; I am more intent upon their happiness than ambitious to enter into a metaphysical discussion of their rights. Their happiness is so nearly connected with ours, that it seems to me absurd to manage any argument so as to set the two sexes at variance by vain contention for superiority. It is not our object to make an invidious division of rights and privileges, but to determine what is most for our general advantage.

* * * *

You apprehend that knowledge must be hurtful to the sex, because it will be the means of their acquiring power. It seems to me impossible that woman can acquire the species of direct power which you dread: the manners of society must totally change before women can mingle with men in the busy and public scenes of life. They must become Amazons before they can effect this change; they must cease to be women before they can desire it. The happiness of neither sex could be increased by this metamorphosis: the object cannot be worth the price. ... If, my dear Sir, it be your object to monopolize power for our sex, you cannot possibly better secure it from the wishes of the other, than by enlightening their minds, and enlarging their views of human affairs. The common fault of all ignorant and ill-educated women is a love for dominion: this they shew in every petty struggle where they are permitted to act in private life. You are afraid that the same disposition should have a larger field for its display; and you believe this temper to be inherent in the sex. I doubt whether any temper be *natural*, as it is called: certainly this disposition need not be attributed to any innate cause; it is the consequence of their erroneous education.

❀ ❀ ❀ ❀

You dislike in the female sex that daring spirit which despises the common forms of society, and which breaks through the delicacy and reserve of female manners. So do I. And the best method to make my pupil respect these things, is to shew her how they are indispensibly connected with the best interests of society, and with their highest pleasures. Till of late, women were kept in Turkish ignorance; every means of acquiring knowledge was discountenanced by fashion, and impracticable even to those who despised fashion: Our books of science were full of unintelligible jargon, and mystery veiled pompous ignorance from public contempt: but now, writers must offer their discoveries to the public in distinct terms, which every body may understand; technical language no longer supplies the place of knowledge, and the art of teaching has been carried to great perfection by the demand for learning: all this is in favour of women. Many things which were thought to be above their comprehension, or unsuited to their sex, have now been found to be perfectly within the compass of their abilities.

❀ ❀ ❀ ❀

I do not desire to make my daughter a musician, a painter, or a poetess; I do not desire to make her a botanist, a mathematician, or a chemist; but I wish to give her the habit of industry and attention, the love of knowledge and the power of reasoning: these will enable her to attain excellence in any pursuit of science or of literature. Her tastes and occupations will, I hope, be determined by her situation, and by the wishes of her friends: she will consider all accomplishments and all knowledge as subordinate to her first object, the contributing to their happiness and her own.

———

19. Ann Yearsley
Anarchy

Furies! Why sleep amid the carnage? – rise!
    Bring up my wolves of war, my pointed spears.
Daggers, yet reeking, banners filled with sighs,
    And paint your cheeks with gore, and lave your locks in tears.

On yon white bosom see that happy child!
    Seize it, deface its infant charms! And say,
Anarchy viewed its mangled limbs and smiled.
    Strike the young mother to the earth! – Away!
This is my era! O'er the dead I go!
    From my hot nostrils minute murders fall!
Behind my burning car lurks feeble Woe!
    Filled with my dragon's ire, my slaves for kingdoms call!
Hear them not, Father of the ensanguined race! –
World! Give my monsters way! – Death! keep thy steady chase!

20. Ann Yearsley
from *Dedicated to Louis XVI*

    Cold was the star
That ruled my natal hour! and pale the beams
That trembled o'er my head, as they distilled
The damps of woe – yet soon! bear witness Heaven!
I loved thee, Contemplation! And, by thee
I was beloved – O mutual bliss! The Night
Threw off her sadness, when with thee I lay
Dissolved in grateful wonder! Worlds on worlds,
Ponderous with their inhabitants came on –

And still another, and another rolled,
Forced by the arm of Time from the dark breast
Of great Eternity; the Infinite
At length shut up my wearied sense, and gave
A guiltless slumber. – Dawn no sooner shed
Her tints in wild profusion from the East,
Than cheered I rose to follow thee. How oft
We paused on ruined towers, watched down the moon,
And listened to the mariner afar,
Who sang across the main? To my young eye
Thou helds't aerial vision. There I saw
Unshapely Matter moving into life;
Myriads of atoms glistening in the wind –
Insects conglobed, and yet so finely formed,
That Zephyr breathed them into being – Tones

Of harmony they gave too thin to touch
The nerve of mortal hearing. Taught by thee,
My soul expanded, soared, and stooped again
To view the animalcula that join
Eternally through minutes, days and years;
Tilling the mighty universe. Thus charmed
By Contemplation, my rough passions sleep;
Whilst heavenly Sympathy, to Nature true,
Droops her white pinions, mourns the ills of War,
And through her tears e'en foes forget to frown.

* * * *

Much soothing do they need who bite their bread
With insult! Wildly grand are they are they whose souls
Rise stubborn from despair! Superior he
Who lulls them to repose! – You'll say, great Sire!
That blessings are divided; and that all
Are not to crowns hereditary heirs.
But since such passions in the heart of man
For ever lurk, be it your tenderest care
Not to provoke them with the barbed dart
Of hot Oppression. For the haughty train,
The elder sons of Gallia, bid them grace
The bosom with a star, within their halls
Hang high their family achievements; lay
Luxurious purple on their pillows, sink
To Sapphic measures, but whilst melting thus,
O! bid them spare a brother's heart! 'Tis vile!
So wantonly to loose the wolves of law
On that defenceless frame whose fortune pleads
Against its wretched owner. Plunge not man
So deeply down within your prison walls,
To linger out the bloom of life! Draw near
This iron grate, and you shall hear the groan
Of a dejected Father! Cold Despair
Shall on your forehead breathe its piteous blast,
And foul contagion spot you! Is it well
To charge this dungeon with the human heart!
Where it must long be perishing? Behold
How dismal spectres sweep along the walls,
Frightening the angel Pity from her stand.

Go; tell your Legislators! were your laws
More lenient, Gallia's crown would closer sit
On him who wears it. Know – though horrid gloom
Wrap the lost captive from a social world;
Not unobserving is that world; the bands
Of Friendship bind the wretched link unseen;
Millions of spirits, who to woe inured,
Shall burst upon the light, when sanguine power
Shall sink abashed, and see her fetters rust.

1796

21. Mary Wollstonecraft
from *Letters Written during a Short Residence in Sweden, Norway and Denmark*

To save the sailors any further toil, I had my baggage instantly removed into [the pilot's] boat; for, as he could speak English, a previous parley was not necessary; though Marguerite's respect for me could hardly keep her from expressing the fear, strongly marked on her countenance, which my putting ourselves into the power of a strange man excited. He pointed out his cottage; and, drawing near to it, I was not sorry to see a female figure, though I had not, like Marguerite, been thinking of robberies, murders, or the other evil which instantly, as the sailors would have said, runs foul of a woman's imagination.

On entering, I was still better pleased to find a clean house, with some degree of rural elegance. The beds were of muslin, coarse it is true, but dazzlingly white; and the floor was strewed over with little sprigs of juniper (the custom, as I afterwards found, of the country), which formed a contrast with the curtains and produced an agreeable sensation of freshness, to soften the ardour of noon. Still nothing was so pleasing as the alacrity of hospitality – all that the house afforded was quickly spread on the whitest linen. – Remember I had just left the vessel, where, without being fastidious, I had continually been disgusted. Fish, milk, butter, and cheese, and I am sorry to add, brandy, the bane of this country, were spread on the board.

After we had dined, hospitality made them, with some degree of mystery, bring us some excellent coffee. I did not know then that it was prohibited.

The good man of the house apologized for coming in continually, but declared that he was so glad to speak English, he could not stay out. He need not have apologized; I was equally glad of his company. With the wife I could only exchange smiles; and she was employed observing the make of our clothes. My hands, I found, had first led her to discover that I was the lady. I had, of course, my quantum of reverences; for the politeness of the north seems to partake of the coldness of the climate, and the rigidity of its iron sinewed rocks. Amongst the peasantry, there is, however, so much of the simplicity of the golden age in this land of flint – so much overflowing of heart, and fellow-feeling, that only benevolence, and the honest sympathy of nature, diffused smiles over my countenance when they kept me standing, regardless of my fatigue, whilst they dropped courtesy after courtesy.

✻ ✻ ✻ ✻

Though my host amused me with an account of himself, which gave me an idea of the manners of the people I was about to visit, I was eager to climb the rocks to view the country, and see whether the honest tars had regained their ship. With the help of the lieutenant's telescope I saw the vessel under-way with a fair though gentle gale. The sea was calm, playful even as the most shallow stream, and on the vast basin I did not see a dark speck to indicate the boat. My conductors were consequently arrived.

Straying further, my eye was attracted by the sight of some heart's-ease that peeped through the rocks. I caught at it as a good omen, and going to preserve it in a letter that had not conveyed balm to my heart, a cruel remembrance suffused my eyes; but it passed away like an April shower. If you are deep read in Shakespeare, you will recollect that this was the little western flower tinged by love's dart, which 'maidens call love in idleness'. The gaiety of my babe was unmixed; regardless of omens or sentiments, she found a few wild strawberries more grateful than flowers or fancies.

The lieutenant informed me that this was a commodious bay. Of that I could not judge, though I felt its picturesque beauty. Rocks were piled on rocks, forming a suitable bulwark to the ocean. Come no further, they emphatically said, turning their dark sides to the waves to augment the idle roar. The view was sterile: still little patches of earth, of the most exquisite verdure, enamelled with the sweetest wild flowers, seemed to promise the goats and a few straggling cows luxurious herbage. How silent and peaceful was the scene. I gazed around with rapture, and felt more of that spontaneous

pleasure which gives credibility to our expectation of happiness, than I
had for a long, long time. I forgot all the horrors I had witnessed in France,
which had cast a gloom over all nature, and suffering the enthusiasm of my
character, too often, gracious God! damped by the tears of disappointed
affection, to be lighted up afresh, care took wing while simple fellow feeling
expanded my heart.

* * * *

   Nothing, in fact, can equal the beauty of the northern summer's evening
and night; if night it may be called that only wants the glare of day, the full
light, which frequently seems so impertinent; for I could write at midnight
very well without a candle. I contemplated all nature at rest; the rocks, even
grown darker in their appearance, looked as if they partook of the general
repose, and reclined more heavily on their foundation. – What, I exclaimed,
is this active principle which keeps me still awake? – Why fly my thoughts
abroad when every thing around me appears at home? My child was sleeping with equal calmness – innocent and sweet as the closing flowers. –
Some recollections, attached to the idea of home, mingled with reflections
respecting the state of society I had been contemplating that evening, made
a tear drop on the rosy cheek I had just kissed; and emotions that trembled
on the brink of ecstasy and agony gave a poignancy to my sensations,
which made me feel more alive than usual.
   What are these imperious sympathies? How frequently has melancholy
and even misanthropy taken possession of me, when the world has disgusted me, and friends have proved unkind. I have then considered myself
as a particle broken off from the grand mass of mankind; – I was alone, till
some involuntary sensation, like the attraction of adhesion, made me feel I
was still part of a mighty whole, from which I could not sever myself – not,
perhaps, for the reflection has been carried very far, by snapping the thread
of an existence which loses its charms in proportion as the cruel experience
of life stops or poisons the current of the heart. Futurity, what hast thou to
give to those who know that there is such a thing as happiness! I speak not
of philosophical contentment, though pain has afforded them the
strongest conviction of it.

* * * *

. . . a sort of weak melancholy . . . hung about my heart at parting from my
daughter for the first time.
   You know that as a female I am particularly attached to her – I feel more
than a mother's fondness and anxiety, when I reflect on the dependent and

oppressed state of her sex. I dread lest she should be forced to sacrifice her heart to her principles, or principles to her heart. With trembling hand I cultivate sensibility, and cherish delicacy of sentiment, lest, while I lend fresh blushes to the rose, I sharpen the thorns that will wound the breast I would fain guard – I dread to unfold her mind, lest it should render her unfit for the world she is to inhabit – Hapless woman! what a fate is thine!

❀ ❀ ❀ ❀

I have often mentioned the grandeur, but I feel myself unequal to the task of conveying an idea of the beauty and elegance of the scene when the spiral tops of the pines are loaded with ripening seed, and the sun gives a glow to their light green tinge, which is changing into purple, one tree more or less advanced, contrasting with another. The profusion with which nature has decked them, with pendant honours, prevents all surprise at seeing, in every crevice, some sapling struggling for existence. Vast masses of stone are thus encircled; and roots, torn up by the storms, become a shelter for a young generation. The pine and fir woods, left entirely to nature, display an endless variety; and the paths in the wood are not entangled with fallen leaves, which are only interesting whilst they are fluttering between life and death. The grey cobweb-like appearance of the aged pines is a much finer form of decay; the fibres whitening as they lose their moisture, imprisoned life seems to be stealing away. I cannot tell why – but death, in every form, appears to me like something getting free – to expand in I know not what element; nay I feel that this conscious being must be as unfettered, have the wings of thought, before it can be happy.

Reaching the cascade, or rather cataract, the roaring of which had a long time announced its vicinity, my soul was hurried by the falls into a new train of reflections. The impetuous dashing of the rebounding torrent from the dark cavities which mocked the exploring eye, produced an equal activity in my mind: my thoughts darted from earth to heaven, and I asked myself why I was chained to life and its misery? Still the tumultuous emotions this sublime object excited, were pleasurable; and, viewing it, my soul rose, with renewed dignity, above its cares – grasping at immortality – it seemed as impossible to stop the current of my thoughts, as of the always varying, still the same, torrent before me – I stretched out my hand to eternity, bounding over the dark speck of life to come.

22. Mary Robinson
from *Sappho and Phaon*

II: The Temple of Chastity

High on a rock, coeval with the skies,
    A temple stands, reared by immortal powers
    To Chastity divine! ambrosial flowers
Twining round icicles, in columns rise,
Mingling with pendent gems of orient dyes!
    Piercing the air, a golden crescent towers,
Veiled by transparent clouds; while smiling hours
Shake from their varying wings – celestial joys!
    The steps of spotless marble, scattered o'er
With deathless roses armed with many a thorn,
    Lead to the altar. On the frozen floor,
Studded with tear-drops petrified by scorn,
    Pale vestals kneel the Goddess to adore,
While Love, his arrows broke, retires forlorn.

X: Describes Phaon

Dangerous to hear, is that melodious tongue,
    And fatal to the sense those murderous eyes,
    Where in a sapphire sheath, Love's arrow lies,
Himself concealed the crystal haunts among!
Oft o'er that form, enamoured have I hung,
    On that smooth cheek to mark the deepening dyes,
    While from that lip the fragrant breath would rise,
That lip, like Cupid's bow with rubies strung!
    Still let me gaze upon that polished brow,
O'er which the golden hair luxuriant plays;
    So, on the modest lily's leaves of snow
The proud sun revels in resplendent rays!
    Warm as his beams the sensate heart shall glow,
Till life's last hour, with Phaon's self decays!

XII: Previous to her Interview with Phaon

Now, o'er the tessellated pavement strew
    Fresh saffron, steeped in essence of the rose,
    While down yon agate column gently flows

A glittering streamlet of ambrosial dew!
My Phaon smiles! the rich carnation's hue,
    On his flushed cheek in conscious lustre glows,
    While o'er his breast enamoured Venus throws
Her starry mantle of celestial blue!
    Breathe soft, ye dulcet flutes among the trees
Where clustering boughs with golden citron twine;
    While slow vibrations, dying on the breeze,
Shall soothe his soul with harmony divine!
    Then let my form his yielding fancy seize,
    And all his fondest wishes, blend with mine.

XXII: Phaon Forsakes Her

Wild is the foaming sea! The surges roar!
And nimbly dart the livid lightnings round!
    On the rent rock the angry waves rebound;
Ah me! the lessening bark is seen no more!
Along the margin of the trembling shore,
    Loud as the blast my frantic cries shall sound,
    My storm drenched limbs the flinty fragments wound,
And o'er my bleeding breast the billows pour!
    Phaon! return! ye winds, O! waft the strain
To his swift bark; ye barbarous waves forbear!
    Taunt not the anguish of a lover's brain
Nor feebly emulate the soul's despair!
    For howling winds, and foaming seas, in vain
Assail the breast, when passion rages there!

XLIII: Her Reflections on the Leucadian Rock before she Perishes

While from the dizzy precipice I gaze,
    The world receding from my pensive eyes,
    High o'er my head the tyrant eagle flies,
Clothed in the sinking sun's transcendent gaze!
The meek-eyed moon, midst clouds of amber plays
    As o'er the purpling plains of light she hies,
    Till the last stream of living lustre dies,
And the cool concave owns her tempered rays!
    So shall this glowing, palpitating soul,
Welcome returning Reason's placid beam,
    While o'er my breast the waves Lethean roll,

To calm rebellious Fancy's feverish dream;
   Then shall my lyre disdain love's dread control,
And loftier passions, prompt the loftier theme!

1797

23. Mary Wollstonecraft
On Poetry, and Our Relish for the Beauties of Nature

A taste for rural scenes, in the present state of society, appears to me to be very often an artificial sentiment, rather inspired by poetry and romances, than a real perception of the beauties of nature; but, as it is reckoned a proof of refined taste to praise the calm pleasure which the country affords, the theme is exhausted; yet, it may be made a question, whether this romantic kind of declamation has much effect on the conduct of those who leave, for a season, the crowded cities in which they were bred.

I have been led into these reflections by observing, when I have resided for any length of time in the country, how few people seem to contemplate nature with their own eyes. I have 'brushed the dew away' in the morning; but, pacing over the printless grass, I have wondered that, in such delightful situations, the sun was allowed to rise in solitary majesty, whilst my eyes alone hailed its beautifying beams. The webs of the evening have still been spread across the hedged path, unless some labouring man, trudging to work, disturbed the fairy structure; yet, in spite of this supineness, on joining the social circle, every tongue rang changes on the pleasures of the country.

Having frequently had occasion to make the same observation, in one of my solitary rambles I was led to endeavour to trace the cause, and likewise to enquire why the poetry, written in the infancy of society, is most natural: which, strictly speaking (for natural is a very indefinite expression) is merely to say, that it is the transcript of immediate emotions, when fancy, awakened by the view of interesting objects, in all their native wildness and simplicity, was most actively at work. At such moments, sensibility quickly furnishes similes, and the sublimed spirits combine with happy facility – images, which, spontaneously bursting on him, it is not necessary coldly to ransack the understanding or memory, till the laborious efforts of judgement exclude present sensations, and damp the fire of enthusiasm.

The effusions of a vigorous mind will, nevertheless, ever inform us how far the faculties have been enlarged by thought, and stored with knowledge. The richness of the soil even appears on the surface; and the result of profound thinking often mixing with playful grace in the reveries of the poet, smoothly incorporates with the ebullitions of animal spirits, when the finely fashioned nerve vibrates acutely with rapture, or when relaxed by soft melancholy, a pleasing languor prompts the long-drawn sigh, and feeds the slowly falling tear.

The poet, the man of strong feelings, only gives us a picture of his mind when he was actually alone, conversing with himself, and marking the impression which nature made on his own heart. If, during these sacred moments, the idea of some departed friend, some tender recollection, when the soul was most alive to tenderness, intruded unawares into his mind, the sorrow which it produces is artlessly, but poetically expressed; and who can avoid sympathizing?

Love of man leads to devotion. Grand and sublime images strike the imagination. God is seen in every floating cloud, and comes from the misty mountains to receive the noblest homage of an intelligent creature – praise. How solemn is the moment, when all affections and remembrances fade before the sublime admiration which the wisdom and goodness of God inspires, when he is worshipped in a temple not made with hands, and the world seems to contain only the mind that formed and contemplates it. These are not the weak responses of ceremonial devotion; nor to express them would the poet need another poet's aid. No: his heart burns within him, and he speaks the language of truth and nature, with resistless energy.

Inequalities, of course, are observable in his effusions; and a less vigorous imagination, with more taste, would have produced more elegance and uniformity. But as passages are softened or expunged, during the cooler moments of reflection, the understanding is gratified at the expense of those involuntary sensations which, like the beauteous tints of an evening sky, are so evanescent, that they melt into new forms before they can be analysed. For, however eloquently we may boast of our reason, man must often be delighted he cannot tell why, or his blunt feelings are not made to relish the beauties which nature, poetry, or any of the imitative arts afford.

The imagery of the ancients appears naturally to have been borrowed from the surrounding objects, and their mythology. When a hero is to be transported from one place to another across pathless wastes, is any vehicle so natural as one of the fleecy clouds, on which he has often gazed, scarcely conscious that he wished to make it his chariot. Again; when nature seems to present obstacles to his progress at almost every step, when the tangled forest and steep mountain stand as barriers, to pass over which, the mind longs for supernatural aid; an interposing deity, created by love or fear, who walks on the waves, and rules the storm, severely felt in the first attempts to cultivate a country, will receive from the impassioned fancy a local habitation and a name.

It would be a philosophical enquiry, and throw some light on the history of the human mind, to trace, as far as our information will allow us, the spontaneous feelings and ideas which have produced the images that now frequently appear unnatural, because they are remote, and disgusting, because they have been servilely copied by poets, whose habits of thinking and views of nature must have been different; for the understanding seldom disturbs the currents of our present feelings, without dissipating the gay clouds which fancy has been embracing; yet, it silently gives the colour to the whole tenor of them, and the reverie is over when truth is grossly violated, or imagery introduced, selected from books, and not from local manners, or popular prejudices.

In a more advanced state of civilization, a poet is rather a creature of art than nature; the books that he peruses in his youth, become a hot-bed, in which artificial fruits are produced, beautiful to a common eye, though they want the true hue and flavour. His images do not flow from imagination, but are servile copies; and, like the works of the painters who copy ancient statues when they draw men and women of their own times, we acknowledge that the features are fine, the proportions just, still they are men of stone; insipid figures, that never convey to the mind the idea of a portrait taken from the life, where the soul gives spirit and homogeneity to the whole form. The silken wings of fancy are shrivelled by rules, and a desire of attaining elegance of diction occasions an attention to words, incompatible with sublime impassioned thoughts.

A boy of abilities, who has been taught the structure of verse at school, and has been roused by emulation to compose rhymes whilst he was reading works of genius, may, by practice, produce pretty verses, and even become what is often termed an elegant poet; though his readers, without well knowing where the fault lies, do not find themselves warmly interested. In the productions of the poets who fasten on their affections, they see grosser defects, and the very images and allusions which shocked their taste; yet they do not appear as puerile or extrinsic in one as the other. Why? Because they did not appear so to the author.

It may sound paradoxical, after observing that those productions want vigour that are the work of imitation, in which the understanding violently directed, if not extinguished, the blaze of fancy, to assert, that though genius be allowed to be only another word for strong imagination, the first observers of nature exercised their judgement much more than their imitators. But they exercised it to discriminate things, whilst their followers were busy borrowing sentiments and arranging words.

Boys who have received a classical education load their memory with words, and the correspondent ideas are, perhaps, never distinctly comprehended. As a proof of this assertion I must mention as a fact, that I have known many young people who could write tolerably smooth verses, and string epithets prettily together, when their prose themes showed the barrenness; or, more justly speaking, how superficial the cultivation must have been, which their understanding had received.

Dr Johnson, I know, has taken some pains to prove, that a strong mind, accidentally led to some particular study in which it excels, is a genius. Not to stop to investigate the causes which produced this happy strength of mind, it is sufficient to remark, that the world has agreed to denominate those men of genius, who have pursued a particular art or science, after the bent of nature has been displayed in obstinate perseverance or fond attachment to a particular study. Dr Johnson, in fact, appears sometimes to be of the same opinion; especially when he observes 'that Thomson looked on nature with the eye which she only gives a poet'.

And, to return to the first object of discussion, the reason why most people are more interested by a scene described by a poet than by a view of nature, probably arises from the want of a lively imagination. The poet contrasts the prospect, and selecting the most picturesque parts in his camera, the judgement is directed, and the whole attention of the languid faculty turned towards the objects which excited the most forcible emotions in the poet's heart, firing his imagination; the reader consequently feels the enlivened description, though he was not able to receive a first impression from the operations of his own mind.

Besides, it may be further observed, that uncultivated minds are only to be moved by forcible representations. To rouse the thoughtless, objects must be contrasted, calculated to excite tumultuous emotions. The unsubstantial picturesque forms which a contemplative man gazes on, and often follows with ardour till mocked by a glimpse of unattainable excellence, appear to them the light vapours of a dreaming enthusiast, who gives up the substance for the shadow. It is not within that they seek amusement, their eyes are rarely turned back on themselves; of course, their emotions, though sometimes fervid, are always transient, and the nicer perceptions which distinguish the man of taste are not felt, or make such a slight impression as scarcely to excite any pleasurable sensations. Is it surprising, then, that fine scenery is often overlooked, by those who may be delighted by the same imagery concentrated and contrasted by the poet? But even this numerous class is exceed by witlings, who, anxious to appear to have wit and taste, do not allow their understandings, or feelings, any liberty: for instead of cultivating their faculties and reflecting on their operations, they are busy collecting prejudices, and are pre-determined to admire what the suffrage of time announces excellent; not to store up a fund of amusement for themselves, but to enable them to talk.

These hints will assist the reader to trace some of the causes why the beauties of nature are not forcibly felt, when civilization and its canker-worm, luxury, have made considerable advances. Those calm emotions are not sufficiently lively to serve as a relaxation to the voluptuary, or even for the moderate pursuers of artificial pleasures. In the present state of society, the understanding must bring the feelings back to nature, or the sensibility must have attained such strength, as rather to be sharpened than destroyed by the strong exercise of passions.

That the most valuable things are liable to the most perversion, is, however, as trite as true. For the same sensibility, or quickness of senses, which makes a man relish the charms of nature, when sensation, rather than reason, imparts delight, frequently makes a libertine of him, by leading him to prefer the tumult of love, a little refined by sentiment, to the calm pleasure of affectionate friendship, in whose sober satisfactions reason mixing her tranquillizing convictions, whispers, that content, not happiness, is the reward, or consequence, of virtue in this world.

———

1798

24. Dorothy Wordsworth
from *Journals*

[Alfoxden] January 20th, 1798.
The green paths down the hill-sides are channels for streams. The young wheat is streaked by silver lines of water running between the ridges, the sheep are gathered together on the slopes. After the wet dark days, the countryside seems more populous. It peoples itself in the sunbeams. The garden, mimic of spring, is gay with flowers. The purple-starred hepatica spreads itself in the sun, and the clustering snow-drops put forth their white heads, at first upright, ribbed with green, and like a rosebud when

completely opened, hanging their heads downwards, but slowly lengthening their slender stems. The slanting woods of an unvarying brown, showing the light through the thin net-work of their upper boughs. Upon the highest ridge of that round hill covered with planted oaks, the shafts of the trees show in the light like the columns of a ruin.

January 21st.

Walked on the hill-tops – a warm day. Sat under the firs in the park. The tops of the beeches of a brown-red, or crimson. Those oaks, fanned by the sea breeze, thick with feathery sea-green moss, as a grove not stripped of its leaves. Moss cups more proper than acorns for fairies.

January 22nd.

Walked through the wood to Holford. The ivy twisted round the oaks like bristled serpents. The day cold – a warm shelter in the hollies, capriciously bearing berries. Query: Are the male and female flowers on separate trees?

* * * *

January 25th.

Went to Poole's after tea. The sky spread over with one continuous cloud, whitened by the light of the moon, which, though her dim shape was seen, did not throw forth so strong a light as to chequer the earth with shadows. At once the clouds seemed to cleave asunder, and left her in the centre of a black-blue vault. She sailed along, followed by multitudes of stars, small, bright, and sharp. Their brightness seemed concentrated (half-moon).

January 26th.

Walked upon the hill-tops; followed the sheep tracks till we overlooked the larger combe. Sat in the sunshine. The distant sheep-bells, the sound of the stream; the woodman winding along the half-marked road with his laden pony; locks of wool still spangled with the dewdrops; the blue-grey sea, shaded with immense masses of cloud, not streaked; the sheep glittering in the sunshine. Returned through the wood. The trees skirting the wood, being exposed more directly to the actions of the sea breeze, stripped of the net-work of their upper boughs, which are stiff and erect, like black skeletons; the ground strewed with the red berries of the holly. Set forward before two o'clock. Returned a little after four.

* * * *

January 29th.

A very stormy day. William walked to the top of the hill to see the sea. Nothing distinguishable but a heavy blackness. An immense bough riven from one of the fir trees.

January 30th.

William called me into the garden to observe a singular appearance about the moon. A perfect rainbow, within the bow one star, only of colours more vivid. The semi-circle soon became a complete circle, and in the course of three or four minutes the whole faded away. Walked to the blacksmith's and the baker's; an uninteresting evening.

✾ ✾ ✾ ✾

[Hamburg, September 19th].

The first impression that an Englishman receives on entering a Hamburg inn is that of filth and smells. I sat down for a few minutes while the company went to look at the apartments. The landlord, landlady, and a party of waiters were preparing plums for preserving or bottling. He looked like an English landlord living on the good things of the house. She, about forty, had her hair full-dressed, spread out and powdered, without cap. We were conducted into Monsr. de Loutre's apartment. On enquiry we found we could have no dinner, for dinner was over. I went upstairs to dress, a *man*-servant brought up a napkin, water etc. My room, at the top of the house, containing a small bed, a chest of drawers, a table, four chairs and a stove at one corner; the floor just washed, but I could see that the process had spread or plastered the coating of dirt; – no carpet – floor painted brown – a large looking glass – 4 marks (a mark is sixteen-pence) the price of this room, and Chester's and Coleridge's. When I returned I found the party below eating cold beef – no cloth spread – no vegetables, but some bad cucumbers pickled without vinegar. Very good wine at 4 sous the bottle. We had afterwards tea and coffee; the bread good, halfpenny rolls, butter not fresh.

[September 20th,] Thursday Morning.

Rouzed by the noises of the market. I could not but observe, notwith-standing the dirt of the houses, that the lower orders of women seemed in general much cleaner in their persons than the same rank in England. This appeared to me on the first view and all the observation I have since made has confirmed me in this opinion.

✾ ✾ ✾ ✾

[September 23rd,] Sunday.

I was unable to go to the Churches, being unwell. We dined at the ordinary at 12 o'clock. An addition of plum tart, I suppose because it was Sunday. William went in the boat to Harburgh at [1/2] past three; fare 4d. In our road to the boat we looked into one of the large churches. Service was just ended. The audience appeared to be simply composed of singing boys dressed in large cocked hats, and a few old women who sat in the aisles. The inferior shops open, women sitting at their doors knitting and sewing, and I saw one woman ironing. Met many bright-looking girls with white caps, carrying black prayer-books in their hands, old men with wigs, one in full dress with a bag and a chapeau de bras – old ladies in London fashions of the years '80 or '82 and 3 – artificial flowers very common in their frizzled heads.

---

25. [Mary Hays]
from *An Appeal to the Men of Great Britain, in Behalf of Women*

In forming the laws by which women are governed, and in the arbitrary opinions which have been taken up and encouraged with regard to them, and which have nailed the fetters of the law down, or supplied their place where they have been entirely silent; have not men in forming these and in continuing them, consulted more their own conveniency, comfort, and dignity, as far as judgement and foresight served them, than that of women; though they are as nearly concerned, and much more likely to be sufferers, as having no hand in forming them?

If men in all ages have done so, – which I believe will hardly be denied by a single individual amongst them, – what dependence can be had for justice in any case where women are concerned, upon judges so partial, so criminally selfish?

To apply then this nearly general censure to the question in hand, let us only consider upon what grounds it is, that men deny to women the privilege, of an education equally improving to the mind, and equally consequential to the happiness of the individual, as that which they think proper to bestow upon themselves?

* * * *

I apprehend, that independent of their maternal character; – I mean as mothers of the human race, which cannot be taken from them, though it is

reduced to as low a pitch in point of consequence as possible; – that independent of this, women are considered in two ways only. – In the lower
classes as necessary drudges – In the higher as the ornaments of society,
the pleasing triflers, who flutter through life for the amusement of men,
rather than for any settled purpose with regard to themselves; and are
accordingly as it suits the caprice of their masters, the objects of adoration,
or of adornment, or of torment, or of a passion unworthy of a name, or a
place, in civilized society. In plain language, women are in all situations
rendered merely the humble companions of men, – the tools of their
necessities, – or the sport of their authority, of their prejudices, and of
their passions. Women viewed in this degrading light, are perhaps as well
off with the trifling and corruptive mode of education generally allowed
them; as with one which would rouse those talents, and increase that desire
after knowledge, with which God and nature has from the beginning, so
liberally endowed them.

But, the question here is, – Are men warranted in forming upon light
grounds, such opinions with regard to women; and in compelling them in
every essential point in life, to act according to these pre-conceived, and
as we think erroneous opinions? The answer from the men, is but too
ready, but too persuasive; for say they – Our judgement disclaims your
pretensions; – we hold our judgement as superior to yours; – and we are
invested with powers to compel, if we cannot persuade.

From such a tribunal then, is there no appeal? – Alas! none.

When men however deign to argue more to the point, they allege, that
when women are educated too much upon an equality with them, it renders
them – presuming and conceited; – unless in their families; – masculine
and consequently disgusting in their manners.

These are very heavy charges indeed; but women do not allow them to
be well founded, nor unanswerable.

The first objection advanced, is – that knowledge and learning render
women presuming and conceited. I beg leave to say that both reason and
experience contradict this assertion; for it has never been proven, that
knowledge in a general view, favoured or produced presumption, though
in particular instances it may no doubt be found to have done so. Much it
must be counselled depends on the subject acted upon, and knowledge
may be compared with respect to its effects on the mind, to wholesome
food upon the body; for a diseased habit will turn the purest aliments to
corruption, instead of nourishment. But this only confirms what has so
often and so well been said, that there is no rule without exception.

This I will not pretend to deny, but that some women who have a great
deal of knowledge, are neither so amiable, not so useful as members of

society, as other who have little, or none, above what is necessary in the most common occurrences in life. But does this not likewise apply to men of the same description? And what does it after all prove? Nothing – but that the most valuable acquisitions may in particular instances, be perverted and misapplied. If this, however, were allowed to be a sufficient objection, we scarcely know any thing which could stand so severe a test. For all sublunary good is liable to be perverted to evil. We may then be permitted to say that upon the whole, knowledge has a direct and natural tendency to promote the love, and the consequent practice of virtue, – to improve the mind, – to exercise and strengthen the judgement, – and to correct the heart. In short, under the guidance of reason and religion, to conduct mankind to every possible perfection. At least if this is not acknowledged, we can give no good reason, why men should adopt the acquisition of it as necessary and ornamental to themselves.

Since this doctrine will not, nor indeed cannot be denied with regard to men; reasoning from analogy, I do not conceive that it can be denied when applied to women. For even allowing what cannot be easily proven, that there is a difference in degree, they are so closely akin, that whatever applies to the one, does to the other, with very slight deviations.

Indeed knowledge, learning, and all solid acquirements, are as yet so very rare among the female sex, that it is by no means surprising if some who really possess those advantages, know it, and feel it. Nor is it surprising, nor perhaps altogether out of nature, though by no means commendable or pleasing, if they at times endeavour to let others know it, and feel it too. Yet to the honour of both sexes let it be said, – to the honour of human nature and learning be it spoken, – instances of proud and presumptuous persons of real abilities and solid acquirements, are but rare, in comparison to the numbers; who are the delight of their friends, the ornaments of society, and the benefactors of mankind. It were possible to enumerate names well known to the world, and dear to their own circle, who are equally admired in an amiable, as in a literary point of view. Suffice it to say, that the experience of the present times as well as of past ages fully justify us in maintaining, that a few exceptions granted, which prove nothing, knowledge does improve every one, man or woman, who is blessed with common sense for a foundation – that presumption and conceit are rather the offspring of ignorance than knowledge – and that knowledge of almost any description is better than ignorance. Always without a doubt however preferring, that kind most suited to situation and circumstances; and which as far as human foresight can judge, is most likely to be useful and ornamental through life.

✳ ✳ ✳ ✳

Thus I have presumed to advance, that there are no attainments at which human nature can arrive, to which women are not equal, and may not be benefited by, as individuals, or in the mass; with those exceptions only, which common sense, which female delicacy, and which peculiar circumstances point out. And were these the only chains imposed upon the sex, every reasonable woman would wear them, not only with docility but with pleasure. But when men try to stamp a marked inferiority on the whole sex, – when they insinuate that they are made of baser materials, or mixed with more alloy, – it is time, perhaps, to endeavour at least, to stop the progress of a species of folly, which has already taken too deep root among mankind; much to the injury of the best interests of society. And which in the end, is equally pernicious to those who inflict the injury, as to those upon whom it is inflicted.

26. Matilda Betham
We Wish not the Mechanic Arts to Scan

We wish not the mechanic arts to scan,
But leave the slavish work to selfish man!
He claims alone the privilege to war,
But 'tis our smiles that must reward the scar!
We need not these heroic dangers brave,
Who hold the laurelled conqueror a slave.
We need not search the world for sordid gain,
While we its proud possessors can enchain,
When their pursuit is only meant to prove,
How much they'd venture to deserve our love;
For wealth and honours they can only prize,
As making them more worthy in our eyes.
Their insufficiency they would supply,
And to these glittering resources fly!
Let the poor boasters then indulge their pride,
And think they o'er the universe preside;
Let them recount their numerous triumphs o'er,
And tell the tales, so often told before;
Their own much-doubted merit to enhance;
And gain the great reward – a favouring glance!
Let them, in bondage, fancy themselves free;
And whilst fast fettered, vaunt their liberty!

Because they do not massy chains behold,
Suppose that they are monarchs uncontrolled!
How vain! to hope 'twould be to them revealed
The flame burns strongest that is most concealed!
Then with what potent, what resistless art,
Those hidden bonds are twined about the heart,
So that the captive wanders unconfined,
And has no sovereign but o'er his mind!
The prize is mutual, eithe power or fame;
We have the substance, *they* may keep the name!

27. Priscilla Wakefield

from *Reflections on the Present Condition of the Female Sex*

It is asserted by Doctor Adam Smith, that every individual is a burthen upon the society to which he belongs, who does not contribute his share of productive labour for the good of the whole. The doctor, when he lays down this principle, speaks in general terms of man, as a being capable of forming a social compact for mutual defence, and the advantage of the community at large. He does not absolutely specify, that both sexes, in order to render themselves beneficial members of society, are equally required to comply with these terms; but since the female sex is included in the idea of the species, and as women possess the same qualities as men, though perhaps in a different degree, their sex cannot free them from the claim of the public for their proportion of usefulness. That the major part of the sex, especially of those among the higher orders, neglect to fulfil this important obligation, is a fact that must be admitted, and points out the propriety of an enquiry into the causes of their deficiency.

The indolent indulgence and trifling pursuits in which those who are distinguished by the appellation of gentlewoman, often pass their lives, may be attributed, with greater probability, to a contracted education, custom, false pride, and idolizing adulation, than to any defect in their intellectual capacities. The contest for equality in the mental capacity of the sexes has been maintained, on each side of the question, with ingenuity; but as judgement only can be formed from facts, as they arise in the present state of things, if the experiments have been fairly tried, the rare instances of extraordinary talents, which have been brought forward to support the system of equality, must yield to irresistible influence of corporeal powers. Which leads to a conclusion, that the intellectual faculties of each sex are wisely adapted to their appropriate purposes, and that, laying aside the invidious terms of superiority and inferiority, the perfection of mind in man and in woman, consists in a power to maintain the distinguishing characteristics of excellence in each. But this concession by no means proves, that, even in this enlightened age and country, the talents of women have ever been generally exerted to the utmost extent of their capacity, or that they have been turned towards the most useful objects; neither does it imply that the cultivation they receive is adequate to bring into action the full strength of those powers which have been bestowed on them by nature. The intellectual faculties of the female mind have been too long confined by narrow and ill-directed modes of education, and thus have been concealed, not only from others, but from themselves, the energies of which they are capable.

Society may be resolved into four classes or degrees: the first compre-hends the nobility, and all those who, either by the influence of high offices or extensive hereditary possessions, rival them in power: the second con-tains those, who by the application of their talents to learning, commerce, manufactures, or agriculture, procure a respectable subsistence approaching to opulence: to the third may be referred those, whose honest and useful industry raises them above want, without procuring for them the means of splendid or luxurious gratification: the fourth is composed of the labouring poor. The rank of women being determined by the accident of their birth, or their connections in marriage, a correspondent arrangement is, with equal propriety, applicable to them, as to the other sex.

An enquiry into the objects of attainment, employments, and pursuits of the different classes of the one sex, will throw light upon those that ought to occupy the corresponding ranks of the other.

Noblemen, and gentlemen of independent property, receive a course of instruction adapted to prepare them for filling up the highest offices in the different departments of the state, consistently with their own dignity and the service of their country; or to maintain the inviolability of our valuable constitution, as distinguished ornaments in the senate, or at the bar. – The learned professions, or the lucrative and respectable avocations of com-mercial life, are sources of honour and wealth to the inferior gentry and merchants. Farmers, tradesmen and artificers, besides the general acquisition of the simpler branches of learning, attain the knowledge of some peculiar art, or branch of commerce, by which they are enabled to gain a competent support.

The necessity of directing the attention of females to some certain occu-pation is not so apparent, because custom has rendered them dependent upon their fathers and husbands for support; but as some of every class experience the loss of those relations, without inheriting an adequate resource, there would be great propriety in preparing each of them, by an education of energy and useful attainments, to meet such disasters, and to be able, under such circumstances, to procure an independence for herself. There is scarcely a more helpless object, in the wide circle of misery which the vicissitudes of civilized society display, than a woman genteelly educated, whether single or married, who is deprived, by any unfortunate accident, of the protection and support of male relations: unaccustomed to struggle with difficulty, unacquainted with any resource to supply an independent maintenance, she is reduced to the depths of wretchedness, and not unfrequently, if she be young and handsome, is driven by despair to those paths which lead to infamy. Is it not time to find a remedy for such evils, when the contentions of nations has produced the most affecting transitions in private life, and transferred the affluent and the noble to the humiliating extremes of want and obscurity? When our streets teem with multitudes of unhappy women, many of whom might have been rescued from their present degradation, or who would perhaps never have fallen into it, had they been instructed in the exercise of some art or profession, which would have enabled them to procure for themselves a respectable support by their own industry.

28. Joanna Baillie
from *Introductory Discourse: Plays on the Passions*

The highest pleasures we receive from poetry, as well as from the real objects which surround us in the world, are derived from the sympathetic interest we all take in beings like ourselves; and I will even venture to say, that were the grandest scenes which can enter into the imagination of man, presented to our view, and all reference to man completely shut out from our thoughts, the objects that composed it would convey to our minds little better than dry ideas of magnitude, colour, and form; and the remembrance of them would rest upon our minds like the measurement and distances of the planets.

If the study of human nature, then, is so useful to the poet, the novelist, the historian, and the philosopher, of how much greater importance must it be to the dramatic writer? To them it is a powerful auxiliary, to him it is the centre and strength of the battle. If characteristic views of human nature enliven not their pages, there are many excellencies with which they can, in some degree, make up for the deficiency, it is what we receive from them with pleasure rather than demand. But in his works no richness of invention, harmony of language, nor grandeur of sentiment will supply the place of faithfully delineated nature. The poet and the novelist may represent to you their great characters from the cradle to the tomb. They may represent them in any mood or temper, and under the influence of any passion which they see proper, without being obliged to put words into their mouths, those great betrayers of the feigned and adopted. They may relate every circumstance however trifling and minute, that serves to develop their tempers and dispositions. They tell us what kind of people they intend their men and women to be, and as such we receive them. If they are to move us with any scene of distress, every circumstance regarding the parties concerned in it, how they looked, how they moved, how they sighed, how the tears gushed from their eyes, how the very light and shadow fell upon them, is carefully described, and the few things that are given them to say along with all this assistance, must be very unnatural indeed if we refuse to sympathize with them. But the characters of the drama must speak directly for themselves. Under the influence of every passion, humour, and impression; in the artificial veilings of hypocrisy and ceremony, in the openness of freedom and confidence of meditation they speak. He who made us hath placed within our breast a judge that judges instantaneously of every thing we say. We expect to find them creatures like ourselves; and if they are untrue to nature, we feel that we are imposed upon; as though the poet had introduced to us for brethren, creatures of a different race, beings of another world.

* * * *

In whatever age or country the Drama might have taken its rise, Tragedy would have been the first-born of its children. For every nation has its great men, and its great events upon record; and to represent their own forefathers struggling with those difficulties and braving those dangers, of which they have heard with admiration, and the effects of which they still, perhaps, experience, would certainly have been the most animating subject for the poet, and the most interesting for his audience, even independently of the natural inclination we all so universally shew for scenes of horror and distress, of passion and heroic exertion. Tragedy would have been the first child of the Drama, for the same reasons that have made the heroic ballad, with all its battles, murders, and disasters, the earliest poetical compositions of every country.

We behold heroes and great men at a distance; unmarked by those

small but distinguishing features of the mind which give a certain individuality to such an infinite variety of similar beings, in the near and familiar
intercourse of life. They appear to us from this view like distant mountains, whose dark outlines we trace in the clear horizon, but the varieties of
whose roughened sides, with heath and brush-wood, and seamed with
many a cleft, we perceive not. When accidental anecdote reveals to us any
weakness or peculiarity belonging to them, we start upon it like a discovery.
They are made known to us in history only, by the great events they are
connected with, and the part they have taken in extraordinary or important
transactions. Even in poetry and romance, with the exception of some love
story interwoven with the main events of their lives, they are seldom more
intimately made known to us. To Tragedy it belongs to lead them forward
to our nearer regard, in all the distinguishing varieties which nearer
inspection discovers; with the passions, the humours, the weaknesses, the
prejudices of men. It is for her to present to us the great and magnanimous
hero, who appears to our distinctive view as a superior being, as a God,
softened down with those smaller frailties and imperfections which enable
us to glory in, and claim kindred to his virtues. It is for her to exhibit to us
the daring and ambitious man, planning his dark designs, and executing
his bloody purposes, marked with those appropriate characteristics which
distinguish him as an individual of that class; and agitated with those
varied passions, which disturb the mind of man when he is engaged in the
commission of such deeds. It is for her to point out to us the brave and
impetuous warrior struck with those visitations of nature, which, in certain
situations will unnerve the strongest arm, and make the boldest heart
tremble. It is for her to shew the tender, gentle, and unassuming mind
animated with that fire which, by the provocation of circumstances, will
give to the kindest heart the ferocity and keenness of a tiger. It is for her to
present to us the great and striking characters that are to be found amongst
men in a way which the poet, the novelist, and the historian can but
imperfectly attempt. But above all, to her, and to her only it belongs to
unveil to us the human mind under the domination of those strong and
fixed passions, which, seemingly unprovoked by outward circumstances,
will from small beginnings brood within the breast, till all the better dispositions, all the fair gifts of nature are borne down before them. Those
passions which conceal themselves from the observation of men; which
cannot unbosom themselves even to the dearest friend; and can, often
times, only give their fullness vent in the lonely desert, or in the darkness
of midnight.

29. Mary Wollstonecraft
from *Hints*

The lover is ever most deeply enamoured, when it is with he knows not what – and the devotion of a mystic has a rude Gothic grandeur in it, which the respectful adoration of a philosopher will never reach. I may be thought fanciful; but it has continually occurred to me, that, though, I allow, reason in this world is the mother of wisdom – yet some flights of the imagination seem to reach what wisdom cannot teach – and, while they delude us here, afford a glorious hope, if not a foretaste, of what we may expect hereafter. He that created us, did not mean to mark us with ideal images of grandeur, the baseless fabric of a vision – No – that perfection we follow with hopeless ardour when the whisperings of reason are heard, may be found, when not incompatible with our state, in the round of eternity. Perfection indeed must, even then, be a comparative idea – but the wisdom, the happiness of a superior state, has been supposed to be intuitive, and the happiest effusions of human genius have seemed like inspiration – the deductions of reason destroy sublimity.

I am more and more convinced, that poetry is the first effervescence of the imagination, and the forerunner of civilization.

When the Arabs had no trace of literature or science, they composed beautiful verses on the subjects of love and war. The flights of imagination, and the laboured deductions of reason, appear almost incompatible.

Poetry certainly flourishes most in the first rude state of society. The passions speak most eloquently, when they are not shackled by reason. The sublime expression, which has been so often quoted, (Genesis, ch. 1, ver. 3) is perhaps a barbarous flight; or rather the grand conception of an uncultivated mind; for it is contrary to nature and experience, to suppose that this account is founded on facts – It is doubtless a sublime allegory. But a cultivated mind would not thus have described the creation – for, arguing from analogy, it appears that creation must have been a comprehensive plan, and that the Supreme Being always uses second causes, slowly and silently to fulfil his purpose. This is, in reality, a more sublime view of that power which wisdom supports: but it is not the sublimity that would strike the impassioned mind, in which the imagination took the place of intellect. Tell a being, whose affections and passions have been more exercised than his reason, that God said, Let there be light! and there was light; and he would prostrate himself before the Being who could thus call things out of nothing, as if they were: but a man in whom reason had taken the place of passion, would not adore, till wisdom was conspicuous as well as power, for his admiration must be founded on principle.

Individuality is ever conspicuous in those enthusiastic flights of fancy, in which reason is left behind, without being lost sight of.

———

1799

30. Anna Seward
To the Poppy

While summer roses all their glory yield
    To crown the votary of love and joy,
    Misfortune's victim hails, with many a sigh,
    Thee, scarlet poppy of the pathless field,
Gaudy, yet wild and lone; no leaf to shield
    Thy flaccid vest, that, as the gale blows high,
    Flaps, and alternate folds around thy head. –
So stands in the long grass a love-crazed maid,
Smiling aghast; while stream to every wind
    Her garish ribbons, smeared with dust and rain;
    But brain-sick visions cheat her tortured mind,
And bring false peace. Thus, lulling grief and pain,
    Kind dreams oblivious from thy juice proceed,
    Thou flimsy, showy, melancholy weed.

———

31. Mary Ann Radcliffe
from *The Female Advocate*

[On well-born women reduced to beggary]
Let us then, if you please, select one of these distressed females, out of the prodigious multitude, and pursue her through the humiliating scene of beggary. . . .

What must be the perturbation of a mind like this, when dire necessity compels the poor, neglected victim to pursue such degrading steps, in order to support a miserable existence! See her trembling limbs, which are scarcely able to support her load of wretchedness, whilst she asks alms from the casual passenger. She who, perhaps, a short time since, charmed her acquaintance with her sprightly conversation and virtuous example, by one adverse stroke, is nevertheless so soon become the contempt, the scorn, and the outcast of mortals! Nor is this wretched doom confined to youth alone; but, by the cruel hand of fate, the poor, dejected mother, as well as the daughter, is condemned to share the same direful misfortunes, and be reduced to the same low state of wretchedness, from which their characters are stigmatized with infamy, and to which they unavoidably fall a sacrifice. . . .

Good heavens, what a scene of woe! when the poor mother and her daughter are turned adrift, to the mercy of an unfeeling world; which neither their genteel education, or delicate constitutions, broken down by poverty and hardships, can prevent. O! what distress, in a situation like this! The mother, the fond mother, in the full bitterness of maternal affection, takes another, and another view of her darling child; perhaps the only pledge of a late kind partner! sees her still laden with the fruits of a pious education at least: views her with unutterable fondness, 'whilst all the soft passions of her tender soul throb through her breast with unavailing grief' at the near approach of their destruction! In vain do they supplicate their former friends, for the voice of censure has pointed them out as infamous! Good God! what grief can equal this? Abandoned by friends, and left to the reproach, contempt, and censure of a cruel world, without a provision, or any probable means of gaining a subsistence, or even the smallest glimpse of a distant hope.

And, though shocking to relate, yet such is the miserable situation of thousands of defenceless women.

❋ ❋ ❋ ❋

However shocking the sentence, what numbers of these poor objects have been dragged away by the ruthless hand of the unfeeling savage, to some loathsome prison, without regard to the more refined or delicate sensations of one or another? Good heavens! there surely needs no Siddonian powers to heighten such a tragic scene. She who, perhaps, was reared with all the gentle softness and maternal care of a fond parent; she, who so lately was looked upon as an ornament to her sex, until the pressures of misfortune compelled her to seek for bread, to be at once confined to a dark prison, there to be obliged to hear all the opprobrious language of the very lowest set of beings, and that under a storm of oaths and imprecations, which, of itself, must pierce her very soul. There to have her ears grated with the rattling of bolts and bars, and all the adamantine fetters of misery. Good God! is it possible we can see our fellow creatures debased so low! Can we see the tender and delicate frame, which was formerly accustomed to ease and tranquillity, and which was formed by nature to participate in others' misfortunes! can we let these innocent and helpless beings pass unnoticed, and not commiserate their distress, and ask, from whence the cause? No! it is impossible the eyes can any longer be shut to their sufferings, or the ears to their piercing cries of 'Have pity on me! Oh! ye, my friends, have pity on me!'

Is not this real distress? Surely there cannot be any thing more wretchedly miserable than the situation of these poor women, who are prohibited from sharing in industry, or the common necessaries of life, or even tasting the very dregs of comfort.

---

32. 'Anne Frances Randall' [Mary Robinson]
from *A Letter to the Women of England, on the Injustice of Mental Subordination*

The embargo upon words, the enforcement of tacit submission, has been productive of consequences highly honourable to the women of the present age. Since the sex have been condemned for exercising the powers of speech, they have successfully taken up the pen and their writings exemplify both energy of mind, and the capability of acquiring the most extensive knowledge. The press will be the monuments from which the genius of British women will rise to immortal celebrity: their works will, in proportion as their educations are liberal, from year to year, challenge an equal portion of fame, with the labours of their classical *male* contemporaries.

In proportion as women are acquainted with the languages they will become citizens of the world. The laws, customs and inhabitants of different nations will be their kindred in the propinquity of nature. Prejudice will be palsied, if not receive its death blow, by the expansion of intellect: and woman being permitted to feel her own importance in the scale of society, will be tenacious of maintaining it. She will know that she was created for something beyond the mere amusement of man; that she is capable of mental energies, and worthy of the most unbounded confidence. Such a system of mental equality, would, while it stigmatized the trifling vain and pernicious race of high fashioned Messalinas, produce such British women, as would equal the Portias and Arrias of history.

Had fortune enabled me, I would build an UNIVERSITY FOR WOMEN; where they should be politely, and at the same time classically educated; the depth of their studies, should be proportioned to their mental powers; and those who were *incompetent to the labours of knowledge*, should be dismissed after a fair trial of their capabilities, and allotted to the more humble paths of life; such as *domestic and useful occupations*. The wealthy parts of the community who neglected to educate their female offspring, at this seminary of learning, should pay a fine, which should be appropriated to the maintenance of the unportioned scholars. In half a century there would be a sufficient number of learned women to fill all the departments of the university, and those who excelled in an eminent degree should receive honorary medals, which they should wear as an ORDER of LITERARY MERIT.

Oh my unenlightened country-women! read, and profit, by the admonition of reason. Shake off the trifling, glittering shackles, which debase you. Resist those fascinating spells which, like the petrifying torpedo, fasten on your mental faculties. Be less the slaves of vanity, and more the converts of reflection. Nature has endowed you with personal attractions: she has also given you the mind capable of expansion. Seek not the visionary triumph of universal conquest; know yourselves equal to greater, nobler, acquirements: and by prudence, temperance, firmness, and reflection, subdue that prejudice which has, for ages past, been your inveterate enemy. Let your daughters be liberally, classically, philosophically, and usefully educated; let them speak and write their opinions freely; let them read and think like rational creatures; adapt their studies to their strength of intellect; expand their minds, and purify their hearts, by teaching them to feel their mental equality with their imperious rulers. By such laudable exertions, you will excite the noblest emulation; you will explode the superstitious tenets of bigotry and fanaticism; confirm the intuitive immortality of the soul, and give them that genuine glow of conscious virtue which will grace them to posterity.

---

33. Hannah More

from *Strictures on the Modern System of Female Education*

It is a singular injustice which is often exercised towards women, first to give them a most defective education, and then to expect from them the most undeviating purity of conduct; – to train them in such a manner as shall lay them open to the most dangerous faults, and then to censure them for not proving faultless. Is it not unreasonable and unjust, to express disappointment if our daughters should, in their subsequent lives, turn out precisely that very character for which it would be evident to an unprejudiced bystander that the whole tenor and scope of their education had been systematically preparing them for?

❋ ❋ ❋ ❋

The *rights of man* have been discussed, till we are somewhat wearied with the discussion. To these have been opposed with more presumption than prudence the *rights of woman*. It follows according to the natural progression of human things that the next stage of that irradiation which our enlighteners are pouring in upon us will produce grave descants on the *rights of children*.

❋ ❋ ❋ ❋

A young lady may excel in speaking French and Italian, may repeat a few phrases from a volume of extracts; play like a professor, and sing like a siren; have her dressing room decorated with her own drawings, tables, stands, screens, and cabinets; nay, she may dance like Sempronia herself, and yet may have been very badly educated. I am very far from meaning to set no value whatever on any or all of these qualifications; they are all of them elegant, and many of them properly tend to the perfecting of a polite education. These things in their measure and degree, may be done, but there are others which should not be left undone. Many things are becoming, but only 'one thing is needful'. Besides, as the world seems to be fully apprized of the value of whatever tends to embellish life, there is less occasion here to insist on its importance.

But, though a well-bred young lady may lawfully learn most of the fashionable arts, yet it does not seem to be the true end of education to make women of fashion *dancers, singers, players, painters, actresses, sculptors, gilders, varnishers, engravers*, and *embroiderers*. Most *men* are commonly destined to some profession, and their minds are consequently turned each to its respective object. Would it not be strange if they were called out to exercise their profession, or set up their trade, with only a little general knowledge of the trades of all other men, and without any previous definite application to their own peculiar calling? The profession of ladies, to which the bent of *their* instruction should be turned, is that of daughters, wives, mothers, and mistresses of families. They should be therefore trained with a view to these several conditions, and be furnished with a stock of ideas, and principles, and qualifications, and habits, ready to be applied and appropriated, as occasion may demand, to each of these respective situations: for though the arts which merely embellish life must claim admiration; yet when a man of sense comes to marry, it is a companion whom he wants, and not an artist. It is not merely a creature who can paint, and play, and dress, and dance; it is a being who can comfort and counsel him; one who can reason and reflect, and feel, and judge, and act, and discourse, and discriminate; one who can assist him in his affairs, lighten his cares, soothe his sorrows, purify his joys, strengthen his principles, and educate his children.

❋ ❋ ❋ ❋

Perhaps there is some analogy between the mental and bodily conformation of women. The instructor therefore should imitate the physician. If the latter prescribe bracing medicines for a body of which delicacy is the disease, the former would do well to prohibit relaxing reading for a mind which is already of too soft a texture, and should strengthen its feeble tone by invigorating reading.

By softness, I cannot be supposed to mean imbecility of understanding, but natural softness of heart, together with that indolence of spirit which is softened by indulging in seducing books, and in the general habits of fashionable life.

I mean not here to recommend books which are immediately religious, but such as exercise the reasoning faculties, teach the mind to get acquainted with its own nature, and to stir up its own powers. . . . [T]he studies here recommended would act upon the constitution of the mind as a kind of alternative, and, if I may be allowed the expression, would help to brace the intellectual stamina.

This is however by no means intended to exclude works of taste and imagination, which must always make the ornamental part, and of course a very considerable part of female studies. It is only suggested that they should not form them entirely. For what is called dry tough reading, independent of the knowledge it conveys, is useful as an habit and wholesome as an exercise. Serious study serves to harden the mind for more trying conflicts; it lifts the reader from sensation to intellect; it abstracts her from the world and its vanities; it fixes a wandering spirit, and fortifies a weak one; it divorces her from matter; it corrects that spirit of trifling which she naturally contracts from the frivolous turn of female conversation, and the petty nature of female employments; it concentrates her attention, assists her in a habit of excluding trivial thoughts, and thus even helps to qualify her for religious pursuits. Yes; I repeat it, there is to woman a Christian use to be made of sober studies; while books of an opposite cast, however unexceptionable they may be sometimes found in point of expression; however free from evil in its more gross and palpable shapes, yet by their very nature and constitution they excite a spirit of relaxation, by exhibiting scenes and ideas which soften the mind; they impair its general powers of resistance, and at best feed habits of improper indulgence, and nourish a vain and visionary indolence, which lays the mind open to error and the heart to seduction.

Women are little accustomed to close reasoning on any subject; still less do they inure their minds to consider particular parts of a subject; they are not habituated to turn a truth round and view it in all its varied aspects and positions; and this perhaps is one cause . . . of the too great confidence they are disposed to place in their opinions. Though their imagination is already too lively, and their judgement naturally incorrect; in educating them we go on to stimulate the imagination, while we neglect the regulation of the judgement. They already want ballast, and we make their education consist in continually crowding more sail than they can carry. Their intellectual powers being so little strengthened by exercise, makes every little business appear a hardship to them: whereas serious study would be useful, were it only that it leads the mind to the habit of conquering difficulties. But it is peculiarly hard to turn at once from the indolent repose of light reading, from the concerns of mere animal life, the objects of sense, or the frivolousness of chit chat; it is peculiarly hard I say, to a mind so softened, to rescue itself from the dominion of self-indulgence, to resume its powers, to call home its scattered strength, to shut out every foreign intrusion, to force back a spring so unnaturally bent, and to devote itself to religious reading, reflection, or self-examination: whereas to an intellect accustomed to think at all, the difficulty of thinking seriously is obviously lessened.

Far be it from me to desire to make scholastic ladies or female dialecticians; but there is little fear that the kind of books here recommended, if thoroughly studied, and not superficially skimmed, will make them pedants or induce conceit; for by showing them the possible powers of the human mind, you will bring them to see the littleness of their own, and to get acquainted with the mind, and to regulate it, does not seem the way to puff it up.

34. Mary Alcock
The Body-Politic

If in the Body-politic you see
Rebellion, rapine, bloodshed, anarchy,
That state you say is lost! So when you find
The body human with distempered mind,

The blood corrupted, and the fever high,
You doubt not to pronounce – that man must die.
    Now in the way of fable we'll suppose
Rebellion in the human frame arose;
Each member loudly sounded forth his merit,
And cried, t'obey the Head showed want of spirit;
'Twas time the Limbs should now assert their part,
And overturn the empire of the Heart.
    The stubborn Knees declared no more they'd bend
For God or King, nor any strength would lend
To bear a Head of such unwieldy size;
To hear and see required not Ears and Eyes;
All parts were equal, and each had a right
T'assume the gift of hearing and of sight.
    Whereat the Feet stepped forth with furious sound
Stamping and swearing they'd not touch the ground;
Henceforth aloft they'd rise erect in air,
And make the daintier Hands the burden bear.
    This said, the Hands indignant caught the alarm,
And struggling tried to separate from the Arm;
Aloud they clapped, and summoned all to fight
To fix their freedom, and enforce their right.
And now Convulsion seized on every part,
Loud beat each Pulse, and terror shook the Heart;
Within was heard a horrid noise and rout,
The Inside claimed the right to be the Out.
The Lungs protested they'd not draw the breath;
They cared not if it brought on instant death;
'Twere better all were lost than they denied
The right to hold a share in the Outside.
    The Stomach roared he soon would stop digestion,
If e'er his outside right was called in question:
The veins declared they'd not perform their part,
Nor longer throw the blood up to the Heart;
The Heart might feed itself, or yield its place
To those who'd fill it with a better grace.
    On this the Liver writhed himself around,
And swore that long, though rotten and unsound,
He'd sought that place; he now would seize the throne,
For he was fit to rule, and he alone.

This roused the Spleen, who on the vitals fed,
Planning by craft the downfall of the Head;
But now o'ercharged with envy, rage, and guile,
In haste he rose, and overset the Bile.
    Thus all within was agony and strife,
Each fresh convulsion seemed to threaten life;
The Limbs distorted rise – they give the blow,
And soon the Head (so honoured once) lay low.
And now behold the Body's wretched state,
Taught by this sad example, ere too late,
That such each Body-politic must be,
Where foul rebellion reigns and anarchy.

1800

35. Dorothy Wordsworth
from *Grasmere Journal*

May 14th, 1800 [Wednesday].
Wm. and John set off, into Yorkshire after dinner at 1/2 past 2 o'clock, cold pork in their pockets. I left them at the turning of the Lowwood bay under the trees. – My heart was so full that I could hardly speak to W. when I gave him a farewell kiss. I sate a long time upon a stone at the margin of the lake, and after a flood of tears my heart was easier. The lake looked to me, I knew not why, dull and melancholy, and the weltering on the shores seemed a heavy sound. I walked as long as I could amongst the stones of the shore. The wood rich in flowers; a beautiful yellow, palish yellow, flower, that looked thick, round, and double, and smelt very sweet – I supposed it was a ranunculus. Crowfoot, the grassy-leaved rabbit-toothed white flower, strawberries, geranium, scentless violets, anemones two kinds, orchises, primroses. The heckberry very beautiful, the crab coming out as a low shrub. Met a blind man, driving a very large beautiful bull, and a cow – he walked with two sticks. Came home by Clappersgate. The valley very green; many sweet views up to Rydale head, when I could juggle away the fine houses; but they disturbed me, even more than when I have been happier; one beautiful view of the Bridge, without Sir Michael's. Sate

down very often, though it was cold. I resolved to write a journal of the time till W. and J. return, and I set about keeping my resolve, because I will not quarrel with myself, and because I shall give Wm. pleasure by it when he comes home again. At Rydale, a woman of the village, stout and well dressed, begged, a half-penny; she had never she said done it before, but these hard times! Arrived at home with a bad headache, set some slips of privett, the evening cold, had a fire, my face now flame-coloured. It is nine o'clock. I shall soon go to bed. A young woman begged at the door – she had come from Manchester on Sunday morn. with two shillings and a slip of paper which she supposed a Bank note – it was a cheat. She had buried her husband and three children within a year and a half – all in one grave – burying very dear – paupers all put in one place – 20 shillings paid for as much ground as will bury a man – a stone to be put over it or the right will be lost – 11/6 each time the ground is opened. Oh! that I had a letter from William!

[May 18th], Sunday.

Went to church, slight showers, a cold air. The mountains from this window look much greener, and I think the valley is more green than ever. The corn begins to show itself. The ashes are still bare, went part of the way home with Miss Simpson. A little girl from Coniston came to beg. She had lain out all night – her step-mother had turned her out of doors. Her father could not stay at home 'she flights so'. Walked to Ambleside in the evening round the lake, the prospect exceedingly beautiful from Loughrigg Fell. It was so green that no eye could be weary of reposing upon it. The most beautiful situation for a house in the field next to Mr. Benson's. It threatened rain all the evening but was mild and pleasant. I was overtaken by 2 Cumberland people on the other side of Rydale who complimented me upon my walking. They were going to sell cloth, and odd things which they make themselves, in Hawkshead and the neighbourhood.

[May 19th,] Monday.

Sauntered a good deal in the garden, bound carpets, mended old clothes. Read *Timon of Athens*. Dried linen. Molly weeded the turnips, John stuck the peas. We had not much sunshine or wind, but no rain till about 7 o'clock, when we had a slight shower just after I had set out upon my walk. I did not return but walked up into the Black Quarter. I sauntered a long time among the rocks above the church. The most delightful situation possible for a cottage, commanding two distinct views of the vale and of the lake, is among those rocks. I strolled on, gathered mosses etc. The quietness and still seclusion of the valley affected me even to producing the deepest melancholy. I forced myself from it. The wind rose before I went to bed.

[May 20th,] Tuesday Morning.

A fine mild rain. After breakfast the sky cleared and before the clouds passed from the hills I went to Ambleside. It was a sweet morning. Everything green and overflowing with life, and the streams making a perpetual song, with the thrushes and all little birds, not forgetting the stonechats. The post was not come in. Walked as far as Windermere, and met him there. No letters, no papers. Came home by Clappersgate. I was sadly tired, ate a hasty dinner and had a bad headache – went to bed and slept at least 2 hours. Rain came on in the evening – Molly washing.

[May 21st,] Wednesday.

Went often to spread the linen which was bleaching – a rainy day and very wet night.

[May 22nd,] Thursday.

A very fine day with showers – dried the linen and starched. Drank tea at Mr. Simpson's. Brought down Batchelor's Buttons (Rock Ranunculus) and other plants – went – part of the way back, a showery mild evening – all the peas up.

[May 23rd,] Friday.

Ironing-till-time. So heavy a rain that I could not go for letters – put by the linen, mended stockings etc.

May 24th. Saturday.

Walked in the morning to Ambleside. I found a letter from Wm and from Mary Hutchinson and Douglas. Returned on the other side of the lakes – wrote to William after dinner, nailed up the beds, worked in the garden, sate in the evening under the trees. I went to bed soon with a bad headache. A fine day.

1800

36. Jane West
from *Letters to a Young Lady*

[On novels]
What effect, shall we enquire, has the general turn of fictitious adventure on an age in which *every* young woman reads, and many confine their

knowledge to this species of misinformation? Does it teach them what things *have been*, or what things *are*? Certainly not; for such beings and such an order of things, never did nor ever can exist. Parents are quite as apt to judge rightly for their children, as children are to form a proper estimate of what is good for themselves; and the chance between the *disinterestedness* of paternal affection, and that of him who plays the lover's part, is in favour of the former. Heroes and heroines, or, in plain English, men and women, never did possess such an accumulation of splendid graces and virtues as are collected together in these false prisms. The unreasonably suspicious lover is sure to make an unreasonably jealous husband. Violent attachments are either never lasting, or the source of unhappiness, being always accompanied with painful irritation of mind. Suitable offers of marriage occur too rarely, for a young woman to expect more from the majority of her followers, than that evanescent admiration which is paid to all who have the reputation of fortune, wit, or beauty. Virtue is more severely tried by a *multiplicity* of petty evils, than by *great* conflicts; and benevolence displays her heavenly nature by minute attentions, oftener, and with more beneficial effect, than by extraordinary exertions. Sudden reverses of fortune are unusual, and so are acts of great liberality. Adventures rarely happen to a prudent woman, and never without injury to her reputation. Licentious intentions are seldom formed without a prospect of success, and the most hardened rake may be awed by unassuming discretion. . . .

The first motions of evil may be resisted, if the thoughts be not permitted to stray towards an unlawful object, or to ponder on the means by which wished ends may be accomplished. They who trifle with temptation expose themselves to the danger of defeat, and deserve the ruin which they sustain. Marriage may be said rather to open than to close the eventful period of female life; since it is by that means that we enter on a scene of enlarged usefulness, activity, and responsibility; nor is marrying the man whom we fondly love an invulnerable protection from the shafts of sorrow; perhaps it is oftener a ready inlet to the pangs of disappointment, or the cares of solicitude.

I could write volumes to expose those false views of human life, which doubtless have accelerated that change of female manners which we all see and deplore. Had not so much idolatrous incense been offered to beauty, grace, and nymph-like elegance; had so many fascinating descriptions never been given of the pleasures, enjoyments, and advantages of rank and fortune, the elegantes of humble life would have been far less numerous, and we should have retained some valuable stuff, capable of being converted into the wives of traders and yeomen. Let not those who confine themselves to this style of reading make a merit of having been at their books. Mischievous reading is worse than unsophisticated ignorance.

———

1801

37. Elizabeth Hamilton
from *Letters on the Elementary Principles of Education*

By far the greater part of those who have hitherto taken upon them to stand forth as champions for sexual equality have done it upon grounds that to me appear indefensible, if not absurd. It is not an equality of moral worth for which they contend, and which is the only true object of regard, nor for an equality of rights with respect to the Divine favour, which alone elevates the human character into dignity and importance; but for an equality of employments and avocations, founded upon the erroneous idea of a perfect similarity of powers. Infected by the prejudices which associate ideas of honour and esteem with knowledge and science, independent of moral virtue, and envious of the short-lived glories of ambition, they desire for their sex an admission into the theatre of public life, and wish to qualify them for it by an education in every respect similar to that of men. Men scoff at their pretence and hold their presumption in abhorrence; but men do not consider, that these pretences, and that presumption, have been caught from the false notions of importance which they have themselves affixed to their own peculiar avocations. Taught from earliest infancy to arrogate to themselves a claim of inherent superiority, this idea attaches itself to all the studies and pursuits which custom has exclusively assigned them. These prejudices operating likewise on the minds of women, it is not surprising that those who perceive in themselves a capacity for attaining as high a degree of intellectual eminence, should aspire to be sharers in those honours which they have been taught, by the pride of men, to regard as supreme distinction. Were both sexes guarded from the admission of early prejudice, and taught to value themselves on no superiority but that of virtue, these vain and idle jealousies would cease; man would become more worthy, and woman more respectable. Were these prejudices annihilated, the virtues of temperance and chastity would not in the mind of man be associated with ideas of contempt, as merely proper to be observed by the inferior part of the species; nor would habits of licentiousness be considered as a light and venial evil, but regarded with the same horror which is happily still attached to female depravity.

Of the licentiousness of one sex, however, the depravity of the other is the natural and certain consequence. Accustomed to acquiesce in the idea of man's superiority in all wisdom and perfection, women cease to respect those laws of decency and reserve which they perceive it the glory of the other sex to set at defiance. They learn to consider the restrictions of chastity as the fetters of worldly prudence; and as those to whom they are accustomed to look up as beings of a superior order, scoff at that religion which teaches purity of heart as well as manners, they likewise learn to regard it with contempt.

* * * *

It has been observed, that women who have reasoned upon subjects of abstract speculation with much skill, have shown in their conduct neither judgement, nor propriety, nor a delicate sense of moral rectitude: that they who have been most remarkable for talents, have not always been most remarkable for virtue: that genius has frequently led to error: and that females who have cultivated the higher powers of the understanding with most success have manifestly neglected the peculiar duties of their sex and situation. It is moreover observed, that though men of talents and learning are generally modest in proportion to the superiority of their attainments, vanity is commonly the companion of every species of superiority in our sex.

Heavy charges! humiliating picture of female imbecility! How shall I answer to my sex for their exhibition? Believe me, my fair Friends, that could I, in analizing the instances which have been here brought forward, trace them to no other source than such an inferiority in the intellectual powers as renders the attainment of the speculative faculties incompatible with the exercise of the active duties, I have too much of the woman in me not to endeavour to keep our own secret. But if to a defective education all the errors alluded to may be fairly traced, I shall instead of censure, hope to receive the meed of approbation.

Often does the ill-judging vanity and pride of parents lay the foundation of such characters as have been above described. The over educated and the uneducated are equally incapacitated from making a proper use of their faculties. The conceptions of the former having been stretched to embrace abstract propositions, at a period when they ought to have been strengthened on the objects of perception, become dull and languid as to those objects; and the judgement having, like the conceptions been exercised upon speculative enquiry, before it had been improved upon simple propositions, has neither soundness nor vigour.

———

38. Mary Robinson
from *Memoirs*

I went to the Oratorio; and, on taking my seat in the balcony-box, the Prince almost instantaneously observed me. He held the printed bill before his face, and drew his hand across his forehead, still fixing his eyes on me. I was confused and knew not what to do. My husband was with me, and I was fearful of his observing what passed. Still the Prince continued to make signs, such as moving his hand on the edge of the box as if writing, and then speaking to the Duke of York, (then Bishop of Osnaburg), who also looked towards me with particular attention.

I now observed one of the gentlemen in waiting bring the Prince a glass of water: before he raised it to his lips he looked at me. So marked was his Royal Highness's conduct that many of the audience observed it; several persons in the Pit directed their gaze at the place where I sat; and, on the following day, one of the diurnal prints observed that there was one passage in Dryden's Ode which seemed particularly interesting to the Prince of Wales, who

> Gazed on the fair
> Who caused his care,
> And sighed, and looked, and sighed again.

However flattering it might have been to female vanity, to know that the most admired and most accomplished Prince in Europe was devotedly attached to me; however dangerous to the heart such idolatry as his Royal Highness, during many months, professed in almost daily letters, which were conveyed to me by Lord Malden, still I declined any interview with his Royal Highness. I was not insensible to all his powers of attraction; I thought him one of the most amiable of men. There was a beautiful ingenuousness in his language, a warm and enthusiastic adoration, expressed in every letter, which interested and charmed me. During the whole Spring till the theatre closed this correspondence continued; every day giving me some new assurance of inviolable affection.

After we had corresponded some months without ever speaking to each other, (for I still declined meeting his Royal Highness, from a dread of the éclat which such a connection would produce, and the fear of injuring him in the opinion of his royal relatives), I received, through the hands of Lord Malden, the Prince's portrait in miniature, painted by the late Mr Meyer. This picture is now in my possession. Within the case was a small heart cut in paper, which I also have; on one side was written, 'Je ne change qu'en mourant'. On the other, 'Unalterable to my Perdita through life'.

During my many months of confidential correspondence, I always offered his Royal Highness the best advice in my power; I disclaimed every sordid and interested thought; I recommended him to be patient till he should become his own master; to wait till he knew more of my mind and manners before he engaged in a public attachment to me and, above all, to do nothing that might incur the displeasure of his Royal Highness's family. I entreated him to recollect that he was young, and led on by the impetuosity of passion; that should I consent to quit my profession and my husband, I should be thrown entirely on his mercy. I strongly pictured the temptations to which beauty would expose him; the many arts that would be practised to undermine me in his affections; the public abuse which calumny and envy would heap upon me; and the misery I should suffer, if, after I had given him every proof of confidence, he should change in his sentiments towards me. To all this I received repeated assurances of inviolable affection; and I most firmly believe that his Royal Highness meant what he professed: indeed, his soul was too ingenuous, his mind too liberal and his heart too susceptible to deceive premeditatedly, or to harbour, even for a moment, the idea of a deliberate deception.

At every interview with Lord Malden I perceived that he regretted the task he had undertaken; but he assured me that the Prince was almost frantic whenever he suggested a wish to decline interfering. Once I remember his Lordship's telling me that the late Duke of Cumberland had made him a visit early in the morning, at his house in Clarges Street, informing him that the Prince was most wretched on my account, and imploring him to continue his services only a short time longer. The Prince's establishment was then in agitation: at this period his Royal Highness still resided in Buckingham House.

A proposal was now made that I should meet his Royal Highness at his apartments, in the disguise of male attire. I was accustomed to perform in that dress, and the Prince had seen me (I believe) in the character of the 'Irish Widow'. To this plan I decidedly objected. The indelicacy of such a step, as well as the danger of detection, made me shrink from the proposal. My refusal threw his Royal Highness into the most distressing agitation, as was expressed by the letter which I received on the following morning. Lord Malden again lamented that he had engaged himself in the intercourse, and declared that he had himself conceived so violent a passion for me that he was the most miserable and unfortunate of mortals.

During this period, though Mr Robinson was a stranger to my epistolary intercourse with the Prince, his conduct was entirely neglectful. He was perfectly careless regarding my fame and my repose; passed his leisure hours with the most abandoned of women, and even my own servants complained of his illicit advances. I remember one, who was plain even to ugliness; she was short, ill-made, squalid, and dirty: once, on my return from a rehearsal, I found this woman was locked with my husband in my chamber. I also knew that Mr Robinson continued his connection with a female who lodged in Maiden Lane, and who was only one of the few that proved his domestic apostasy.

His indifference naturally produced an alienation of esteem on my side, and the increasing adoration of the most enchanting of mortals hourly reconciled my mind to the idea of a separation. The unbounded assurances of lasting affection which I received from his Royal Highness in many scores of the most eloquent letters, the contempt which I experienced from my husband, and the perpetual labour which I underwent for his support, at length began to weary my fortitude. Still I was reluctant to become the theme of public animadversion, and still I remonstrated with my husband on the unkindness of his conduct.

1802

39. Amelia Opie
The Dying Daughter to her Mother

Mother! when these unsteady lines
Thy long-averted eyes shall see,
This hand that writes, this heart that pines
Will cold, quite cold, and tranquil be.

That guilty child so long disowned
Can then, blessed thought! no more offend;
And, shoulds't thou deem my crimes atoned,
O deign my orphan to befriend: –

That orphan, who with trembling hand
To thee will give my dying prayer; –
Canst thou my dying prayer withstand,
And from my child withhold thy care?

O raise the veil which hides her cheek,
Nor start her mother's face to see,
But let her look thy love bespeak, –
For once that face was dear to thee.

Gaze on, – and thou'lt perchance forget
The long, the mournful lapse of years,
Thy couch with tears of anguish wet,
And e'en the guilt which caused those tears.

And in my pure and artless child
Thou'lt think her mother meets thy view;
Such as she was when life first smiled,
And guilt by name alone she knew.

Ah! then I see thee o'er her charms
A look of fond affection cast;
I see thee clasp her in thine arms,
And in the present lose the past.

But soon the dear illusion flies;
The sad reality returns;
My crimes again to memory ride,
And ah! in vain my orphan mourns.

Till suddenly some keen remorse,
Some deep regret, her claims shall aid,
For wrath that held too long its course,
For words of peace too long delayed.

For pardon (most, alas! denied
When pardon might have snatched from shame)
And kindness, hadst thou kindness tried,
Had checked my guilt, and saved my fame.

And then thou'lt wish, as I do now,
Thy hand my humble bed had smoothed,
Wiped the chill moisture off my brow,
And all the wants of sickness soothed.

For oh! the means to soothe my pain
My poverty has still denied;
And thou wilt wish, ah! wish in vain,
Thy riches had those means supplied.

Thou'lt wish, with keen repentance wrung,
I'd closed my eyes upon thy breast,
Expiring while thy faltering tongue
Pardon in kindest tones expressed.

O sounds which I must never hear!
Through years of woe my fond desire!
O mother, spite of all most dear!
Must I unblessed by thee expire?

Thy love alone I call to mind,
And all thy past disdain forget, –
Each keen reproach, each frown unkind,
That crushed my hopes when last we met.

But when I saw that angry brow,
Both health and youth were still my own:
O mother! couldst thou see me now,
Thou wouldst not have the heart to frown.

But see! my orphan's cheek displays
Both youth, and health's carnation dyes,
Such as on mine in happier days
So fondly charmed thy partial eyes.

Grief o'er her bloom a veil now draws,
Grief her loved parent's pangs to see;
And when thou thinks't upon the cause,
That paleness will have charms for thee:

And thou wilt fondly press that cheek,
Bid happiness its bloom restore,
And thus in tenderest accents speak,
'Sweet orphan, thou shalt mourn no more'.

But wilt thou thus indulgent be?
O! am I not by hope beguiled?
The long long anger shown to me,
Say, will it not pursue my child?

And must she suffer for my crime?
Ah! no! – forbid it, gracious Heaven!
And let thy goodness speed the time
When she'll be loved, and I forgiven!

1803

40. Dorothy Wordsworth
from *A Tour Made in Scotland*

Came to a bark hut by the shores, and sat for some time under the shelter
of it. While we were here a poor woman with a little child by her side
begged a penny of me, and asked where she could 'find quarters in the village'. She was a travelling beggar, a native of Scotland, had often 'heard of
that water', but was never there before. This woman's appearance, while
the wind was rustling about us, and the waves breaking at our feet, was
very melancholy: the waters looked wide, the hills many, and dark, and far
off – no house but at Luss. I thought what a dreary waste must this lake be
to such poor creatures, struggling with fatigue and poverty and unknown
ways!

We ordered tea when we reached the inn, and desired the girl to light us
a fire; she replied, 'I dinna ken whether she'll gie fire', meaning her mistress. We told her we did not wish her mistress to *give* fire, we only desired
her to let *her* make a fire and we would pay for it. The girl brought in the
tea-things, but no fire, and when I asked if she was coming to light it, she
said 'her mistress was not varra willing to gie fire'. At last, however, on our

insisting upon it, the fire was lighted: we got tea by candlelight, and spent a comfortable evening. I had seen the landlady before we went out, for, as had been usual in all the country inns, there was a demur respecting beds, notwithstanding the house was empty, and there were at least half-a-dozen spare beds. Her countenance corresponded with the unkindness of denying us a fire on a cold night, for she was the most cruel and even hateful-looking woman I ever saw. She was overgrown with fat, and was sitting with her feet and legs in a tub of water for the dropsy (probably brought on by whisky-drinking). The sympathy which I felt and expressed for her, on seeing her in this wretched condition (for her legs were swollen as thick as mill-posts), seemed to produce no effect; and I was obliged, after five minutes' conversation, to leave the affair of the beds undecided. C. had some talk with her daughter, a smart lass in a cotton gown, with a bandeau round her head, without shoes and stockings. She told C. with some pride that she had not spent all her time at Loss, but was then fresh from Glasgow.

It came on a very stormy night; the wind rattled every window in the house, and it rained heavily. Wm. and C. had bad beds, in a two-bedded room in the garrets, though there were empty rooms on the first floor, and they were disturbed by a drunken man, who had come to the inn when we were gone to sleep.

❧ ❧ ❧

Presently after C. joined us, and we determined to go to the island. I was sorry that the man who had been talking with us was not our boatman; Wm. by some chance had engaged another. We had two rowers and a strong boat; so I felt myself bold, though there was a great chance of a high wind. The nearest point of Inch-ta-vannach is not perhaps more than a mile and a quarter from Luss; we did not land there, but rowed round the end, and landed on that side which looks towards our favourite cottages, and their own island, which, wherever seen, is still their own. It rained a little when we landed, and I took my cloak, which afterwards served us to sit down upon in our road up the hill, when the day grew much finer, with gleams of sunshine. This island belongs to Sir James Colquhaun, who has made a convenient road that winds gently to the top of it.

We had not climbed far before we were stopped by a sudden burst of prospect, so singular and beautiful that it was like a flash of images from another world. We stood with our backs to the hill of the island, which we were ascending, and which shut out Ben Lomond entirely, and all the upper part of the lake, and we looked towards the foot of the lake, with islands without beginning and without end. The sun shone, and the distant hills were visible, some through sunny mists, others in gloom with patches of sunshine; the lake was lost under the low and distant hills, and the islands lost in the lake, which was all in motion with travelling fields of light, or dark shadows under rainy clouds. There are many hills, but no commanding eminence at a distance to confine the prospect, so that the land seemed endless as the water.

What I had heard of Loch Lomond, or any other place in Great Britain, had given me no idea of anything like what we beheld: it was an outlandish scene – we might have believed ourselves in North America. The islands were of every possible variety of shape and surface – hilly and level, large and small, bare, rocky, pastoral, or covered with wood. Immediately under my eyes lay one large flat island, bare and green, so flat and low that it scarcely appeared to rise above the water, with straggling peat-stacks and a single hut upon one of its out-shooting promontories (for it was of a very irregular shape, though perfectly flat). Another, its next neighbour, and still nearer to us, was covered over with heath and coppice-wood, the surface undulating, with flat or sloping banks towards the water, and hollow places, cradle-like valleys, behind. These two islands, with Inch-ta-vannach, where we were standing, were intermingled with the water, I might say interbedded and interveined with it, in a manner that was exquisitely pleasing. There were bays innumerable, straits or passages like calm rivers, landlocked lakes, and, to the main water, stormy promontories. The solitary hut on the flat green island seemed unsheltered and desolate, and yet not wholly so, for it was but a broad river's breadth from the covert of the wood of the other island. Near to these is a miniature, an islet covered with trees, on which stands a small ruin that looks like the remains of a religious house; it is overgrown with ivy, and were it not that the arch of a window or gateway may be distinctly seen, it would be difficult to believe that it was not a tuft of trees growing in the shape of a ruin, rather than a ruin overshadowed by trees. When we had walked a little further we saw below us, on the nearest large island, where some of the wood had been cut down, a hut, which we conjectured to be a bark hut. It appeared to be on the shore of a little forest lake, enclosed by Inch-ta-vannach (where we were), and the woody island on which the hut stands.

1805

41. Mary Tighe
from *Psyche; or The Legend of Love*

Allowed to settle on celestial eyes
Soft Sleep exulting now exerts his sway,
From Psyche's anxious pillow gladly flies
To veil those orbs, whose pure and lambent ray
The powers of heaven submissively obey.
Trembling and breathless then she softly rose
And seized the lamp where it obscurely lay,
With hand too rashly daring to disclose
The sacred veil which hung mysterious o'er her woes.

Twice, as with, agitated step she went,
The lamp expiring shone with doubtful gleam,
As though it warned her from her rash intent:
And twice she paused, and on its trembling beam
Gazed with suspended breath, while voices seem
With murmuring sound along the roof to sigh;
As one just waking from a troublous dream,
With palpitating heart and straining eye,
Still fixed with fear remains, still thinks the danger nigh.

Oh, daring Muse! wilt thou indeed essay
To paint the wonders which that lamp could show?
And canst thou hope in living words to say
The dazzling glories of that heavenly view?
Ah! well I ween, that if with pencil true
That splendid vision could be well expressed,
The fearful awe imprudent Psyche knew
Would seize with rapture every wondering breast,
When Love's all potent charms divinely stood confessed.

All imperceptible to human touch,
His wings display celestial essence light,
The clear effulgence of the blaze is such,
The brilliant plumage shines so heavenly bright
That mortal eyes turn dazzled from the sight;

A youth he seems in manhood's freshest years;
Round his fair neck, as clinging with delight,
Each golden curl resplendently appears,
Or shades his darker brow, which grace majestic wears.

Or o'er his guileless front the ringlets bright
Their rays of sunny lustre seem to throw
That front than polished ivory more white!
His blooming cheeks with deeper blushes glow
Than roses scattered o'er a bed of snow:
While on his lips distilled in balmy dews,
(Those lips divine that even in silence know
The heart to touch), persuasion to infuse
Still hangs a rosy charm that never vainly sues.

The friendly curtain of indulgent sleep
Disclosed not yet his eyes' resistless sway,
But from their silky veil there seemed to peep
Some brilliant glances with a softened ray,
Which o'er his features exquisitely play,
And all his polished limbs suffuse with light.
Thus through some narrow space the azure day
Sudden its cheerful rays diffusing bright,
Wide darts its lucid beams, to gild the brow of night.

His fatal arrows and celestial bow
Beside the couch were negligently thrown,
Nor needs the god his dazzling arms, to show
His glorious birth, such beauty round him shone
As sure could spring from Beauty's self alone;
The gloom which glowed o'er all of soft desire,
Could well proclaim him Beauty's cherished son;
And Beauty's self will oft these charms admire,
And steal his witching smile, his glance's living fire.

Speechless with awe, in transport strangely lost
Long Psyche stood with fixed adoring eye;
Her limbs, immovable, her senses tossed
Between amazement, fear, and ecstasy,
She hangs enamoured o'er the Deity.

Till from her trembling hand extinguished falls
The fatal lamp – He starts – and suddenly
Tremendous thunders echo through the halls,
While ruin's hideous crash bursts o'er the affrighted walls.

Dread horror seizes on her sinking heart,
A mortal chillness shudders at her breast,
Her soul shrinks fainting from death's icy dart,
The groan scarce uttered dies but half expressed,
And down she sinks in deadly swoon oppressed;
But when at length, awaking from her trance,
The terrors of her fate stand all confessed,
In vain she casts around her timid glance,
The rudely frowning scenes her former joys enhance.

No traces of those joys, alas, remain!
A desert solitude alone appears.
No verdant shade relieves the sandy plain,
The wide-spread waste no gentle fountain cheers,
One barren face the dreary prospect wears;
Nought through the vast horizon meets her eye
To calm the dismal tumult of her fears,
No trace of human habitation nigh,
A sandy wild beneath, above a threatening sky.

1806

42. Mary Robinson
Stanzas to a Friend who wished to have my Portrait

E'en from the early days of youth,
I've blessed the sacred voice of truth –
   And candour is my pride:
I always speak what I believe;
I know not if I can deceive –
   Because I never tried.

I'm often serious, sometimes gay,
Can laugh the fleeting hours away,
    Or weep for others' woe:
I'm proud! this fault you cannot blame,
Nor does it tinge my cheek with shame:
    Your friendship made me so.

I'm odd, eccentric, fond of ease,
Impatient, difficult to please;
    Ambition fires my breast:
Yet not for wealth or titles vain;
Let but the laurel deck my strain,
    And dullness take the rest.

In temper quick, in friendship nice;
I doat on genius, shrink from vice,
    And scorn the flatterer's art:
With penetrating skill can see,
Where, masked in sweet simplicity,
    Lies hid the treacherous heart.

If once betrayed, I scarce forgive;
And though I pity all that live,
    And mourn for every pain,
Yet could I never court the great,
Or worship fools, whate'er their state;
    For falsehood I disdain.

I'm jealous, for I fondly love;
No feeble flame my heart can prove,
    Caprice ne'er dimmed its fires:
I blush to see the human mind,
For nobler, prouder claims designed,
    The slave of low desires.

Reserved in manner, where unknown;
A little obstinate, I own,
    And apt to form opinion;
Yet, envy never broke my rest,
Not could self-interest bow my breast
    To folly's base dominion.

No gaudy trappings I display,
Nor meanly plain, nor idly gay,
　　Yet swayed by fashion's rule;
For singularity, we find,
Betrays to every reasoning mind,
　　The *pedant* or the *fool*.

I fly the rich, the sordid crowd,
The little great, the vulgar proud,
　　The ignorant and base:
The sons of genius homage pay,
And own their sovereign right to sway –
　　Lords of the human race.

When coxcombs tell me I'm divine,
I plainly see the weak design,
　　And mock a tale so common:
Howe'er the flattering strain may flow,
My faults, alas! too plainly show,
　　I'm but a mortal woman!

Such is my portrait now believe;
My pencil never can deceive,
　　And know me what I paint.
Taught in affliction's rigid school,
I act from principle, not rule,
　　No sinner, yet no saint.

1807

43. Anne Grant
from *Letters from the Mountains*

I have seen Mary Wollstonecraft's book, which is so run after here, that
there is no keeping it long enough to read it leisurely, though one had
leisure. It has produced no other conviction in my mind, but that of the
author's possessing considerable abilities, and greatly misapplying them.

To refute her arguments would be to write another and a larger book; for there is more pains and skill required to refute ill-founded assertions, than to make them. Nothing can be more specious and plausible, for nothing can delight Misses more than to tell them they are as wise as their masters. Though, after all, they will in every emergency be like Trinculo in the storm, when he crept under Caliban's gabardine for shelter. – I consider this work as every way dangerous. First, because the author to considerable powers adds feeling, and I dare say a degree of rectitude of intention. She speaks from conviction on her own part, and has completely imposed on herself before she attempts to mislead you. Then because she speaks in such a strain of seeming piety, and quotes Scripture in a manner so applicable and emphatic, that you are thrown off your guard, and surprised into partial acquiescence, before you observe that the deduction to be drawn from her position, is in direct contradiction, not only to Scripture, reason, the common sense and universal custom of the world, but even to parts of her own system, and many of her own assertions. Some women of a good capacity, with the advantage of superior education, have no doubt acted and reasoned more consequentially and judiciously than some weak men; but, take the whole sex through, this seldom happens; and were the principal departments, where strong thinking and acting become necessary, allotted to females, it would evidently happen so much the more rarely, that there would be little room for triumph, and less for inverting the common order of things, to give room for the exercise of female intellect.

* * * *

Mary W. and some others put me in mind of a kitten we had last winter, who, finding a small tea-pot without a lid, put in its head, but not finding it so easy to take it out again, she broke the pot in the struggle; her head, however, still remained in the opening, and she retained as much of the broken utensil round her neck, as made a kind of moveable pillory. She ran about the house in alarm and astonishment. She did not know what was the matter; felt she was not like other cats, but had acquired a greater power of making a disturbance, which she was resolved to use to the very utmost, and so would neither be quiet herself, or suffer any one else to remain so. I leave the application to you. Our powers are extremely well adapted to the purposes for which they are intended; and if now and then faculties of a superior order are bestowed upon us, they too are, no doubt, given for good and wise purposes, and we have as good a right to use them as a linnet has to sing; but this so seldom happens, and it is of so little consequence whether it happens or not, that there is no reason why Scripture, custom, and nature, should be set at defiance, to erect up a system of education for qualifying women to act parts which Providence has not assigned to the sex. Where a woman has those superior powers of mind to which we give the name of genius, she will exert them under all disadvantages. . . . Certainly in the present state of society, when knowledge is so very attainable, a strong and vigorous intellect may soon find its level. Creating hot-beds for female genius, is merely another way of forcing exotic productions, which, after all, are mere luxuries, indifferent in their kind, and cost more time and expense than they are worth. As to superiority of mental powers, Mrs. W. is doubtless the empress of female philosophers; yet what has she done for philosophy, or for the sex, but closed a ditch, to open a gulf? There is a degree of boldness in her conceptions, and masculine energy in her stile, that is very imposing. There is a gloomy grandeur in her imagination, while she explores the regions of intellect without chart or compass, which gives one the idea of genius wandering through chaos. Yet her continual self contradiction, and quoting, with such seeming reverence, that very Scripture, one of whose first and clearest principles it is the avowed object of her work to controvert; her considering religion as an adjunct to virtue, so far and no farther than suits her hypothesis; the taking up and laying down of revelation with the same facility; make me think of a line in an old song,

> One foot on sea and one on shore,
> To one thing constant never.

What, as I said before, has she done? showed us all the miseries of our condition; robbed us of the only sure remedy for the evils of life, the sure hope of a blessed immortality; and left for our comfort the rudiments of crude, unfinished systems, that crumble to nothing whenever you begin to examine the materials of which they are constructed. Come, let us for a moment shut the Bible, and listen to Mary. Let us suppose intellect equally divided between the sexes. We may deceive the understanding, but it would be a very bold effort of sophistry to attempt to impose on the senses. We know too well that our imaginations are more awake, our senses more acute, our feelings more delicate, than those of our *tyrants*. Say, then, we are otherwise equal. These qualities or defects would still leave the advantage on their side; we should much oftener resolve and act, before we called reason to counsel, than they would. Besides, I foresee that the balance will go in the old fashioned way at last, if Mary carries her point. When the desired revolution is brought about, will not the most sanguine advocates of equality be satisfied, in the first national council, with having an equal number of each sex elected? Now I foresee that when this is done (as girls, or very old women, will not be eligible for the duties of legislation, and mothers have certainly a greater stake in the commonwealth) a third of the senate members will be lying-in, recovering, or nursing; for you can never admit the idea of a female philosopher giving her child to be nursed. Whatever other changes may be found proper, I hope they will retain the wool-sacks in the upper house, and add some more. The membresses of course will bring their infants into the house; this will interrupt no debate; for children that suck in philosophy with their milk, will not cry like the vulgar brats under the old regime, but they may possibly sleep during a long debate, and then the wool-sacks will be very convenient to lay them upon. There is no end either of reasoning or ridicule on this truly ridiculous subject. If the powers of a very superior female mind prove so inadequate to its own purposes, when thus absurdly exerted, what will become of those who adopt her vanity and scepticism, without her knowledge and genius to support them?

———

44. Elizabeth Inchbald
from *On Novel Writing*

If the critical knowledge of an art was invariably combined with the successful practice of it, I would here proudly take my rank among artists, and give instructions on the art of writing novels. – But though I humbly confess that I have not the slightest information to impart, that may tend to produce a good novel; yet it may not be wholly incompatible with the useful design of your publication, if I show – how to avoid writing a very bad one.

Observe, that your hero and heroine be neither of them too bountiful. The prodigious sums of money which are given away every year in novels, ought, in justice, to be subject to the property tax; by which regulation, the national treasury, or every such book, would be highly benefited.

Beware how you imitate Mrs. Radcliffe, or Maria Edgeworth; you cannot equal them; and those readers who most admire their works, will most despise yours.

Take care to reckon up the many times you make use of the words 'Amiable', 'Interesting', 'Elegant', 'Sensibility', 'Delicacy', 'Feeling'. Count each of these words over before you send your manuscript to be printed, and be sure to erase half the number you have written; – you may erase again when your first proof comes from the press – again, on having a revise – and then mark three or four, as mistakes of the printer, in your Errata.

Examine likewise, and for the same purpose, the various times you have made your heroine blush, and your hero turn pale – the number of times he has pressed her hand to his 'trembling lips' and she his letters to her 'beating heart' – the several times he has been 'speechless' and she 'all emotion', the one 'struck to the soul'; the other 'struck dumb'.

The lavish use of 'tears,' both in 'showers' and 'floods,' should next be scrupulously avoided; though many a gentle reader will weep on being told that others are weeping, and require no greater cause to excite their compassion.

Consider well before you introduce a child into your work. To maim the characters of men and women is no venial offence; but to destroy innocent babes is most ferocious cruelty: and yet this savage practice has, of late, arrived at such excess, that numberless persons of taste and sentiment have declared – they will never read another novel, unless the advertisement which announces the book, adds (as in advertisements for letting lodgings) *There are no children.*

When you are contriving that incident where your heroine is in danger of being drowned, burnt, or her neck broken by the breaking of an axle-tree – for without perils by fire, water, or coaches, your book would be incomplete – it might be advisable to suffer her to be rescued from impending death by the sagacity of a dog, a fox, a monkey, or a hawk; any one to whom she cannot give her hand in marriage; for whenever the deliverer is a fine young man, the catastrophe of your plot is foreseen, and suspense extinguished.

Let not your ambition to display variety cause you to produce such a number of personages in your story, as shall create perplexity, dissipate curiosity, and confound recollection. But if, to show your powers of invention, you are resolved to introduce your reader to a new acquaintance in every chapter, and in every chapter snatch away his old one; he will soon have the consolation to perceive – they are none of them worth his regret.

Respect virtue – nor let her be so warm or so violent as to cause derision; – nor vice so enormous as to resemble insanity. No one can be interested for an enthusiast – nor gain instruction from a madman.

And when you have written as good a novel as you can – compress it into three or four short volumes at most; or the man of genius whose moments are precious, and on whose praise your fame depends, will not find time to read the production, till you have committed suicide in consequence of its ill reception with the public.

45. Charlotte Smith
from *Beachy Head*

An early worshipper at Nature's shrine,
I loved her rudest scenes – warrens, and heaths,
And yellow commons, and birch-shaded hollows,
And hedge rows, bordering unfrequented lanes
Bowered with wild roses, and the clasping woodbine
Where purple tassels of the tangling vetch
With bittersweet, and bryony inweave,
And the dew fills the silver bindweed's cups –
I loved to trace the brooks whose humid banks
Nourish the harebell, and the freckled pagil;
And stroll among o'ershadowing woods of beech,
Lending in summer, from the heats of noon
A whispering shade; while haply there reclines
Some pensive lover of uncultured flowers,
Who, from the tumps with bright green mosses clad,
Plucks the wood sorrel, with its light thin leaves,
Heart-shaped, and triply folded; and its root
Creeping like beaded coral; who there
Gathers, the copse's pride, anemones,
With rays like golden studs on ivory laid
Most delicate: but touched with purple clouds,
Fit crown for April's fair but changeful brow.

Ah! hills so early loved! in fancy still
I breathe your pure keen air; and still behold
Those widely spreading views, mocking alike
The poet and the painter's utmost art.
And still, observing objects more minute,
Wondering remark the strange and foreign forms
Of sea-shells; with the pale calcareous soil,
Mingled, and seeming of resembling substance
Tho' surely the blue ocean, (from the heights
Where the downs westward trend, but dimly seen)
Here never ruled its surge. Does Nature then
Mimic, in wanton mood, fantastic shapes
Of bivalves, and inwreathed volutes, that cling
To the dark sea-rock of the watery world?

Or did this range of chalky mountains, once
Form a vast basin, where the ocean waves
Swelled fathomless? What time these fossil shells,
Buoyed on their native element, were thrown
Among the imbedding calx: when the huge hill
Its giant bulk heaved, and in strange ferment
Grew up a guardian barrier, 'twixt the sea
    And the green level of the sylvan weald.

———

1808

46. Felicia Hemans

from *England and Spain; or, Valour and Patriotism*

Hail, Albion! hail, thou land of freedom's birth!
Pride of the main, and phoenix of the earth!
Thou second Rome, where mercy, justice dwell,
Whose sons in wisdom as in arms excel:
Thine are the dauntless bands, like Spartans brave,
Bold in the field, triumphant on the wave;
In classic elegance and arts divine,
To rival Athens' fairest palm is thine;
For taste and fancy from Hymettus fly,
And richer bloom beneath thy varying sky.
Where Science mounts in radiant car sublime
To other worlds beyond the sphere of time!
Hail, Albion! hail! to thee has fate denied
Peruvian mines and rich Hindostan's pride,
The gems that Ormuz and Golconda boast,
And all the wealth of Montezuma's coast:
For thee no Parian marbles brightly shine,
No glowing suns mature the blushing vine;
No light Arabian gales their wings expand,
To waft Sabaean incense o'er the land;
No graceful cedars crown thy lofty hills,
No trickling myrrh for thee its balm distils;

Not from thy trees the lucid amber flows,
And far from thee the scented cassia blows:
Yet fearless Commerce, pillar of thy throne,
Makes all the wealth of foreign climes thy own;
From Lapland's shore to Afric's fervid reign,
She bids thy ensigns float above the main;
Unfurls her streamers to the favouring gale,
And shows to other worlds her daring sail:
Then wafts their gold, their varied stores to thee,
Queen of the trident! empress of the sea!

O thou, the sovereign of the noble soul!
Thou source of energies beyond control!
Queen of the lofty thought, the generous deed,
Whose sons unconquered fight, undaunted bleed, –
Inspiring Liberty! thy worshipped name
The warm enthusiast kindles to a flame;
Thy charms inspire him to achievements high,
Thy look of heaven, thy voice of harmony.
More blest with thee to tread perennial snows,
Where ne'er a flower, ne'er a zephyr blows;
Where Winter, binding nature in his chain,
In frost-work palace holds perpetual reign;
Than, far from thee, with frolic step to rove
The green savannas and the spicy grove;
Scent the rich balm of India's perfumed gales,
In citron-woods and aromatic vales:
For oh! fair Liberty, when thou art near,
Elysium blossoms in the desert drear!
    Where'er thy smile its magic power bestows,
There arts and taste expand, there fancy glows;
The sacred lyre its wild enchantment gives,
And every chord to swelling transport lives;
There ardent Genius bids the pencil trace
The soul of beauty and the lines of grace;
With bold Promethean hand, the canvas warms,
And calls from stone expression's breathing forms.

1809

47. Sydney Owenson, Lady Morgan
from *Patriotic Sketches of Ireland*

It was requisite . . . I should leave my native country to learn the turpitude, degradation, ferocity and inconsequence of her offspring: the miseries of her present, and the falsity of the recorded splendours of her ancient state. – This ungracious information I acquired during a short tour through a sister isle; and it was in the course of one of the many conversations which occurred on the subject of my always termed, 'unhappy country', that a hint casually suggested, formed the origin of a little work, which has since appeared under the title of the Wild Irish Girl.

Yet I came to the self-devoted task, with a diffidence proportional to the ardour which instigated me to the attempt; for as a woman, a young woman, and an Irish woman; I felt all the delicacy of undertaking a work which had for the professed theme of its discussion, circumstances of national import, and national interest.

But although I meant not to appear on the list of opposition as a fairy amazon, armed with a pebble and a sling, against a host of gigantic preju- dices: although to compose a national defence, to ward off the shaft of opprobrium hurled at the character of my country, to extenuate the effects or expose the cause of its popular discontents, was as incompatible with my sex and years, as with my trivial talent, and limited powers; yet I was still aware that in the historic page, recent details, and existing circum- stances of Irish history, lived many a record of Irish virtue, Irish genius, and Irish heroism, which the simplicity of truth alone was sufficient to delineate; many a tale of pathos which a woman's heart could warmest tell, and truest tell, and many a trait of romantic colouring and chivalrous refinement, which woman's fancy fondest contemplates and best depicts.

* * * *

To minds which slavery has not broken, nor oppression debased, the consciousness of political inferiority and national inconsequence must ever bring with it a sensitive pride, a tenacious reserve, a suspicious timidity, and an irritability of spirit, which are only to be dissipated by the concili- ating advances of that superior influence under which a series of certain events has placed them: and when two parties are internally divided by a difference in religious faith, by an inequality of political establishment, and externally coalesced by local circumstances and certain ties of determination common to both; where prerogative rests on one side, and submission on the other; the natural suspicions, the cautious vigilant diffidence of the subordinate party, are only to be seduced into amity, or warmed into confidence, by the open, ingenuous, volunteering liberality of the supreme power.

But in that dominant sect . . . dwells there that mild, that generous, and all conciliating spirit of charity . . . ? Dwells there among those who vaunt their own abhorrence of fanaticism and bigotry, that pure and sole religion which, in considering the great and only Object of universal worship of mankind, neither derides nor reviles the medium through which it flows? . . . Does it feel for the political subjection of a compatriot, but not established sect; endeavour to counteract the effects of an erroneous and fatal policy . . . , and by endeavouring to produce that compatriot felicity, that national unanimity and brotherly love, over which a fanatical dogma, or intolerant law, has no jurisdiction? If these interrogations can be answered by an undeniable affirmative of actual demonstration, what has Ireland to fear? what has Ireland to wish?

———

1810

48. Lucy Aikin
from *Epistles on the Character and Conditions of Women*

Let me in the first place disclaim entirely the absurd idea that the two sexes can be, or ought ever to be, placed in all respects on a footing of equality. Man, when he abuses his power may justly be considered as a tyrant; but his power itself is no tyranny, being founded not on usurpation, but on certain unalterable necessities; . . . sanctioned, not by prescription alone, but by the fundamental laws of human nature. As long as the bodily constitution of the species shall remain the same, man must in general assume those public and active offices of life which confer authority, whilst to woman will usually be allotted such domestic and private ones as imply a degree of subordination.

Nothing therefore could, in my opinion, be more foolish than the attempt to engage our sex in a struggle for stations that they are physically unable properly to fill; for power of which they must always want the

means to possess themselves. No! instead of aspiring to be inferior men, let
us content ourselves with becoming noble women.

❋ ❋ ❋ ❋

Sons of fair Albion, tender, brave, sincere
(Be this the strain) an earnest suppliant hear!
Feel that when heaven evolved its perfect plan,
Crowned with its last best gift transported Man,
It formed no creature of ignoble strain,
Of heart unteachable, obtuse of brain
(Such had not filled the solitary void,
Nor such his soul's new sympathies employed,)
But one all eloquent of eye, of mien;
Intensely human; exquisitely keen
To feel, to know: Be generous then, unbind
Your barbarous shackles, loose the female mind;
Aid its new flights, instruct its wavering wing,
And guide its thirst to wisdom's purest spring:
Sincere as generous, with fraternal heart
Spurn the dark satirist's unmanly part;
Scorn too the flatterer's, in the medium wise,
Nor feed those follies that yourselves despise.
For you, bright daughters of a land renowned,
By Genius blest, by glorious Freedom crowned;
Safe in a polished privacy, content
To grace, not shun, the lot that Nature lent,
Be yours the joys of home, affection's charms,
And infants clinging with caressing arms:
Yours too the boon, of taste's whole garden free,
To pluck at will her bright Hesperian tree,
Unchecked the wreath of each fair Muse assume,
And fill your lap with amaranthine bloom.
Press eager on; of this great art possessed,
To seize the good, to follow still the best,
Ply the pale lamp, explore the breathing page,
And catch the soul of each immortal age.

❋ ❋ ❋ ❋

Thus self-endowed, thus armed for every state,
Improve, excel, surmount, subdue, your fate!
So shall at length enlightened Man efface

That slavish stigma seared on half the race,
His rude forefathers' shame; and pleased confess,
'Tis yours to elevate, 'tis yours to bless;
Your interest one with his; your hopes the same
Fair peace, in life, in death undying fame,
And bliss in worlds beyond, the species' general aim.
'Rise', shall he cry, 'O Woman, rise! be free!
My life's associate, now partake with me;
Rouse thy keen energies, expand thy soul,
And see, and feel, and comprehend the whole;
My deepest thoughts, intelligent, divide
When right confirm me, and when erring guide;
Soothe all my cares, in all my virtues blend,
And be, my sister, be at length my friend.'

---

49. Anna Barbauld
from *On the Origin and Progress of Novel Writing*

A collection of novels has a better chance of giving pleasure than of commanding respect. Books of this description are condemned by the grave,
and despised by the fastidious; but their leaves are seldom found unopened,
and they occupy the parlour and the dressing-room while productions of
higher name are often gathering dust upon the shelf. It might not be perhaps difficult to show that this species of composition is entitled to a
higher rank than has been generally assigned to it. Fictitious adventures, in
one form or another, have made a part of the polite literature of every age
and nation. These have been grafted upon the actions of their heroes; they
have been interwoven with their mythology; they have been moulded upon
the manners of the age, – and, in return, have influenced the manners of
the succeeding generation by the sentiments they have infused and the
sensibilities they have excited.

Adorned with the embellishments of poetry, they produce the epic;
more concentrated in the story, and exchanging narrative for action, they
become dramatic. When allied with some great moral end . . . they may be
termed didactic. They are often made the vehicles of satire. . . .They take
a tincture from the politics of the times, and are made use of successfully
to attack or recommend the prevailing systems of the day. When the range
of this kind of writing is so extensive, and its effects so great, it seems
evident that it ought to hold a respectable place among the productions of

genius; nor is it easy to say why the poet, who deals in one kind of fictions, should have so high a place allotted to him in the temple of fame; and the romance-writer so low a one as in the general estimation he is confined to. To measure the dignity of a writer by the pleasure he affords his readers is not perhaps using an accurate criterion; but the invention of a story, the choice of proper incidents, the ordnance of the plan, occasional beauties of description, and above all, the power exercised over the reader's heart by filling it with the successive emotions of love, pity, joy, anguish, transport, or indignation, together with the grave impressive moral resulting from the whole, imply talents of the highest order, and ought to be appreciated accordingly. A good novel is an epic in prose, with more of character and less (indeed in modern novels nothing) of the supernatural machinery.

❋ ❋ ❋ ❋

[On women's novels]: Why is it that women when they write are apt to give a melancholy tinge to their compositions? Is it that they suffer more, and have fewer resources against melancholy? Is it that men, mixing at large in society, have a brisker flow of ideas, and, seeing a greater variety of characters, introduce more of the business and pleasure of life into their compositions? Is it that humour is a scarcer product of the mind than sentiments, and more congenial to the stronger powers of man? Is it that women nurse those feelings in secrecy and silence, and diversify the expression of them with endless shades of sentiment, which are more transiently felt, and with fewer modifications of delicacy, by the other sex? The remark, if true, doubtless has many exceptions; but the productions of several ladies, both English and French, seems to countenance it.

❋ ❋ ❋ ❋

Reading is the cheapest of all pleasures: it is a domestic pleasure. Dramatic exhibitions give a more poignant delight, but they are seldom enjoyed in perfection, and never without expense and trouble. Poetry requires in the reader a certain elevation of mind and a practised ear. It is seldom relished unless a taste be formed for it pretty early. But the humble novel is always ready to enliven the gloom of solitude, to soothe the languor of debility and disease, to win the attention from pain or vexatious occurrences, to take man from himself (at many seasons the worst company he can be in) and, while the moving picture of life passes before him, to make him forget the subject of his own complaints. It is pleasant to the mind to sport in boundless regions of possibility; to find relief from the sameness of every-day occurrences by expatiating amidst brighter skies and fairer fields; to exhibit love that is always happy, valour that is always successful; to feed the appetite for wonder by a quick succession of marvellous events; and to distribute, like a ruling providence, rewards and punishments which fall just where they ought. . . .

But it is not necessary to rest the credit of these works on amusement alone, since it is certain they have had a very strong effect in infusing principles and moral feelings. It is impossible to deny that the most glowing and impressive sentiments of virtue are to be found in many of these compositions, and have been deeply imbibed by their youthful readers. They awaken a sense of finer feelings than the commerce of ordinary life inspires. . . . Many a maxim of prudence is laid up in the memory from these stories, ready to operate when occasion offers.

* * * *

[N]otwithstanding the many paltry books of this kind published in the course of every year, it may be safely affirmed that we have more good writers in this walk living at the present time, than at any period since the days of Richardson and Fielding. A very great proportion of these are ladies: and surely it will not be said that either taste or morals have been losers by their taking the pen in hand. The names of D'Arblay, Edgeworth, Inchbald, Radcliffe, and a number more will vindicate this assertion.

1811

50. Elizabeth Hamilton
from *Observations on the Power of Imagination*

Imagination is not a simple faculty, but a complex power, in which all the faculties of the mind occasionally operate. I now propose to show, that the operation of these faculties upon the power of imagination, bears an exact proportion to the degree in which the objects of these faculties have been objects of attention; or, in other words, to the degree in which these several faculties have been previously cultivated. There can be no doubt, that the imagination of the person in whom they have all been cultivated will be rich and vigorous. In the combinations which it forms, the operations of quick discernment, ready apprehension, sound judgement, taste, and reason, will be equally conspicuous. From minds thus endowed have proceeded all such works of genius as have contributed to the delight and improvement of successive ages. In all these extraordinary instances, however, the faculties will not only be found to have been universally cultivated, but to have been endowed by nature with an uncommon degree of strength and vigour. Where nature has been less liberal, it will not be possible, by the most assiduous cultivation of the faculties, to render the produce of the imagination eminently sublime or beautiful. But, even where there are no pretensions to superior genius, the imagination that has been enriched by a variety of ideas, will not only prove a source of perpetual enjoyment to the possessor, but a delight to all who have the happiness of his acquaintance. When, in persons thus endowed, the talent of conversation has also been cultivated, such is the pleasure derived from their company, that they may, without hyperbole, be termed the sun-beams of social life.

Let us now view the power of imagination as it operates under less favourable auspices.

In the mind of the person whose primary faculties have been no farther cultivated, than as impelled by necessity, or excited by some selfish impulse, the imagination may be equally active as in minds of a superior order; but, when the attention has never been directed towards subjects of an intellectual nature, we may easily conceive how little its utmost activity can produce. In such instances, the combinations formed by the imagination will, when the passions do not interfere, be like the dreams of children, made up of incongruous assemblages of external objects; but when any of the passions predominate, those images, however incoherent, will from that passion take their form and colouring; which will easily be accounted for, when we consider how naturally the object of every passion attracts and occupies the attention.

* * * *

And here it may be proper to remark, that as in every exercise of imagination attention is directed towards the ideas which the mind has received from observation or description, constant employment, if it be of a kind that demands attention, must necessarily impede the exercise of imagination, as idleness must, on the contrary, promote its exercise. Wherever, therefore, imagination prevails, we may be certain that there industry does not flourish; and where habits of industry are prevalent, there we need not expect to meet with many proofs of imagination. But as, among the various avocations of busy life, there are some which make comparatively little demand upon attention, and as imagination will ever, in such instances, be found extremely active, of great importance to society to provide against the evils which this activity must produce, where it has no materials to work upon but such as are of an inflammable nature. In this consideration we have an unanswerable argument for paying that attention to the education of the lower orders, which is essential towards enabling them to store the mind with such ideas as may be contemplated with advantage to the moral character; and, while they occupy the imagination, may elevate the feelings and improve the heart.

With regard to the higher classes, who enjoy the privilege of leisure as a birthright, imagination must, in their minds, have an almost perpetual operation; and according to the degree in which all the faculties have been exercised, and the desires regulated, will the operation be salutary or otherwise. Where the attention has been habitually directed to mean and unworthy objects, it is by objects of the same description that the imagination will be solely occupied. And those who, from base and sordid views, seek to gratify the imaginations of persons of this description, must exhibit such pictures as accord with the depraved habits of their minds. It is shocking to reflect how frequently genius has stooped to this ignoble office! We may, however, conclude, that the poet or the painter who thus employs the powers of invention to cater for the corrupt imaginations of the vulgar great, does not possess that intellectual vigour essential to the production of whatever is truly admirable or excellent. The judgement must be very defective that does not quickly perceive, that neither fame, not glory, nor honour, attach to such talents, when they forsake the service of virtue.

If imagination be so active in the idle as I have represented it, whence comes it that the idle are so generally dull? In answer to this question it may be observed, that as the indolent and uncultivated have few ideas, though imagination may be occupied in forming new combinations of these, they are seldom worthy of being communicated. They are even, for want of variety, tiresome to those who form them, and consequently render the spirits flat and joyless. Such persons, though they have no true relish for the pleasures of social intercourse, are always ready to bestow their weariness on strangers. At home they have no resources, but to re-dream the dreams that have already been dreamed; at home they are consequently wretched.

Among uneducated women of all ranks and situations, we may find numerous examples to illustrate the truth of the above remark.

I have, in a former section, in treating of the effects of attention in awakening the perceptions, pointed out the consequences which result from having the attention habitually occupied by dress. The pleasure which we naturally derive from the beauty of colours, from novelty, and variety, may sufficiently account for the facility with which the love of ornament is thus inspired. It is not, however, until it seizes the imagination, that it becomes a passion. But when in an empty mind the love of dress thus predominates, how melancholy is the result! Could the combinations produced in the imaginations of such persons be exposed to view, what heaps of foil and feathers, what glittering store of jewels and embroidery, would meet our dazzling eyes! When these brilliant reveries are unbroken by the rude voice of conscience calling to the performance of active duties, it is astonishing to what lengths they may be carried. I have myself known more than one instance of women, whose imaginations, from childhood to old age, have been thus occupied, and to whose minds these day-dreams have afforded a chief source of enjoyment; and this without any stimulus from the desire of admiration! Let that desire be added, and the effect upon the imagination will be incalculably increased.

From the pains taken to direct the thoughts of young women to matrimony, it is not surprising that the idea of matrimony should, in some instances, engross their whole attention. From the time that the attention is thus absorbed by one object, no improvement of the faculties can, for reasons before stated, possibly take place. The mind must consequently, thenceforth, remain stationary; while the one predominant idea, uncontrolled by the judgement or reason, keeps possession of the imagination. To imagination all things are possible: – under its deluding influence the homely girl sees men who are most sensible to the power of beauty captivated by her charms; the vulgar is led to the altar by the man of taste; and the poor makes conquest after conquest of lords, nabobs, and contractors! Instances have been known to occur, of persons not naturally deficient in understanding, who, for thirty or five and thirty years of their lives, have incessantly pursued such phantoms of felicity; and this without having experienced, for one of all the various objects that from time to time engaged their thoughts, a single spark of either esteem or affection.

What a waste of the intellectual faculties do such instances exhibit! What regret must it produce in every thinking mind, to behold this utter annihilation of all those mental energies, which, had the attention in early life been properly directed, would have been rendered instrumental to the happiness of the individual and of society.

It is true, that while the mind is engaged in forming these visions of happiness it experiences a certain gratification. Life may, however, extend far beyond the period in which it is possible, even for the most visionary, to indulge in these chimeras; whereas imagination, in the cultivated, affords enjoyment to life's latest verge.

* * * *

From circumstances apparently trivial, a word casually uttered, an object accidentally presented to view, a lively imagination will rapidly, from association, create a picture, whose origin it may perhaps be impossible to trace. This picture of its own creating it may contemplate with delight, and if the objects that compose it be of their natures noble and dignified, and calculated to produce in the mind a state of elevation somewhat similar to that produced by the contemplation of truth, the pleasurable effects of the emotion may continue to be felt, even after the cause that gave rise to them has been forgotten. The pleasure experienced by an uncultivated mind in the indulgence of its reveries, is, on the contrary, transient; never extending farther than to the moment in which the dream is broken. But in minds destitute of cultivation, the combinations of imagination are frequently worse than useless, they are positively pernicious. They debase the mind, by rendering it familiar with low and grovelling objects, and even while the conduct remains without reproach, deprave the character by polluting the purity of the heart. It cannot be denied, that these opposite effects naturally and inevitably flow from the opposite nature of the objects to which attention has been habitually directed.

In female education, as it is generally conducted, the imagination is stimulated, while the stock of ideas is yet too scanty to afford a supply of wholesome materials for its operations. And here it may be proper to remark, that it is not by attention to the objects of perception that this active faculty is first awakened. Though powerfully affected by visible objects, I question whether, by the contemplation of visible objects merely, the imagination was ever yet excited. It is by the description of objects, and not by their actual presence, that the spark is kindled, which, in the language of poetry, is described as a spark from heaven!

———

51. Mary Tighe
Written at Scarborough, August, 1799

As musing pensive in my silent home
    I hear far off the sullen ocean's roar,
    Where the rude wave just sweeps the level shore,
Or bursts upon the rocks with whitening foam,
I think upon the scenes my life has known;
    On days of sorrow, and some hours of joy;
    Both which alike time could so soon destroy!
And now they seem a busy dream alone;

While on the earth exists no single trace
    Of all that shook my agitated soul,
      As on the beach new waves for ever roll
And fill their past forgotten brother's place:
      But I, like the worn sand, exposed remain
      To each new storm which frets the angry main.

1812

52. Anna Barbauld
from *Eighteen Hundred and Eleven: A Poem*

And think'st thou, Britain, still to sit at ease,
An island Queen amidst thy subject seas,
While the vexed billows, in their distant roar,
But soothe thy slumbers, and but kiss thy shore?
To sport in wars, while danger keeps aloof,
Thy grassy turf unbruised by hostile hoof?
So sing thy flatterers; but, Britain, know,
Thou who hast shared the guilt must share the woe.
Nor distant is the hour; low murmurs spread,
And whispered fears, creating what they dread;
Ruin, as with an earthquake shock, is here,
There, the heart-witherings of unuttered fear,
And that sad death, where most affection bleeds,
Where sickness, only of the soul, precedes.
Thy baseless wealth dissolves in air away,
Like mists that melt before the morning ray:
No more on crowded mart or busy street
Friends, meeting friends, with cheerful hurry greet;
Sad, on the ground thy princely merchants bend
Their altered looks, and evil days portend,
And fold their arms, and watch with anxious breast
The tempest blackening in the distant West.

Yes, thou must droop; thy Midas dream is o'er;
The golden tide of Commerce leaves thy shore,
Leaves thee to prove the alternate ills that haunt
Enfeebling Luxury and ghastly Want;
Leaves thee, perhaps, to visit distant lands,
And deal the gifts of heaven with equal hands.
Yet, O my country, name beloved, revered,
By every tie that binds the soul endeared,
Whose image to my infant senses came
Mixed with Religion's light and Freedom's holy flame!
If prayers may not avert, if 'tis thy fate
To rank amongst the names that once were great,
Not like the dim, cold crescent shalt thou fade,
Thy debt to Science and the Muse unpaid;
Thine are the laws surrounding states revere,
Thine the full harvest of the mental year,
Thine the bright stars in glory's sky that shine,
And arts that make it life to live are thine.
If westward streams the light that leaves thy shores,
Still from thy lamp the streaming radiance pours.
Wide spread thy race from Ganges to the pole,
O'er half the western world thy accents roll:
Nations beyond the Appalachian hills
Thy hand has planted and thy spirit fills:
Soon as their gradual progress shall impart
The finer sense of morals and of art,
Thy stores of knowledge the new states shall know,
And think thy thoughts, and with thy fancy glow;
Thy Lockes, thy Paleys shall instruct their youth,
Thy leading star direct their search for truth;
Beneath the spreading platan's tent-like shade,
Or by Missouri's rushing waters laid,
'Old father Thames' shall be the poet's theme,
Of Hagley's woods the enamoured virgin dream,
And Milton's tones the raptured ear enthral,
Mixed with the roaring of Niagara's fall;
In Thomson's glass the ingenious youth shall learn
A fairer face of Nature to discern;
Nor of the bards that swept the British lyre
Shall fade one laurel, or one note expire.

❋ ❋ ❋ ❋

London exalts: – on London Art bestows
Her summer ices and her winter rose;
Gems of the East her mural crown adorn,
And Plenty at her feet pours forth her horn;
While even the exiles her just laws disclaim,
People a continent, and build a name:
August she sits, and with extended hands
Holds forth the book of life to distant lands.
    But fairest flowers expand but to decay;
The worm is in thy core, thy glories pass away;
Arts, arms and wealth destroy the fruits they bring;
Commerce, like beauty, knows no second spring.
Crime walks thy streets, Fraud earns her unblessed bread,
O'er want and woe thy gorgeous robe is spread,
And angel charities in vain oppose:
    With grandeur's growth the mass of misery grows.

1814

53. Dorothy Wordsworth
from *A Narrative Concerning George and Sarah Green*

Alas! a love of sales had always been their failing, being perhaps the only
public meetings in this neighbourhood where social pleasure is to be
had without the necessity of expending money, except, indeed, our annual
fair, and on that day I can recollect having more than once seen Sarah
Green among the rest with her cheerful countenance – two or three little-
ones about her; and their youngest brother or sister, an infant, in her arms.
These things are now remembered; and the awful event checks all disposition to harsh comments; perhaps formerly it might be said, and with
truth, the woman had better been at home; but who shall assert that this
same spirit which led her to come at times among her neighbours as an
equal, seeking like them society and pleasure, that this spirit did not assist
greatly in preserving her in cheerful independence of mind through the
many hardships and privations of extreme poverty? The children, though
very ragged, were always cleanly, and are as pure and innocent, and in
every respect as promising children as any I ever saw. The three or four

latest born, it is true, look as if they had been checked in their growth for want of full nourishment; but none appear unhealthy except the youngest, a fair and beautiful Infant. It looks sickly, but not suffering; there is a heavenly patience in its countenance; and, while it lay asleep in its cradle three days after its mother's death, one could not look upon it without fanciful thoughts that the babe had been sent into this life but to be her companion, and was ready to follow her in tranquil peace.

It would not be easy to give you an idea of the suspense and trouble in every face before the bodies were found: it seemed as if nothing could be done, nothing else thought of, till the unfortunate pair were brought again to their own house: – the first question was, 'Have you heard anything from the fells?' On the second evening I asked a young man, a next-door neighbour of ours, what he should do tomorrow? 'Why, to be sure, go out again,' he replied, and I believe that though he left a profitable employment (he is by trade a shoemaker), he would have persevered daily if the search had continued many days longer, even weeks.

My sister Mary and I went to visit the orphans on the Wednesday morning: we found all calm and quiet – two little boys were playing on the floor – the infant was asleep; and two of the old man's up-grown daughters wept silently while they pursued the business of the house: but several times one of them went out to listen at the door – 'Oh!' said they, 'the worst for us is yet to come! We shall never be at rest till they are brought home; and that will be a dreadful moment.' – Their grief then broke out afresh; and they spoke of a miserable time, above twenty years ago, when their own mother and brother died of a malignant fever: nobody would come near them, and their father was forced himself to lay his wife in her coffin. 'Surely,' they often repeated, 'this is an afflicted house!' – and indeed in like manner have I since frequently heard it spoken of by persons less nearly concerned, but who still retain a vivid remembrance of the former affliction. It is, when any unusual event happens, affecting to listen to the fireside talk in our cottages; you then find how faithfully the inner histories of families, their lesser and greater cares, their peculiar habits, and ways of life are recorded in the breasts of their fellow-inhabitants of the vale; much more faithfully than it is possible that the lives of those, who have moved in higher stations and had numerous friends in the busy world, can be preserved in remembrance, even when their doings and sufferings have been watched for the express purpose of recording them in written narratives. I heard a woman, a week ago, describe in as lively a manner the sufferings of George Green's family, when the former two funerals went out of the house, as if that trouble had been the present trouble. Among other things she related how friends and acquaintances, as is the custom here when any one is sick, used to carry presents; but, instead of going to comfort the family with their company and conversation, laid their gifts upon a wall near the house, and watched till they were taken away.

It was, as I have said, upon the Wednesday that we went to visit the orphans. A few hours after we had left them John Fisher came to tell us that the men were come home with the dead bodies. A great shout had been uttered when they were found; but we could not hear it as it was on the Langdale side of the mountains.

The pair were buried in one grave on the Friday afternoon – my sister and I attended the funeral. A great number of people of decent and respectable appearance were assembled at the house. I went into the parlour where the two coffins were placed with the elder of the mourners sitting beside them: the younger girls gathered about the kitchen fire, partly amused, perhaps, by the unusual sight of so many persons in their house; the baby and its sister Jane (she who had been left by the mother with the care of the family) sat on a little stool in the chimney-corner, and, as our Molly said, after having seen them on the Tuesday, 'they looked such an innocent pair!' The young nurse appeared to have touches of pride in her important office; for every one praised her for her notable management of the infant, while they cast tender looks of sorrow on them both. The child would go to none but her – , and while on her knee its countenance was perfectly calm – more than that: I could have fancied it to express even thoughtful resignation.

We went out of doors, and were much moved by the rude and simple objects before us – the noisy stream, the craggy mountain down which the old man and his wife had hoped to make their way on that unhappy night – the little garden, untilled – with its box-tree and a few peeping flowers! The furniture of the house was decayed and scanty; but there was one oaken cupboard that was so bright with rubbing that it was plain it had been prized as an ornament and a treasure by the poor woman then lying in her coffin.

Before the bodies were taken up a three-penny loaf of bread was dealt out to each of the guests: Mary was unwilling to take hers, thinking that the orphans were in no condition to give away anything; she immediately, however, perceived that she ought to accept of it, and a woman, who was near us, observed that it was an ancient custom now much disused; but probably, as the family had lived long in the vale, and had done the like at funerals formerly, they thought it proper not to drop the custom on this occasion. The funeral procession was very solemn – passing through the solitary valley of Easedale, and, altogether, I never witnessed a more moving scene. As is customary here, there was a pause before the bodies were borne through the church-yard gate, while part of a psalm was sung, the men standing with their heads uncovered. In the church the two coffins were placed near the altar, and the whole family knelt on the floor on each side of the father's coffin, leaning over it. The eldest daughter had been unable to follow with the rest of the mourners, and we had led her back to the house before she got through the first field; the second fainted by the graveside; and their brother stood like a statue of despair silent and motionless; the younger girls sobbed aloud. Many tears were shed by persons who had known little of the deceased; and all the people who were gathered together appeared to be united in one general feeling of sympathy for the helpless condition of the orphans. After the funeral the family returned to their melancholy home. There was a sale of the furniture on the Thursday following; and the next day the house was left empty and silent.

---

54. Isabella Lickbarrow
Introductory Address: To the Muse

Beloved companion of my early years !
My friend in solitude, my secret joy!
Dear were the soothing whispers of thy voice,
Dear were thy visits in my lonely hours,
When like a smiling angel, sent to bless,
Thy presence could beguile the sense of grief.
With thee, through many a devious wood's deep shade
And various featured vale, along the banks
Of rock-imprisoned rivers have I roamed;
Oft when the welcome day of ease arrived,
Freed from confinement, and depressive toil,
With heart elated, as the exulting stag
When ranging o'er his mountain pastures free,
I've strayed to meet thee in thy favourite haunts,
The heights which rise o'er Kendal's lovely vale.
There, far from observation's curious eye,
Lightly I bounded o'er the elastic turf,
Ascending every rocky hillock's brow,
My heart expanding as I looked around,
Thus sweetly passed the summer's eve away,
Till sunk behind dark Langdale's distant pike,

The setting sun threw his diverging rays
In bending arches o'er the azure plain.
In secret shades alone I wooed thee then
By stealth, nor to the world durst tell my love;
But now, when in the face of day I've owned
Our secret friendship, say wilt thou repay
With kindness my long faithful love to thee ?
Our fate decreed, together we must try
The favour of the world, or bear its frowns.
How dear is to the anxious parent's heart
The reputation of a darling child!
Dear to the husband is the honoured name
Of her he loves – and dear is thine to me.
And ah! how keenly will my bosom feel,
If with an eye severe and harsh reproofs,
A frowning world should scan thy numerous faults,
And with unfeeling censures blot thy name.
Together then we'll seek some lonely spot,
Some willow-fringed stream, where thou shalt weave
Such chaplets as despairing lovers wear,
To bind our brows, and breathe in mournful strains
Thy funeral dirge – then silent sleep for ever,
While my warm heart shall grow as cold and chill
As flinty rocks encrusted o'er with ice.

———

55. Claire Clairmont
from *Journals*

Tuesday Aug 30th.

Rise at five – Breakfast – Go down to the Quay – Do not get on board till 1/2 past seven – The morning cold & cloudy – now & then rain – The Rhine begins to get broad a few leagues from Basle – Its banks are very beautiful – Verdantly sloping down to meet its waves & covered with young willows – Islands rise on the surface of the water they are numerous & covered with groves – We saw a sea-mew & wondered much how it came in a place so many miles from the sea – We stopped for about an hour on a small green hill to dine as we had taken provisions – I gathered some of the most beautiful grass I ever beheld – The wind had been against us the whole day & was violent – The clouds fleeted fast away &

the sun broke forth in the afternoon – on both sides of the Rhine there was in the distance two high ridges of black hills – About four o'clock we landed at Brisaac a town in Baden – The watermen said they could not proceed with so strong a wind against us – We were afraid we should be obliged to delay our journey & sleep here but in about an hour they came with the news that the wind was changed & we hastened on board – Shelley reads aloud the *Letters from Norway* – This is one of my very favourite books – the language is so very flowing & eloquent & it is altogether a beautiful poem – We witnessed one of the finest sun sets – The West was a long continued strip of yellow dying away with a lovely pink which again mellowed itself imperceptibly into an amazing horizon of the deepest purple – The Rhine was extremely rapid – The waves borrowed the divine colours of the sky – Never were tints so numerous or so perpetually varied – The undulating motion of the waves rolling ever one over the other produced the same effect as if snakes were creeping perpetually onwards – I now thought of Coleridge's *Ancient Mariner* – 'Beyond the shadow of the ship – I watched the water snakes' – l am convinced that the descriptions contained in that poem are more copied from nature than one is at first aware of – The Rhine appeared narrow here for it is covered with islands which produce the same effect as if you were passing through a narrow defile. The shore on the right were black hills – now rocky – then woody & sometimes gently declined into grassy slopes – We passed a ruined castle situated on the top of a black hill. The ruins suited with the scene – every thing seemed declining – the sun had hid his beams – the trees were gaining a dark hue & the mountains were receding. We slept at Schoff Hock – M's birthday – 17.

* * * *

Friday Oct 7th.

Peacock at breakfast – read *Political Justice*. Shelley Mary & Peacock walk out in the fields – – I go by myself in the squares – Dine at six. Peacock goes at eight – Mary goes to bed – Shelley & myself sit over the fire ... at one the conversation turned upon those unaccountable and mysterious feelings about supernatural things that we are sometime subject to – Shelley looks beyond all passing strange – a look of impressive deep & melancholy awe – I cannot describe it I well know how I felt – I ran upstairs to bed – I placed the candle on the drawers & stood looking at a pillow that lay in the very middle of the bed – I turned my head round to the window & then back again to the bed – the pillow was no longer there – it had been removed to the chair – I stood thinking for two moments – how did this come? Was it possible that I had deluded myself so far as to place it there myself & then forget the action? This was not likely – Every passed at it were in a moment [sic] – I ran down stairs – Shelley heard me & came out of his room – He gives the most horrible description of my countenance – I did not feel in the way he thinks I did – We sat up all night – I was ill – At day break we examined the room & found every thing in the state I described –

Saturday Oct 8th.

Rise at twelve – Not well – Walk with Shelley & Mary into the fields – Sit by the fire all day in a melancholy mood – Go to bed at nine.

* * * *

Friday Oct. 14

Get up late – go down in a very ill humour – quarrel with Shelley – but to know one's faults is to mend them – perhaps this morning though productive of very painful feelings has in reality been of more essential benefit to me than any I ever yet passed – How hateful it is to quarrel – to say a thousand unkind things – meaning none – things produced by the bitterness of disappointment – (I hate these feelings) – Walk home through the Regent's Park – leave them & go home by myself. Peacock calls – laughs at us. . . . Shelley comes into my room & thinks he was to blame – but I don't – how I like good kind explaining people.

1815

56. Mary Ann Lamb
On Needlework

In early life I passed eleven years in the exercise of my needle for a livelihood. Will you allow me to address your readers, among whom might perhaps be found some of the kind patronesses of my former humble labours, on a subject widely connected with female life – the state of needlework in this country.

To lighten the heavy burden which many ladies impose upon themselves is one object I have in view; but, I confess, my strongest motive is to excite attention towards the industrious sisterhood to which I once belonged.

From books I have been informed of the fact, upon which *The British Lady's Magazine* chiefly founds its pretensions, namely, that women have of late been rapidly advancing in intellectual improvement. Much may have been gained for that class of females for whom I wish to plead. Needlework and intellectual improvement are naturally in a state of warfare. But I am afraid the root of the evil has not as yet been struck at. Workwomen of every description were never in so much distress for want of employment.

Among the present circle of my acquaintance I am proud to rank many that may truly be called respectable; nor do the female part of them, in their mental attainments, at all disprove the prevailing opinion of that intellectual progression which you have taken as the basis of your work; yet I affirm that I know not a single family where there is not some essential drawback to its comfort which may be traced to needle-work done at home, as the phrase is for all needle-work performed in a family by some of its own members, and for which no remuneration in money is received or expected.

In money alone, did I say? I would appeal to all the fair votaries of voluntary housewifery whether, in the matter of conscience, any one of them ever thought she had done as much needle-work as she ought to have done. Even fancy work, the fairest of the tribe! – how delightful the arrangement of her materials! the fixing upon her happiest pattern, how pleasing an anxiety! how cheerful the commencement of the labour she enjoins! But that lady must be a true lover of the art, and so industrious a pursuer of a predetermined purpose, that it were pity her energy should not have been directed to some wiser end, who can affirm she neither feels weariness during the execution of a fancy piece, nor takes more time than she had calculated for the performance.

Is it too bold an attempt to persuade your readers that it would prove an incalculable addition to general happiness, and the domestic comfort of both sexes, if needle-work were never practised but for a remuneration in money? As nearly, however, as this desirable thing can be effected, so much more nearly will women be upon an equality with men as far as respects the mere enjoyment of life. As far as that goes, I believe it is every woman's opinion that the condition of men is far superior to her own.

'They can do what they like,' we say. Do not these words generally mean, they have time to seek out whatever amusements suit their tastes? We dare not tell them we have no time to do this; for, if they should ask in what manner we dispose of our time, we should blush to enter upon a detail of the minutiae which compose the sum of a woman's daily employment. Nay, many a lady who allows not herself one quarter of an hour's positive leisure during her waking hours, considers her own husband as the most industrious of men, if he steadily pursue his occupation till the hour of dinner, and will be perpetually lamenting her own idleness.

Real business and *real leisure* make up the portions of men's time – two sources of happiness which we certainly partake of in a very inferior degree. To the execution of employment, in which the faculties of the body or mind are called into busy action, there must be a consoling importance attached, which feminine duties (that generic term for all our business) cannot aspire to.

In the most meritorious discharges of those duties, the highest praise we can aim at is to be accounted the help-mates of *man*; who, in return for all he does for us, expects, and justly expects, us to do all in our power to soften and sweeten life.

In how many ways is a good woman employed, in thought or action, through the day, in order that her *good man* may be enabled to feel his leisure hours *real substantial holiday*, and perfect respite from the cares of business! Not the least part to be done to accomplish this end is to fit herself to become a conversational companion; that is to say, she has to study and understand the subjects on which he loves to talk. This part of our duty, if strictly performed, will be found by far our hardest part. The disadvantages we labour under from an education differing from a manly one make the hours in which we *sit and do nothing* in men's company too often any thing but a relaxation; although, as to pleasure and instruction, time so passed may be esteemed more or less delightful.

To make a man's home so desirable a place as to preclude his having a wish to pass his leisure hours at any fireside in preference to his own, I should humbly take to be the sum and substance of woman's domestic ambition. I would appeal to our *British ladies*, who are generally allowed to be the most zealous and successful of all women in the pursuit of this object, – I would appeal to them who have been most successful in the performance of this laudable service, in behalf of father, son, husband, or brother, whether an anxious desire to perform this duty well is not attended with enough of *mental* exertion, at least, to incline them to the opinion that women may be more properly ranked among the contributors to, than the partakers of, the undisturbed relaxation of man.

If a family be so well ordered that the master is never called in to its direction, and yet he perceives comfort and economy well attended to, the mistress of that family (especially if children form a part of it) has, I apprehend, as large a share of womanly employment as ought to satisfy her own sense of duty; even though the needle-book and thread-case were quite laid aside, and she cheerfully contributed her part to the slender gains of the corset-maker, the milliner, the dress-maker, the plain-worker, the embroidress, and all the numerous classifications of females supporting themselves by *needle-work*, that great staple commodity which is alone appropriated to the self-supporting part of our sex.

Much has been said and written on the subject of men engrossing to themselves every occupation and calling. After many years of observation and reflection, I am obliged to acquiesce in the notion that it cannot well be ordered otherwise.

If at the birth of girls it were possible to foresee in what cases it would be their fortune to pass a single life, we should soon find trades wrested from their present occupiers, and transferred to the exclusive possession of our sex. The whole mechanical business of copying writings in the law department, for instance, might very soon be transferred with advantage to the poorer sort of women, who with very little teaching would soon beat their rivals of the other sex in facility and neatness. The parents of female children, who were known to be destined from their birth to maintain themselves through the whole course of their lives with like certainty as their sons are, would feel it a duty incumbent on themselves to strengthen the minds, and even the bodily constitutions, of their girls, so circumstanced, by an education which, without affronting the preconceived habits of society, might enable them to follow some occupation now considered above the capacity or too robust for the constitution of our sex. Plenty of resources would then lie open for single women to obtain an independent livelihood, when every parent would be upon the alert to encroach upon some employment, now engrossed by men, for such of their daughters as would then be in exactly the same predicament as their sons now are. Who, for instance, would lay by money to set up his sons in trade; give premiums, and in part maintain them through a long apprenticeship; or, which men of moderate incomes frequently do, strain every nerve in order to bring them up to a learned profession; if it were in a very high degree probable that, by the time they were twenty years of age, they would be taken from this trade or profession, and maintained during the remainder of their lives by the *person whom they should marry*. Yet this is precisely the situation in which every parent, whose income does not very much exceed the moderate, is placed with respect to his daughters. Even where boys have gone through a laborious education, superinducing habits of steady attention, accompanied with the entire conviction that the business which they learn is to be the source of their future distinction, may it not be affirmed that the persevering industry required to accomplish this desirable end causes many a hard struggle in the minds of young men, even of the most hopeful disposition? What then must be the disadvantages under which a very young woman is placed who is required to learn a trade, from which she can never expect to reap any profit, but at the expense of losing that place in society, to the possession of which she may reasonably look forward, inasmuch as it is by far the most *common lot*, namely, the condition of a *happy* English wife?

As I desire to offer nothing to the consideration of your readers but what, at least as far as my own observation goes, I consider as truths confirmed by experience, I will only say that, were I to follow the bent of my own speculative opinion, I should be inclined to persuade every female over whom I hoped to have any influence to contribute all the assistance in her power to those of her own sex who may need it, in the employments they at present occupy, rather than to force them into situations now filled wholly by men. With the mere exception of the profits which they have a right to derive from their needle, I would take nothing from the industry of man which he already possesses.

'A penny saved is a penny earned,' is a maxim not true, unless the penny be saved in the same time in which it might have been earned. I, who have known what it is to work for *money earned*, have since had much experience in working for *money saved*; and I consider, from the closest calculation I can make, that a *penny saved* in that way bears about a true proportion to a *farthing earned*. I am no advocate for women, who do not depend on themselves for a subsistence, proposing to themselves to *earn money*. My reasons for thinking it not advisable are too numerous to state – reasons deduced from authentic facts, and strict observations on domestic life in its various shades of comfort. But, if the females of a family, *nominally* supported by the other sex, find it necessary to add something to the common stock, why not endeavour to do something by which they may produce money *in its true shape*?

It would be an excellent plan, attended with very little trouble, to calculate every evening how much money has been saved by needle-work *done in the family*, and compare the result with the daily portion of the yearly income. Nor would it be amiss to make a memorandum of the time passed in this way, adding also a guess as to what share it has taken up in the thoughts and conversation. This would be an easy mode of forming a true notion, and getting at the exact worth of this species of *home* industry, and perhaps might place it in a different light from any in which it has hitherto been the fashion to consider it.

Needle-work, taken up as an amusement, may not be altogether unamusing. We are all pretty good judges of what entertains ourselves, but it is not so easy to pronounce upon what may contribute to the entertainment of others. At all events, let us not confuse the motives of economy with those of simple pastime. If saving be no object, and long habit have rendered needle-work so delightful an avocation that we cannot think of relinquishing it, there are the good old contrivances in which our grand-dames were used to beguile and lose their time – knitting, knotting, netting, carpet working, and the like ingenious pursuits, – those so-often-praised but tedious works, which are so long in the operation, that purchasing the labour has seldom been thought good economy, yet, by a certain fascination, they have been found to chain down the great to a self-imposed slavery, from which they considerately, or haughtily, excuse the needy. These may be esteemed lawful and lady-like amusements. But, if those works, more usually denominated useful, yield greater satisfaction, it might be a laudable scruple of conscience, and no bad test to herself of her own motive, if a lady, who had no absolute need, were to give the money so saved to poor needle-women belonging to those branches of employment from which she has borrowed these shares of pleasurable labour.

1816

57. Mary Shelley
from *History of a Six Weeks' Tour*

[France.]
Exhausted with sickness and fatigue, I walked over the sands with my companions to the hotel. I heard for the first time the confused buzz of voices speaking a different language from that to which I had been accustomed; and saw a costume very unlike that worn on the opposite side of the channel; the women with high caps and short jackets; the men with earrings; ladies walking about with high bonnets or *coiffures* lodged on the top of the head, the hair dragged up underneath, without any stray curls to decorate the temples or cheeks. There is, however, something very pleasing in the manners and appearance of the people of Calais, that prepossesses you in their favour. A national reflection might occur, that when Edward III took Calais, he turned out the old inhabitants, and peopled it almost entirely with our own countrymen; but unfortunately the manners are not English.

We remained during that day and the greater part of the next at Calais: we had been obliged to leave our boxes the night before at the English custom-house, and it was arranged that they should go by the packet of the following day, which, detained by contrary wind, did not arrive until night. S*** and I walked among the fortifications on the outside of the town; they consisted of fields where the hay was making. The aspect of the country was rural and pleasant.

❀ ❀ ❀ ❀

We resolved to walk through France; but as I was too weak for any considerable distance, and my sister could not be supposed to be able to walk as far as S*** each day, we determined to purchase an ass, to carry our portmanteau and one of us by turns. Early, therefore, on Monday August 8th, S*** and C*** went to the ass market, and purchased an ass, and the rest of the day, until four in the afternoon, was spent in preparations for our departure; during which, Madame L'Hote paid us a visit, and attempted to dissuade us from our design. She represented to us that a large army had been recently disbanded, that the soldiers and officers wandered idle about the country, and that *les Dames seroient certainement enlevees*. But we were proof against her arguments, and packing up a few necessaries, leaving the rest to go by the diligence, we departed in a fiacre from the door of the hotel, our little ass following.

We dismissed the coach at the barrier. It was dusk, and the ass seemed totally unable to bear one of us, appearing to sink under the portmanteau, although it was small and light. We were, however, merry enough, and thought the leagues short. We arrived at Charenton about ten.

Charenton is prettily situated in a valley, through which the Seine flows, winding among banks variegated with trees. On looking at this scene, C*** exclaimed, 'Oh! this is beautiful enough; let us live here.' This was her exclamation on every new scene, and as each surpassed the one before, she cried, 'I am glad we did not stay at Charenton, but let us live here.'

Finding our ass useless, we sold it before we proceeded on our journey, and bought a mule, for ten Napoleons. About nine o'clock we departed. We were clad in black silk. I rode on the mule, which carried also our portmanteau; S*** and C**, followed, bringing a small basket of provisions. At about one we arrived at Gros Bois, where, under the shade of trees, we ate our bread and fruit, and drank our wine, thinking of Don Quixote and Sancho.

58. Jane Taylor
from *Prejudice*

In yonder red-brick mansion, tight and square,
Just at the town's commencement, lives the mayor,
Some yards of shining gravel, fenced with box,
Lead to the painted portal – where one knocks:
There, in the left-hand parlour, all in state,
Sit he and she, on either side the grate.
But though their goods and chattels, sound and new,
Bespeak the owners *very well to do*,
His worship's wig and morning suit betray
Slight indications of an humbler day.

That long low shop where still the name appears,
Some doors below, they kept for forty years
And there, with various fortunes, smooth and rough,
They sold tobacco, coffee, tea, and snuff.
There labelled drawers display their spicy row, –
Clove, mace, and nutmeg: from the ceiling low,
Dangle long *twelves* and *eights*, and slender rush,
Mixed with the varied forms of *genus brush*;
Cask, firkin, bag, and barrel, crowd the floor,
And piles of country cheeses guard the door.
The frugal dames came in from far and near,
To buy their ounces and their quarterns here.
Hard was the toil, the profits slow to count,
And yet the mole-hill was at last a mount;
Those petty gains were hoarded day by day,
With little cost, for not a child had they;
Till long proceeding on the saving plan,
He found himself a *warm, fore-handed man*:
And being now arrived at life's decline,
Both he and she, they formed a bold design,
(Although it touched their prudence to the quick)
To turn their savings into stone and brick.
How many an ounce of tea and ounce of snuff,
There must have been consumed to make enough!

At length with paint and paper, bright and gay,
The box was finished, and they went away.

But when their faces were no longer seen
Amongst the canisters of *black* and *green*
– Those well-known faces, all the country round –
'Twas said that had they levelled to the ground
The two old walnut trees before the door,
The customers would not have missed *them* more.
Now, like a pair of parrots in a cage
They live, and civic honours crown their age:
Thrice, since the Whitsuntide they settled there,
Seven years ago, has he been chosen mayor;
And now you'd scarcely know they were the same;
Conscious he struts, of power, and wealth, and fame,
Proud in official dignity, the dame,
And extra stateliness of dress and mien,
During the mayoralty, is plainly seen
With nicer care bestowed to puff and pin
The august lappet that contains her chin.

Such is her life; and like the wise and great,
The mind has journeyed hand in hand with fate;
Her thoughts, unused to take a longer flight
Than from the left-hand counter to the right,
With little change, are vacillating still
Between his worship's glory and the till.
The few ideas moving, slow and dull,
Across the sandy desert of her skull,
Still the course must follow; to and fro,
As first they traversed three-score years ago;
From whence not all the world could turn them back,
Or lead them out upon another track.
What once was right or wrong, or high or low
In her opinion, always must be so: –
You might, perhaps, with reasons new and pat,
Have made *Columbus* think the world was flat;
There might be times of energy worn out,
When his own theory would Sir Isaac doubt;
But not the powers of argument combined,
Could make this dear good woman change her mind,
Or give her intellect the slightest clue.
To that vast world of things she never knew.
Were but her brain dissected, it would show

Her stiff opinions fastened in a row,
Ranged duly, side by side, without a gap
Much like the plaiting on her Sunday cap.

1817

59. Anne Lister
from *Diaries*

Tuesday 13 May [Halifax]
Between 1 & 2, the 1st 7 propositions of the 1st book of Euclid, with which
I mean to renew my acquaintance & to proceed diligently in the hope that,
if I live, I may some time attain a tolerable proficiency in mathematical
studies. I would rather be a philosopher than a polyglot, & mean to turn my
attention, eventually & principally, to natural philosophy. For the present,
I mean to devote my mornings, before breakfast to Greek, & afterwards, till
dinner, to divide the time equally between Euclid & arithmetic till I have
waded thro' Walkingham, when I shall recommence my long neglected
algebra. I must read a page or 2 of French now & then when I can. The
afternoons & evenings are set apart for general reading, for walking, 1/2 an
hour, or 3/4, practice on the flute.

* * * *

Thursday 28 August [Halifax]
   Did nothing but dream of Miss Browne &, tho' I woke at 6, yet had not
resolution to get up but lay dozing & thinking of the fair charmer. She is
certainly very pretty. She seemed evidently not displeased with my attention & I felt all possible inclination to be as foolish as ever I was in former
days. In fact, I shall be much better out of the way of the lovely Maria (for
such is her name) than in it. Mended the leather covering of my stays till
breakfast time.

* * * *

Saturday 13 September [Halifax (Haugh-end)]
   A thousand reflections and recollections crowded on me last night. The
last time I slept in this room & this bed, it was with Marianne, in 1815, the

summer of. Surely no one ever doted on one another as I did then on her. I fondly thought my love & happiness would last for ever. Alas, how changed. She has married a blackguard for the sake of his money. We are debarred all intercourse. I am not always satisfied with her. I am often miserable & often wish to try to wean my heart from her & fix more pro-pitiously. There seems little chance of our ever getting together. Tho' I believe she loves me as yet exclusively, my confidence is not invulnerable.

———

1818

60. Elizabeth Hamilton
from *Journals*

Went again with Dr Bell to the National School. I took my place in the lowest class and said my lesson with the rest. After the children have learnt to make every letter quickly in sand, they are put into this class, and are taught to form syllables. The first girl calls out *a*; after an interval sufficient to count six the second calls out *b*; after a like interval, the third calls out *ab*, &c. If any girl does not know the letter or syllable which it is her turn to say, the next is tried, and the first one who can say takes place of all who cannot. If any girl is observed trifling, she is instantly called on. – In the highest class, the children read selections from Scripture; and, in addition to the other exercises, are examined by the monitor on the meaning of what they read. Nothing can be more striking than the eagerness of attention which the children show, although no other punishment is inflicted for idleness than loss of place in the class. The lowest class being found the most difficult to train, the best teacher is reserved for it. The mistress goes continually from class to class, speaking to the children, reproving or applauding them by name.

❋ ❋ ❋ ❋

Proceeded by a circuitous road through Stourbridge and Hales Owen to Birmingham, the ugly and the dull! We passed a poor manufacturing village called *Mud-City*, inhabited by creatures whose savage habits made them till lately the terror of travellers. They owe their present half-civilization to the charity of Mr Hill, a neighbouring squire, who has built and endowed a church and has established a school among this horde of barbarians. He has a large family of his own, whom may God prosper!

A vile hole this Birmingham! Yesterday I overheard one of the animals from it, a young one too! propose to cut down the Hagley Oaks. 'They might go to the king's yards', said the creature; 'I am sure they are of no use here'.

. . . Tried to see Thomason's manufactory. Nobody was at work; first, because it was Monday, and all last week's wages were not spent; secondly, because it was a *wake*. All was sombre as a church-yard; not even girls eating gingerbread, and boys squeaking on half-penny trumpets. In the evening we laboured through many of the streets of this wearisome town; found out a circulating library, and, on depositing the price, were entrusted with four volumes of trash. Mercifully! occupation makes most places alike.

. . . Left Birmingham in the morning; the country seems pretty, so far as the smoke of 10,000 furnaces would allow us to see it.

At Coleport, we visited Rose's china manufactory; it is upon a still larger scale than that at Worcester, but is still carried out in the same manner. Here we saw many women employed in painting the china; but we were told, that, though they serve the same apprenticeship as the men, under the same teacher, their work is always inferior. Here also we saw the *printing* of a process quite new to me. On a plate, properly engraved, the colour is laid, heated, and well rubbed in; a sheet of cambric paper, prepared with a secret composition, is then printed from this plate. This paper is cut to fit the cup, saucer, &c. and pressed closely to it; the biscuit is then washed in cold water; when the paper peels off, the pattern remains perfectly impressed.

❋ ❋ ❋

The road to Edinburgh is right Scotch; though bleak and dreary, it is judicious and substantial. But oh! it is untold how dismally bare this country seems after four months' acquaintance with 'merry England'! I sigh over the thoughts of an Englishman's impressions on visiting mother Scotland, as Shem and Japhet did over their parent! No wonder if we be a reflecting, frugal race! the gay images of spring, and the luxuriance of summer, never intrude upon us, suggesting frolic and profusion! No wonder if we be hospitable! where one eternal winter constantly reminds us to draw together, and be social.

61. Anne Lister
from *Diaries*

Wednesday 26 August [Halifax]
Got to the old church this evening a few minutes before the lecture began.
Managed this on purpose in the hope of seeing Miss Browne, who generally
goes. Alas! I am doomed to disappointment & . . . I concluded she must
have set off to Harrogate according to her mother's desire. I either am, or
fancy I am, in love with the girl. At least, I think more of her than ever &
felt quite low and vapourish at not seeing her. I wonder if she ever thinks
of me, or if she has the least spark of anything like regard for me?

1819

62. Anne Lister
from *Diaries*

Thursday 18 February [Halifax]
[Miss Browne] owned she had strange thoughts but could not help thinking
she wished I had been a gent; that perhaps she should not have known me.
'Oh, oh', thought I. I replied perhaps she had not more strange thoughts
than other people & that, if I had been a gent, I thought Mr Kelly would
have had a poor chance. She had wondered what I saw in her & thought
perhaps it was her vanity made her believe I liked her. 'No, no', said I. 'I
have given you reason enough.' . . . She begins to like me more than she is,
perhaps, aware . . . I must mind I do not get into a scrape.

63. Eleanor Butler
from *Diaries*

Thursday February 25th
Perfect Spring day – soft – smiling – verdant – employed in planting
hollies . . .

* * * *

Friday May 8th

Painter's son with a party of nine permitted to see this place; a set of ill behaved fools. There is a Miss Fothergill rather pretty of twenty eight walking alone all over Italy.

❀ ❀ ❀ ❀

September (undated)

. . . a luncheon of grouse sandwich – pine apple – peaches and apricots. Ruabon Vicarage – Refreshments under the trees – so convenient – the seats under the clumps of oak – so happily disposed – the tent for dinner so well ordered – so plentiful – such a profusion of fruit – the weather so delicious – every person so well pleased . . . An African from the kingdom of Morocco came to sell spices – made him sing . . .

❀ ❀ ❀ ❀

December 25th

Beautiful French perfumes from Nightingale Shrewsbury – the gift of my beloved.

1820

64. Anne Lister
from *Diaries*

Tuesday 4 April 1820 [Halifax]

After coming up, M– was to look over some of our old letters. In getting them, happened to stumble on some memoranda I made in 1817 on her conduct, her selfishness in marrying, the waste and distraction of my love, etc. Began reading these and went on thoughtlessly till I heard a book fall from her hands &, turning round, saw her motionless & speechless, in tears. Tried very soothing & affectionate means. She had never known before how I loved her or what her marriage had cost me. Had she known she could not have done it & and it was evident that repentance now pressed heavily. . . . She grieved over what I had suffered & would never doubt me again. I am indeed persuaded and satisfied of her love.

1821

65. Anne Lister
from *Diaries*

Monday 29 January [Halifax]

Cutting curl papers half an hour . . . Arranging and putting away my last
year's letters. Looked over & burnt several very old ones from indifferent
people . . . Burnt . . . Mr Montagu's farewell verses that no trace of any
man's admiration may remain. I love, & only love, the fairer sex & thus
beloved by them in turn, my heart revolts from any other love than theirs.

Monday 23 July [Newcastle, Staffs]

We talked all last night & only closed our eyes to doze about half-hour,
just before getting up. Went to M– but somehow did not manage a good
kiss. Refused to promise till I had really felt that she was my wife. Went to
her a second time. Succeeded better & then bound ourselves to each other
by an irrevocable promise for ever, in pledge of which, turned on her finger
the gold ring I gave her several years ago & also her wedding ring which
had not been moved off her finger since her marriage. She seems devoted
to me & I can & shall trust her now . . . It has occurred to me – can C– have
given her a venereal disease?

Saturday 28 July [Newcastle, Staffs]

M– & I talked matters over. We have agreed to solemnize our promise
of mutual faith by taking the sacrament together when next we meet at
Shibden, not thinking it more proper to use any more still binding ceremony during C–'s life.

———

66. Mary Hays
from *Caroline, Wife of George IV*

Upon condition that she consented to her own degradation, yielded up
her rank and name, remained forever an exile, and forfeited every title to
esteem and respect, she was to be graciously allowed, out of the purse of
the English nation, an ample income, with which she might indulge in
dissolute gratification where and in what manner she thought fit. Rejecting
this liberal proposition, and presuming to set her foot upon English land,

she was immediately to take her trial at the bar of the country, as an adul-
teress and unfaithful wife.

She demurred not a moment, but indignantly decided on the spot.
Execution was as rapid as resolve had been prompt: accepting what
accommodation offered itself at the instant, a few hours brought her to the
shores of that country, where so many painful recollections, so many bitter
feelings and associations of humiliation and anguish, could not fail to be
revived. One lady of respectability and honour, and formerly of her household, who had passed over to the continent to rejoin, in her fallen fortunes,
a mistress whom she respected and to whose person she was attached, and
a worthy citizen of London, were her companions on the voyage.

Magnanimously stifling her emotions, uncertain of the fate awaiting her,
of her reception with the nation, of the strength and number of her enemies,
with little other support than what conscious rectitude might afford her,
the queen of England, as a stranger and a fugitive, landed from a packet on
British shores.

✸✸✸✸

Nearly exhausted with emotion and fatigue, the queen entered London,
and, without a palace or residence of her own to receive her, accepted
graciously and gratefully the asylum offered her by the respectable citizen
who accompanied her on the voyage.

✸✸✸✸

The queen, her magnanimity, her cause, now became the focus of
public attention; defamation exerted her hundred tongues; slander poured
her poison into every open ear; the ardent on both sides prejudiced the
cause; reasoning is a slow process of which feeling gets the start; the candid
paused, the wise doubted, and waited for evidence on which to proceed.

Burke, had he now lived, would have retracted his assertion, that the age
of chivalry had passed away; it revived, in all its impassioned fervour,
amidst the soberest and gravest people in the civilized world. Every manly
mind shrank from the idea of driving, by protracted and endless persecu-
tions, a desolate unprotected female from her family, her rank, from society
and from the world. Woman considered it as a common cause against the
despotism and tyranny of man. Morals are of no sex, duties are reciprocal
between being and being, or they are abrogated by nature and reason.
Brute force may subjugate, but in knowledge only is real strength, and to
truth and justice is the last and only legitimate appeal. With the feudal
institutions fell the childish privileges and degrading homage paid to the

sex; and to equity not gallantry do they now prefer their claim. Oppression and persecution, it is true, still linger, but old things appear to be passing away; and, in another century, probably, should the progress of knowledge bear any proportion to its accelerated march during the latter half of the past, all things will become new. We live in eventful times, and at a critical period of the world. Happy those who understand the signs of the times; who seek not to oppose to a flood feeble mounds and inadequate barriers; but who suffer its waters gently to flow and expand through prepared appropriate reservoirs and channels, carrying fertility as they glide.

✷ ✷ ✷ ✷

And now another embarrassment arose. Upon the presumption of the truth of the facts alleged against the accused, of what description was her crime, under what law was it to be denounced, and what was its allotted punishment? It was not treason, because, in cases of this nature, it was declared by high law authority, that the woman could be implicated only through the man, and the man in question owed no allegiance to this country, of which he was not a subject. It was no political offence, because time, circumstance, and place, rendered nugatory any apprehension of future evil being its result. It was no act of infidelity against a husband whose conduct left him without any right of appeal. No law existed to condemn a nominal wife placed in similar circumstances. If it was allowed to be a breach of morals, yet no legal penalty was annexed to such a breach. Incontinence, whether in man or woman, is a moral offence and a violation of the most important branch of temperance, but it carries with it no civil disenfranchisement, and its punishment is left to public opinion, to the usages and customs established in social intercourse, – and heavy enough upon woman does this chastisement fall. If higher virtues are to be expected from queens, on account of the eminence of their situation, and the greater importance of their example, the same reasoning, and the same rule, surely applies to kings. The case were novel, no precedent existed, unless we went back to the days of Henry VIII of wife-killing memory. Catherine of Russia made no pretence to chastity, but she was not the less a great sovereign. Our own Elizabeth, our virgin queen of glorious memory, has not, on this subject, left a fame like unsunned snow.

What then was to be done? Why, a new law was to be made, an ex post facto law, after the alleged commission of the crime. And, previously, to render condemnation more sure, a private and secret tribunal was to try the cause upon evidence of accusation only; and thus, having pre-judged the business, and prejudiced the public mind by a declaration of that pre-judgement, these very men, with their minds thus biased, were to take their places among the judges to whom the final award was to be referred. More, much more, might be said and urged on the same subject; but to enter into details of this extraordinary trial is not the purpose of this present memoir.

✻ ✻ ✻ ✻

The trial commenced and proceeded. The overwhelming evidence that was to crush the accused was a torrent of odious obscenity, from the mouths of discarded servants, foreigners of the lowest classes, without credit or character, persons whose interest defamation had been rendered. The daily journals carried through the country a poison pestiferous and malignant: never had the morals of the people been so endangered. To dwell upon the subject would be too disgusting.

The great talents enlisted in the cause of the queen had ample room to display themselves. The malice, venality, falsehoods and contradictions, which they had to oppose, were rendered manifest in the light of day: persons of undoubted honour, of respectability, of rank, gave their unbought testimony: all was open, clear, and full: of guilt not a vestige of evidence remained.

✻ ✻ ✻ ✻

The queen was in the house, waiting the sentence, in a adjoining apartment. Her friend and advocate came to inform her of the result: she heard it with firmness, and seizing a pen, signed a protest, 'Caroline Regina, in despite of my enemies'.

But those enemies proved themselves capable of shame. The advocate returned with the protest, and THE BILL WAS ABANDONED. He hastened back to inform the august subject of the bill of the turn which affairs had taken. She stood motionless, with mingled feelings. He seized her hand and led her, unresisting, to her carriage, lest the joy of the expecting populace should impede and overpower her. She bowed her thanks, burst into tears, and the carriage rapidly conveyed her away.

The triumph was complete, the joy of the public sincere and full. It manifested itself by tears, by shouts, by acclamations, by illuminations, by every other variety, and in every other mode, by which national enthusiasm and popular sympathy are wont, on extraordinary occasions, to demonstrate their ardour and sincerity.

67. Sydney Owenson, Lady Morgan
from *Italy*

Whoever has wandered far and seen much, has learned to distrust the promises of books; and (in respect of the most splendid efforts of human labour) must have often felt how far the unworn expectation starts beyond its possible accomplishment. But *nature* never disappoints. Neither the memory nor the imagination of authorship can go beyond the fact she dictates, or the image she presents. If general feelings can be measured by individual impressions, Italy, with all her treasures of art, and associations of history, has nothing to exhibit, that strikes the traveller like the Alps which meet his view on his ascent to the summit of Mount Cenis, or of the Simplon. That is a moment in which the imagination feels the real poverty of its resources, the narrow limits of its range. An aspect of the material world then presents itself, which genius, even in its highest exaltation, must leave to original creation, as unimitated and inimitable. The sensation it produces is too strong for pleasure, too intense for enjoyment. There, where all is so new, novelty loses its charm; – where all is so safe, conscious security is no proof against *horrible imaginings*; and those splendid evidences of the science and industry of man, which rise at every step, recede before the terrible possibilities with which they mingle, and which may render the utmost precaution of talent and philanthropy unavailable. It is in vain that the barrier rises and the arch springs; that the gulf is platformed and the precipice screened – still the eye closes and the breath is suspended, while danger, painted in the unmastered savagery of remote scenes, creates an ideal and proximate peril. Here experience teaches the falsity of the trite maxim, that the mind becomes elevated by the contemplation of nature in the midst of her grandest works, and engenders thoughts '*that wander through eternity*'. The mind in such scenes is stricken back upon its own insignificance. Masses like these sublime deformities, starting out of the ordinary proportions of nature, in their contemplation reduce man to what he is – an atom. In such regions nothing is in conformity with him, all is at variance with his end and being, all is commemorative of those elementary convulsions, which sweep away whatever lives and breathes, in the general wreck of inanimate matter. Engines and agents of the destructive elements that rage around them, these are regions fitted only to raise the storm and to launch the avalanche; to cherish the whirlwind, and attract the bolt; until some convulsive throe within their mystic womb, awakens fiercer contentions: then they heave and shift, and burst and burn, again to subside, cool down, and settle into awful stillness and permanent desolation; at once the wreck and the monument of changes which scoff at human record, and trace in characters that admit no controversy the fallacy of calculations and the vanity of systems. Well may the countless races of successive ages have left the mysteries of the Alps unexplored, their snows untracked: but immortal glory be the meed of them, the brave, bold spirits, whose unaccommodated natures, in these regions, where 'cold performs the effect of fire,' braved dangers in count-less forms, to oppose the invading enemies of their country's struggling rights; who climbing where the eagle had not soared, nor the chamois dared to spring, raised the shout of national independence amidst echoes which had never reverberated, save to the howl of the wolf, or the thunder of the avalanche. Gratitude as eternal as the snows of Mount Blanc to them or him, who grappled with obstacles coeval with creation, levelled the pinnacle and blew up the rock, pierced the granite and spanned the tor-rent, disputing with nature in all her potency her right to separate man from man and made straight in the desert an highway for progressive civilization!

* * * *

In 1814, Genoa, like the rest of Italy, believed that the Allies were serious in their promises of liberation; and that the legitimate Crusaders against *illegitimate despotism* meant nothing more than to restore that liberty, whose loss they so affectingly deplored. England personally stood pledged to Genoa! – *She* had voluntarily interposed in its behalf – she had sent the flower of her nobles and her gentry, as friends and guests to hear the tale of domestic griefs, and to steal the confidence of the citizens by a show of sympathy and a pledge of protection. These gentlemen were received into the palaces of the aristocracy, into the houses of the people; and doors, that so rarely open to the stranger's knock in Genoa, flew off their hinges to welcome the British guest. When the British officers rode into their gates, bearing the white flag consecrated by the holy word of '*independence*,' the people, always true to strong emotion, by whatever cause it is promoted, kissed their garments, and rent the air with *vivats* to their honour.

Every heart was open; every tongue was loud; opinions long hidden were revealed; hopes long nourished were confessed; all, of every class, gave themselves up with frankness to their English liberators. When there was nothing more to extort, the English, in their turn, gave up the Genoese to their ancient foe, their inveterate rival, and long-detested neighbour – the King of Sardinia and of Jerusalem.

* * * *

To the last moment, the English continued to feast in the houses, and to swarm in the streets of Genoa. They parted at night from the palaces of the Strada Nuova and Balbi, leaving their hosts to dream over their recovered independence. In the morning they delivered them up, bound hand and foot, to the enemy. Lord William Bentinck's flag of '*Independenza!*' was taken down from the steeples and high places at sun-rise, – before noon, the arms of Sardinia blazoned in their stead; – and yet the Genoese did not rise up *en masse* and massacre the English – the violators of a trust so sacred! To the glory of the Genoese be it recorded, that even in their bitterest moments of disappointment and suffering, they did not accuse the British military of misconduct or treachery: they saw that they were, like themselves, the dupes of the masters they served – the blind agents of a dark and infamous policy. How just they were in this conviction, time has since shown, and time will still after prove. Many a brave English soldier now tells the tale of Genoese ruin, and of the part he was induced to play, with the crimson hues of shame rising on that brow where shame never sat before: many a grateful English heart has voluntarily returned to that Genoese roof, under which he first entered an unconscious agent of treason against the rites of hospitality; and sought and found there that forgiveness it could not grant to itself.

1822

68. Harriet Martineau
On Female Education

In discussing the subject of female education, it is not so much my object to inquire whether the natural powers of women be equal to those of men, as to show the expediency of giving proper scope and employment to the powers which they do possess. It may be as well, notwithstanding, to inquire whether the difference be as great as is generally supposed between the mental structure of men and of women.

Doubtless the formation of the mind must depend in a great degree on the structure of the body. From this cause the strength of mind observable in men is supposed to arise; and the delicacy of the female to be in agreement with the bodily frame. But it is impossible to ascertain how much may depend on early education; nor can we solve our doubts on this head by turning our view to savage countries, where, if bodily strength be nearly equal between the two sexes, their minds are alike sunk in ignorance and darkness. In our own country, we find that as long as the studies of children of both sexes continue the same, the progress they make is equal. After the rudiments of knowledge have been obtained, in the cultivated ranks of society, (of which alone I mean to speak,) the boy goes on continually increasing his stock of information, it being his only employment to store and exercise his mind for future years; while the girl is probably confined to low pursuits, her aspirings after knowledge are subdued, she is taught to believe that solid information is unbecoming her sex; almost her whole time is expended on light accomplishments, and thus before she is sensible of her powers, they are checked in their growth, chained down to mean objects, to rise no more; and when the natural consequences of this mode of treatment arise, all mankind agree that the abilities of women are far inferior to those of men. But in the few instances where a contrary mode of treatment has been pursued, where fair play has been given to the faculties, even without much assistance, what has almost invariably been the result? Has it not been evident that the female mind, though in many respects differently constituted from that of man, may be well brought into comparison with his? If she wants his enterprising spirit, the deficiency is made up by perseverance in what she does undertake; for his ambition, she has a thirst for knowledge; and for his ready perception, she has unwearied application.

It is proof sufficient to my mind, that there is no natural deficiency of power, that, unless proper objects are supplied to women to employ their faculties, their energies are exerted improperly. Some aim they must have, and if no good one is presented to them, they must seek for a bad one.

We may find evidence in abundance of this truth in the condition of women before the introduction of Christianity.

Before the revelation of this blessed religion, (doubly blessed to the female sex,) what was their situation? They were either sunk almost to the level of the brutes in mental darkness, buried in their own homes, the slaves instead of the companions of their husbands, only to be preserved from vice by being excluded from the world, or, not being able to endure these restraints, employing their restless powers and turbulent passions in the pursuit of vicious pleasures and sensual gratifications. And we cannot wonder that this was the case, when they were gifted with faculties which they were not permitted to exercise, and were compelled to vegetate from year to year, with no object in life and no hope in death. Observe what an immediate change was wrought by the introduction of Christianity. Mark the zeal, directed by knowledge, of the female converts, of so many of whom St Paul makes honourable mention as his friends, on account of their exertions in the great cause. An object was held out for them to obtain, and their powers were bent to the attainment of it, instead of being engaged in vice and folly. The female character has been observed to improve since that time, in proportion as the treasures of useful knowledge have been placed within the reach of the sex.

I wish to imply by what I have said, not that great stores of information are as necessary to women as to men, but that as much care should be taken of the formation of their minds. Their attainments cannot in general be so great, because they have their own appropriate duties and peculiar employments, the neglect of which nothing can excuse; but I contend that these duties will be better performed if the powers be rationally employed. If the whole mind be exercised and strengthened, it will bring more vigour to the performance of its duties in any particular province.

The first great objection which is made to enlightening the female mind is, that if engaged in the pursuit of knowledge, women neglect their appropriate duties and peculiar employments.

2nd. That the greatest advances that the female mind can make in knowledge, must still fall far short of the attainments of the other sex. 3rd. That the vanity so universally ascribed to the sex is apt to be inflated by any degree of proficiency in knowledge, and that women therefore become forgetful of the subordinate station allotted them by law, natural and divine.

To the first objection I answer, that such a pursuit of knowledge as shall lead women to neglect their peculiar duties, is not that cultivation of mind for the utility of which I am contending. But these duties may be well performed without engaging the whole time and attention. If 'great thoughts constitute great minds', what can be expected from a woman whose whole intellect is employed on the trifling cares and comparatively mean occupations, to which the advocates for female ignorance would condemn her? These cares and these occupations were allotted to women to enable them to smooth our way through life; they were designed as a means to this end, and should never be pursued as the end itself. The knowledge of these necessary acts is so easily acquired, and they are so easily performed, that an active mind will feel a dismal vacuity, a craving after something nobler and better to employ the thoughts in the intervals of idleness which must occur when these calls of duty are answered, and if nothing nobler and better is presented to it, it will waste its energies in the pursuit of folly, if not of vice, and thus continually perpetuate the faults of the sex.

Some will perhaps say, 'if household occupations are insufficient to exercise the mind, the wide field of charity is open to the employment of its energies.' It is so. But how inefficient is benevolence when not directed by knowledge! And how comparatively faint will be the exertions in the cause, when the views are bounded, the motives narrow and even selfish, (for ignorance is the mother of selfishness,) and charity pursued more as a present employment, than with the desire of doing permanent good to the objects of its benevolence! How different is this from the charity of an enlightened mind, of a mind which, enlarged by knowledge, can comprehend extensive views, can design not only the present relief of misery, but can look forward to the permanent improvement of its kind; which, understanding the workings of the mind, and able to profit by the experience of others, can choose the best means for the attainment of certain ends, and thus by uniting knowledge and judgement with benevolence, can make its efforts doubly efficient! But even if the calls of charity be answered, and feminine duties performed, yet much leisure remains for other pursuits; and what should these pursuits be? Surely, such as will make social intercourse more delightful, such as will furnish innocent recreation at home, such as will cheer the hours of dullness, and furnish pleasant subjects for the thoughts to turn to in times of sickness or of sorrow.

It must be allowed by all, that one of woman's first duties is to qualify herself for being a companion to her husband, or to those with whom her lot in life is cast. She was formed to be a domestic companion, and such an one as shall give to home its charms, as shall furnish such entertainment that her husband need not be driven abroad for amusement. This is one of the first duties required from a woman, and no time can be misemployed which is applied to the purpose of making her such a companion, and I contend that a friend like this cannot be found among women of uncultivated minds. If their thoughts are continually occupied by the vanities of the world, if that time which is not required for the fulfilment of household duties, is spent in folly, or even in harmless trifles in which the husband has no interest, how are the powers of pleasing to be perpetuated, how is she to find interesting subjects for social converse? Surely these desirable objects are best promoted by the hours of leisure being devoted to the acquirement of useful knowledge, such knowledge as may excite the reflective powers, enlarge and steady the mind, and raise it, nearly at least, to the level of the other sex. Thus there may be companionship between the sexes, and surely no woman who aspires to and labours for this end can be accused of neglecting her peculiar duties. But for this object to be completely gained, the work must be begun early. The powers should be cultivated from infancy, and the mind taught to feel pleasure in seeking for information, always in subservience to more important avocations. If the soul be early contracted by too great an attention to trifles, if it be taught that ignorance is to be its portion, no later endeavours will be of any avail to ennoble it.

If we consider woman as the guardian and instructress of infancy, her claims to cultivation of mind become doubly urgent. It is evident that if the soul of the teacher is narrow and contracted, that of the pupil cannot be enlarged. If we consider that the first years of childhood exert an influence over the whole future life, we cannot be too careful to preserve our children from the effects of ignorance and prejudice on their young minds. It has been frequently and justly observed, that almost all men, remarkable for talents or virtue, have had excellent mothers, to the early influence of whose noble qualities, the future superiority of their children was mainly to be ascribed. If this be true, what might not be hoped from the labours of a race of enlightened mothers, who would early impress on their children's minds lessons of piety and wisdom, and who would make the first sentiments of their souls noble and enlarged, who would take in at one comprehensive view all that was to be done to render them what they ought to be, and who would render their first instructions subservient to the objects to be afterwards pursued! If such were to be the foundation of character, what might not the superstructure be!

It may be said that many minds have been great, capable of conceiving and executing noble designs, without any advantages of education. It is certainly true, but these minds have been too aspiring to be chained down by the fetters of ignorance; they have become great in spite of disadvantages, and not in consequence of them; and had their powers been cultivated, their efforts would probably have been better directed and doubly successful. But the best proof, that all the usefulness and all the feminine qualities of women may remain unimpaired, notwithstanding the acquisition of knowledge, may be gained by referring to our own observation and experience. I have known young women whose whole time was occupied by the care of a numerous family of brothers and sisters, stealing a few minutes daily from their breakfast hour, to study the Greek tongue, for the purpose of reading the Testament in the original language; and in no degree did this pursuit interfere with their active duties; so little so, that it was even unknown by most of their own family. They attained their object and enjoyed the satisfaction of settling their religious belief for themselves, without a diminution of their usefulness as women. I do not mean by this that I would have all women instructed in the learned languages. This would be needless, and for those of inferior talents the time would be wasted. I only wish to show that even such deep knowledge as these ladies possessed, did not lead them to appropriate their time too much to selfish

purposes. I have also known a young lady, who, notwithstanding the disadvantages of a defective early education, has made wonderful progress in
knowledge of various kinds, especially in the study of the human mind –
and yet she superintends a large domestic establishment, has founded a
school, which is supported entirely by her exertions, and she is ever ready
with her fund of sensible, unassuming and natural conversation to answer
the calls of those who depend much on her for their entertainment in the
domestic circle. I have known another lady, blest with affluence, employing
the powers of her well-exercised mind in the furtherance of projects of
extensive benevolence; projects which would often have failed, had they
not been executed by one early accustomed to give her time to enlightened
industry, to exercise her reason, and to feed her mind with useful knowledge. Benevolent dispositions, regulated by such a judgement, and supported by motives of piety, have been productive of an immense sum of
good; and I may mention in favour of my argument, that her powers of
usefulness have been employed in teaching the poor the arts of household
economy, of which this lady is a perfect mistress. Many other instances
could I bring, if my limits would permit, but I trust that what I have said
will convince others as well as myself, that the acquisition of knowledge
does not necessarily lead to the neglect of woman's appropriate duties.

With respect to the second objection, viz., That the greatest advances
which the female mind can make in knowledge must fall far short of the
attainments of the other sex, – I allow that the acquirements of women can
seldom equal those of men, and it is not desirable that they should. I do
not wish to excite a spirit of rivalry between the sexes; I do not desire that
many females should seek for fame as authors. I only wish that their
powers should be so employed that they should not be obliged to seek
amusements beneath them, and injurious to them. I wish them to be companions to men, instead of playthings or servants, one of which an ignorant
woman must commonly be. If they are called to be wives, a sensible mind
is an essential qualification for the domestic character; if they remain
single, liberal pursuits are absolutely necessary to preserve them from the
faults so generally attributed to that state, and so justly and inevitably,
while the mind is buried in darkness.

If it be asked what kind and degree of knowledge is necessary to preserve
women from the evils mentioned as following in the train of ignorance, I
answer that much must depend on natural talent, fortune and station; but
no Englishwoman, above the lower ranks of life, ought to be ignorant of
the Evidences and Principles of her religious belief, of Sacred History, of
the outline at least of General History, of the Elements of the Philosophy
of Nature, and of the Human Mind; and to these should be added the

knowledge of such living languages, and the acquirement of such accomplishments, as situation and circumstances may direct.

With respect to the third objection viz., that the vanity so universally ascribed to the sex is apt to be inflated by any degree of proficiency in knowledge, and that women, therefore, become forgetful of the subordinate station assigned them by law, natural and divine: the most important part of education, the implanting of religious principles must be in part neglected, if the share of knowledge which women may appropriate, should be suffered to inflate their vanity, or excite feelings of pride. Christian humility should be one of the first requisites in female education, and till it is attained every acquirement of every kind will become a cause of self exaltation, and those accomplishments which are the most rare, will of course be looked upon with the most self-complacency. But if the taste for knowledge were more generally infused, and if proficiency in the attainments I have mentioned were more common, there would be much less pedantry than there is at present; for when acquirements of this kind are no longer remarkable, they cease to afford a subject for pride. I suppose, when knowledge was rare among men, many of those who had made some proficiency were as pedantic as the blue-stockings of the present day. As the spread of information extended there was less cause for conceit, and the case would be the same with the female sex. This is a fact, which is proved from year to year, for female education is rapidly improving, and the odious pedantry to which it at first gave rise is less observable, and will, ere long, I hope, be more a name than a reality.

Let woman then be taught that her powers of mind were given her to be improved. Let her be taught that she is to be a rational companion of the other sex among whom her lot in life is cast, that her proper sphere is, *home* – that there she is to provide not only for the bodily comforts of man, but that she is to enter also into community of mind with him; she is to strengthen him in the hour of trial; to cheer him in times of despondence; to exert herself for his improvement and her own; to encourage him in rational pursuits, both by her example and sympathy; that she is to be the participator in his happiness, the consoler of his sorrows, the support of his weakness, and his friend under all circumstances. For this purpose she must exert her own faculties, store her mind, strengthen her reason, and so far enrich her natural powers by cultivation, as to be capable of performing the important duties which fall to her lot. Let her preserve her natural feminine gentleness, her perfect innocence. Let her become mistress of all the little arts, of all the important trifles, (if I may so express myself) which render home a scene of comfort; but let not these be made the end instead of the means. Like our attendant planet, let her, while she is the constant companion of man, throw sufficient light from the sun of knowledge to cheer him in his hours of darkness, and he will find that the progress she makes towards this great luminary will not interfere with the companionship she owes to him.

When this is done, when woman is allowed to claim her privileges as an intellectual being, the folly, the frivolity, and all the mean vices and faults which have hitherto been the reproach of the sex, will gradually disappear. As she finds nobler objects presented to her grasp, and that her rank in the scale of being is elevated, she will engraft the vigorous qualities of the mind of man on her own blooming virtues, and insinuate into his mind those softer graces and milder beauties, which will smooth the ruggedness of his character.

Surely, this is the natural state of woman, and to this perfection will they rise, if the improvement of the female mind proceeds with the same rapidity which we have now reason to anticipate. See what has already been done. In the present age, and in our own country, we can reckon among those who have rendered important services to society at large, as well as to their own circle of friends, the names of More, Barbauld, Hamilton, Edgeworth, Carter, Talbot, Elizabeth Smith, Chapone, Grant, Aikin and Cappe. Most of these ladies have written on the noblest subjects which can exercise the human mind, religion and morality, and have thus proved that the cultivation of the powers of the female mind is favourable instead of injurious to these important interests.

I cannot better conclude than with the hope, that these examples of what may be done may excite a noble emulation in their own sex, and in ours such a conviction of the value of the female mind, as shall overcome our long-cherished prejudices, and induce us to give our earnest endeavours to the promotion of woman's best interests.

＞—＜

1823

69. Felicia Hemans
The Voice of Spring

I come, I come! ye have called me long –
I come o'er the mountains with light and song!
Ye may trace my step o'er the wakening earth

By the winds which tell of the violet's birth,
By the primrose-stars in the shadowy grass,
By the green leaves opening as I pass.

I have breathed on the South, and the chestnut-flowers
By thousands have burst from the forest-bowers,
And the ancient graves and the fallen fanes
Are veiled with wreaths on Italian plains; –
But it is not for me, in my hour of bloom
To speak of the ruin or the tomb!

I have looked on the hills of the stormy North,
And the larch has hung all his tassels forth,
The fisher is out on the sunny sea,
And the reindeer bounds o'er the pasture free,
And the pine has a fringe of softer green,
And the moss looks bright where my foot hath been.

I have sent through the wood-paths a glowing sigh,
And called out each voice of the deep blue sky;
From the night-bird's lay through the starry time,
In the groves of the soft Hesperian clime
To the swan's wild note by the Iceland lakes,
When the dark fir-branch into verdure breaks.

From the streams and founts I have loosed the chain,
They are sweeping on to the silvery main,
They are flashing down from the mountain brows,
They are flinging spray o'er the forest boughs,
They are bursting fresh from their sparry caves,
And the earth resounds with the joy of waves!

Come forth, O ye children of gladness! come!
Where the violets lie may be now your home.
Ye of the rose-lip and dew-bright eye,
And the bounding footstep, to meet me fly!
With the lyre, and the wreath, and the joyous lay,
Come forth to the sunshine – I may not stay.

Away from the dwellings of care-worn men,
The waters are sparkling in grove and glen!

Away from the chamber and sullen hearth,
The young leaves are dancing in breezy mirth!
Their light stems thrill to the wild-wood strains,
And youth is abroad in my green domains.

But ye! – ye are changed since ye met me last!
There is something bright from your features passed!
There is that come over your brow and eye
Which speaks of a world where the flowers must die!
– Ye smile! but your smile has a dimness yet:
Oh! what have you looked on since last we met?

Ye are changed, ye are changed! and I see not here
All whom I saw in the vanished year!
There were graceful heads, with their ringlets bright,
Which tossed in the breeze with a play of light;
There were eyes in whose glistening laughter lay
No faint remembrance of dull decay!

There were steps that flew o'er the cowslip's head,
As if for a banquet all earth were spread;
There were voices that rang through the sapphire sky,
And had not a sound of mortality!
Are they gone? is their mirth from the mountains passed?
Ye have looked on death since ye met me last!

I know whence the shadow comes o'er you now –
Ye have strewn the dust on the sunny brow!
Ye have given the lovely to earth's embrace –
She has taken the fairest of beauty's race,
With their laughing eyes and their festal crown:
They are gone from amongst you in silence down!

They are gone from amongst you, the young and fair,
Ye have lost the gleam of their shining hair!
But I know a land where there falls no blight –
I shall find them there, with their eyes of light!
Where Death midst the blooms of the morn may dwell,
I tarry no longer – farewell, farewell!

The summer is coming, on soft winds borne –
Ye may press the grape, ye may bind the corn!
For me, I depart to a brighter shore –
Ye are marked by care, ye are mine no more;
I go where the loved who have left you dwell,
   And the flowers are not Death's. Fare ye well, farewell!

1824

70. Mary Shelley
On Ghosts

I look for ghosts – but none will force
Their way to me, 'tis falsely said
That there was ever intercourse
Between the living and the dead.
                    Wordsworth.

What a different earth do we inhabit from that on which our forefathers
dwelt! The antediluvian world, strode over by mammoths, preyed upon by
the megatherion, and peopled by the offspring of the Sons of God is a
better type of the earth of Homer, Herodotus, and Plato, than the hedged-
in cornfields and measured hills of the present day. The globe was then
encircled by a wall which paled in the bodies of men, while their feathered
thoughts soared over the boundary; it had a brink, and in the deep profound
which it overhung, men's imaginations, eagle-winged, dived and flew, and
brought home strange tales to their believing auditors. Deep caverns har-
boured giants; cloudlike birds cast their shadows upon the plains; while
far out at sea lay islands of bliss, the fair paradise of Atlantis or El Dorado
sparkling with untold jewels. Where are they now? The Fortunate Isles
have lost the glory that spread a halo round them; for who deems himself
nearer to the golden age, because he touches at the Canaries on his voyage
to India? Our only riddle is the rise of the Niger; the interior of New
Holland, our only terra incognita; and our sole mare incognitum, the
north-west passage. But these are tame wonders, lions in leash; we do not
invest Mungo Park, or the Captain of the Hecla, with divine attributes; no
waters of the unknown river bubble up from hell's fountains, no strange

and weird power is supposed to guide the ice-berg, nor do we fable that a stray pick-pocket from Botany Bay has found the gardens of the Hesperides within the circuit of the Blue Mountains. What have we left to dream about? The clouds are no longer the charioted servants of the sun, nor does he any more bathe his glowing brow in the bath of Thetis; the rainbow has ceased to be the messenger of the Gods, and thunder is no longer their awful voice, warning man of that which is to come. We have the sun which has been weighed and measured, but not understood; we have the assemblage of the planets, the congregation of the stars, and the yet unshackled ministration of the winds: – such is the list of our ignorance.

Nor is the empire of the imagination less bounded in its own proper creations, than in those which were bestowed on it by the poor blind eyes of our ancestors. What has become of enchantresses with their palaces of crystal and dungeons of palpable darkness? What of fairies and their wands? What of witches and their familiars? and, last, what of ghosts, with beckoning hands and fleeting shapes, which quelled the soldier's brave heart, and made the murderer disclose to the astonished noon the veiled work of midnight? These which were realities to our forefathers, in our wiser age –

> – Characterless are grated
> To dusty nothing.

Yet is it true that we do not believe in ghosts? There used to be several traditionary tales repeated, with their authorities, enough to stagger us when we consigned them to that place where that is which 'is as though it had never been.' But these are gone out of fashion. Brutus's dream has become a deception of his over-heated brain, Lord Lyttleton's vision is called a cheat; and one by one these inhabitants of deserted houses, moonlight glades, misty mountain tops, and midnight churchyards, have been ejected from their immemorial seats, and small thrill is felt when the dead majesty of Denmark blanches the cheek and unsettles the reason of his philosophic son.

But do none of us believe in ghosts? If this question be read at noon-day, when –

> Every little corner, nook, and hole,
> Is penetrated with the insolent light –

at such a time derision is seated on the features of my reader. But let it be twelve at night in a lone house; take up, I beseech you, the story of the

Bleeding Nun; or of the Statue, to which the bridegroom gave the wedding ring, and she came in the dead of night to claim him, tall, white, and cold; or of the Grandsire, who with shadowy form and breathless lips stood over the couch and kissed the foreheads of his sleeping grand-children, and thus doomed them to their fated death; and let all these details be assisted by solitude, flapping curtains, rushing wind, a long and dusky passage, an half open door – O, then truly, another answer may be given, and many will request leave to sleep upon it, before they decide whether there be such a thing as a ghost in the world, or out of the world, if that phraseology be more spiritual. What is the meaning of this feeling?

For my own part, I never saw a ghost except once in a dream. I feared it in my sleep; I awoke trembling, and lights and the speech of others could hardly dissipate my fear. Some years ago I lost a friend, and a few months afterwards visited the house where I had last seen him. It was deserted, and though in the midst of a city, its vast halls and spacious apartments occasioned the same sense of loneliness as if it had been situated on an uninhabited heath. I walked through the vacant chambers by twilight, and none save I awakened the echoes of their pavement. The far mountains (visible from the upper windows) had lost their tinge of sunset; the tranquil atmosphere grew leaden coloured as the golden stars appeared in the firmament; no wind ruffled the shrunk-up river which crawled lazily through the deepest channel of its wide and empty bed; the chimes of the Ave Maria had ceased, and the bell hung moveless in the open belfry: beauty invested a reposing world, and awe was inspired by beauty only. I walked through the rooms filled with sensations of the most poignant grief. He had been there; his living frame had been caged by those walls, his breath had mingled with that atmosphere, his step had been on those stones, I thought: – the earth is a tomb, the gaudy sky a vault, we but walking corpses. The wind rising in the east rushed through the open casements, making them shake; – methought, I heard, I felt – I know not what – but I trembled. To have seen him but for a moment, I would have knelt until the stones had been worn by the impress, so I told myself, and so I knew a moment after, but then I trembled, awe-struck and fearful. Wherefore? There is something beyond us of which we are ignorant. The sun drawing up the vaporous air makes a void, and the wind rushes in to fill it, – thus beyond our soul's ken there is an empty space; and our hopes and fears, in gentle gales or terrific whirlwinds occupy the vacuum; and if it does no more, it bestows on the heart a belief that influences do exist to watch and guard us, though they be impalpable to the coarser faculties.

I have heard that when Coleridge was asked if he believed in ghosts, –

he replied that he had seen too many to put any trust in their reality – and the person of the most lively imagination that I ever knew echoed this reply. But these were not real ghosts (pardon, unbelievers, my mode of speech) that they saw; they were shadows, phantoms unreal; that while they appalled the senses, yet carried no other feeling to the mind of others than delusion, and were viewed as we might view an optical deception which we see to be true with our eyes, and know to be false with our understandings. I speak of other shapes. The returning bride, who claims the fidelity of her betrothed; the murdered man who shakes to remorse the murderer's heart; ghosts that lift the curtains at the foot of your bed as the clock chimes one; who rise all pale and ghastly from the churchyard and haunt their ancient abodes; who, spoken to, reply; and whose cold unearthly touch makes the hair stand stark upon the head; the true, old-fashioned, foretelling, flitting, gliding ghost, – who has seen such a one?

I have known two persons who at broad daylight have owned that they believed in ghosts, for that they had seen one. One of these was an Englishman, and the other an Italian. The former had lost a friend he dearly loved, who for awhile appeared to him nightly, gently stroking his cheek and spreading a serene calm over his mind. He did not fear the appearance, although he was somewhat awe-stricken as each night it glided into his chamber, and

Ponsi del letto in su la sponda manca.

This visitation continued for several weeks, when by some accident he altered his residence, and then he saw it no more. Such a tale may easily be explained away; – but several years had passed, and he, a man of strong and virile intellect, said that 'he had seen a ghost.'

The Italian was a noble, a soldier, and by no means addicted to super-stition: he had served in Napoleon's armies from early youth, and had been to Russia, had fought and bled, and been rewarded, and he unhesitatingly, and with deep relief, recounted his story.

This Chevalier, a young, and (somewhat a miraculous incident) a gallant Italian, was engaged in a duel with a brother officer, and wounded him in the arm. The subject of the duel was frivolous; and distressed therefore at its consequences he attended on his youthful adversary during his consequent illness, so that when the latter recovered they became firm and dear friends. They were quartered together at Milan, where the youth fell desperately in love with the wife of a musician, who disdained his passion, so that it preyed on his spirits and his health; he absented himself from all amusements, avoided all his brother officers, and his only consolation was to pour his love-sick plaints into the ear of the Chevalier who strove in vain to inspire him either with indifference towards the fair disdainer, or to inculcate lessons of fortitude and heroism. As a last resource he urged him to ask leave of absence; and to seek, either in change of scene, or the amusement of hunting, some diversion to his passion. One evening the youth came to the Chevalier, and said, 'Well, I have asked leave of absence, and am to have it early to-morrow morning, so lend me your fowling-piece and cartridges, for I shall go to hunt for a fortnight.' The Chevalier gave him what he asked; among the shot there were a few bullets. 'I will take these also,' said the youth, 'to secure myself against the attack of any wolf, for I mean to bury myself in the woods'.

Although he had obtained that for which he came, the youth still lingered. He talked of the cruelty of his lady, lamented that she would not even permit him a hopeless attendance, but that she inexorably banished him from her sight, 'so that,' said he, 'I have no hope but in oblivion.' At length he rose to depart. He took the Chevalier's hand and said, 'You will see her to-morrow, you will speak to her, and hear her speak; tell her, I entreat you, that our conversation to-night has been concerning her, and that her name was the last that I spoke.' 'Yes, yes' cried the Chevalier, 'I will say any thing you please; but you must not talk of her any more, you must forget her.' The youth embraced his friend with warmth, but the latter saw nothing more in it than the effects of his affection, combined with his melancholy at absenting himself from his mistress, whose name, joined to a tender farewell, was the last sound that he uttered.

When the Chevalier was on guard that night, he heard the report of a gun. He was at first troubled and agitated by it, but afterwards thought no more of it, and when relieved from guard went to bed, although he passed a restless, sleepless night. Early in the morning some one knocked at his door. It was a soldier, who said that he had got the young officer's leave of absence, and had taken it to his house; a servant had admitted him, and he had gone up stairs, but the room door of the officer was locked, and no one answered to his knocking, but something oozed through from under the door that looked like blood. The Chevalier, agitated and frightened at this account, hurried to his friend's house, burst open the door, and found him stretched on the ground – he had blown out his brains, and the body lay a headless trunk, cold, and stiff.

The shock and grief which the Chevalier experienced in consequence of this catastrophe produced a fever which lasted for some days. When he got well, he obtained leave of absence, and went into the country to try to divert his mind. One evening at moonlight, he was returning home from a walk, and passed through a lane with a hedge on both sides, so high that he could not see over them. The night was balmy – : the bushes gleamed with fireflies, brighter than the stars which the moon had veiled with her silver light. Suddenly he heard a rustling near him, and the figure of his friend issued from the hedge and stood before him, mutilated as he had seen him after his death. This figure he saw several times, always in the same place. It was impalpable to the touch, motionless, except in its advance, and made no sign when it was addressed. Once the Chevalier took a friend with him to the spot. The same rustling was heard, the same shadow stepped forth, his companion fled in horror, but the Chevalier staid, vainly endeavouring to discover what called his friend from his quiet tomb, and if any act of his might give repose to the restless shade.

Such are my two stories, and I record them the more willingly, since they occurred to men, and to individuals distinguished the one for courage and the other for sagacity. I will conclude my 'modern instances,' with a story told by M. G. Lewis, not probably so authentic as these, but perhaps more amusing. I relate it as nearly as possible in his own words.

'A gentleman journeying towards the house of a friend, who lived on the skirts of an extensive forest, in the east of Germany, lost his way. He wandered for some time among the trees, when he saw a light at a distance. On approaching it he was surprised to observe that it proceeded from the interior of a ruined monastery. Before he knocked at the gate he thought it proper to look through the window. He saw a number of cats assembled round a small grave, four of whom were at that moment letting down a coffin with a crown upon it. The gentleman startled at this unusual sight, and, imagining that he had arrived at the retreats of fiends or witches, mounted his horse and rode away with the utmost precipitation. He arrived at his friend's house at a late hour, who sat up waiting for him. On his arrival his friend questioned him as to the cause of the traces of agitation visible in his face. He began to recount his adventures after much hesitation, knowing that it was scarcely possible that his friend should give faith to his relation. No sooner had he mentioned the coffin with the crown upon it, than his friend's cat, who seemed to have been lying asleep before the fire, leaped up, crying out, "Then I am king of the cats"; and then scrambled up the chimney, and was never seen more.'

1825

71. Harriette Wilson
from *Memoirs*

I shall not say why and how I became, at the age of fifteen, the mistress of
Lord Craven. Whether it was love, or the severity of my father, the depravity of my own heart, or the winning arts of the noble lord, which induced
me to leave my paternal roof, and place myself under his protection, does
not, now, much signify; or, if it does, I am not in the humour to gratify
curiosity in this matter.

I resided in the Marine Parade, at Brighton, and I remember that Lord
Craven used to draw cocoa trees, and his fellows, as he called them, on the
best vellum paper, for my amusement. Here stood the enemy, he would say,
and here, my love, are my fellows. There are cocoa trees, &c. It was, in fact,
a dead bore. All these cocoa trees, and fellows, at past eleven o'clock at
night, could have no peculiar interest for a child, like myself, so lately in the
habit of retiring early to rest. One night, I recollect, I fell asleep; and, as I
often dream, I said, yawning, and half awake, Oh Lord! oh Lord! Craven
has got me into the West Indies again. In short I soon found I had made
but a bad speculation, by going, from my father, to Lord Craven. I was even
more afraid of the latter, than I had ever been of the former. Not that there
was any particular harm in the man, beyond his cocoa trees, but we never
suited, nor understood each other.

I was not depraved enough to determine, immediately, on a new choice,
and yet I often thought about it. How indeed, could I do otherwise, when
the Honorable Frederick Lamb was my constant visitor, and talked to me
of nothing else? However, in justice to myself, I must declare, that the idea
of deceiving Lord Craven, while I was under his roof, never once entered
into my head. Frederick was then very handsome, and certainly tried, and
with all his strength, to convince me that constancy to Lord Craven, was
the greatest nonsense in the world. I firmly believe that Frederick Lamb
sincerely loved me, and deeply regretted that he had no fortune to invite
me to share with him.

Lord Melbourne his father, was a good man. Not one of your stiff-laced,
moralizing fathers, who preach chastity and forbearance to their children.
Quite the contrary, he congratulated his son on the lucky circumstances of
his friend Craven having such a fine girl with him. No such thing,
answered Frederick Lamb, I am unsuccessful there. Harriette will have
nothing to do with me. Nonsense! rejoined Melbourne in great surprise, I

never heard anything half so ridiculous, in all my life. The girl must be mad!! She looks mad. I thought so the other day, when I met her galloping about, with her feathers blowing, and her thick, dark hair about her ears.

I'll speak to Harriette for you, added his lordship, after a long pause, and then continually repeating to himself, in an under tone, not have my son indeed! six feet high! a fine, straight, handsome, noble young fellow! I wonder what she would have!

In truth, I scarcely knew myself; but something I determined on: so miserably tired was I of Craven, and his cocoa trees, and his sailing boats, and his ugly, cotton nightcaps, Surely, I would say, all men do not wear those shocking cotton nightcaps; else all women's illusions had been destroyed on the first night of their marriage!

I wonder, thought I, what sort of nightcap the Prince of Wales wears? Then I went on to wonder, whether the Prince of Wales would think me so beautiful, as Frederick Lamb did? Next I reflected that Frederick Lamb was younger than the Prince; but then again, the Prince of Wales!

✳ ✳ ✳ ✳

My new French maid has just been telling me a great deal about her late mistress, Lady Caroline Lamb. Her ladyship's only son is, I understand, in a very bad state of health. Lady Caroline has, therefore, hired a stout, young doctor, to attend him . . . The poor child: being subject to violent attacks in the night, Lady Caroline is often to be found, after midnight, in the doctor's bedchamber. I do not mean you to understand this ironically, as the young Frenchwoman says herself, there, very likely, is nothing in it, although the servants tell a story about a little silk stocking, very like her ladyships, being found one morning, quite at the bottom of the Doctor's bed! . . . She is the meanest woman on earth, and the greatest tyrant generally speaking. . . . [She] ate and drank enough for a porter, and, when the doctor forbade wine, she was in the habit of running into her dressing room, to *dedommager* herself, with a glass or two of eau de vie vielle, de cognac. . . .

Take her ladyship altogether, this comical woman must be excellent company. I only wish I had the honour of being her acquaintance. Not that I think much of her first novel, Glenarvon; and she is, really, not quite mad enough, to excuse her writing, in her husband's lifetime, while under his roof, the history of her love and intrigue, with Lord Byron!! The letters are really his lordship's for he told me so himself! . . . But enough of her ladyship, of whose nonsense, the world is tired. I admire her talents, and wish she would make better use of them.

72. Maria Jane Jewsbury
from *Woman's Love*

It would be easy to enumerate the authors who have described Woman as otherwise than 'in love'. It would be too easy to enumerate the books in which Woman is prominently brought forwards in any of the great relative characters of life; – as the daughter, the wife, the mother, the sister, the matron, or the friend; and yet wherever she is so introduced by a master hand, the absorbing interest of the book centres in her. Fifty other females may have, or want lovers, and we care nothing for them or their troubles. It is her actions, her faith, her love, and her sufferings, which sink into our hearts, ay, and abide there, long after we have closed the book.

✷ ✷ ✷ ✷

Who has not (whilst reading the plays at least) felt more for the lovely and loving Desdemona than the lovely and loving Juliet? for Imogen, the neglected wife, than for Ophelia, the neglected mistress? And to leave off putting cases, who does not sympathise more strongly in those true tales which history has preserved for us of Woman's Love, manifested in the relative duties and relative characters of life, than in any of the creations of the sublimest genius, the purest fancy? . . . These and a thousand other instances which shine, and will shine on the page of history 'as the stars for ever and ever', come home to the human heart with a far deeper and diviner influence, than all the loves of mere lovers. The reasons are plain. Pure and fervent as their love might be, it is still selfish; possessing to no higher motive than personal will and pleasure. It has not yet become sacred as a duty, and settled as a habit; not has it yet passed through long years of need, sickness, sorrow, and adversity, and come out impressed with the broad seal of constancy. Lovers' love may exhibit the 'freshness and the glory of a dream'; but it is from the nature of things unproved, and therefore from books as from real life, we have far deeper satisfaction in contemplating that love which has passed its trial hour, undimmed, and undiminished.

There is another reason: If we cannot all invent, we can all observe; and he must be singularly unfortunate in his society, who does not know living instances of women whose love bears analogy, at least, to that of which we have been speaking. His sphere is indeed confined, to say no worse of it, if he knows no woman who could, were it her duty, die with a husband and for a child – no wife who has found the devoted specious lover change into the unworthy, brutal husband, and yet has endured her lot with

unrepining patience, and met the world with smiles of seeming cheerful-
ness. . . . And, higher and harder task, denied herself the privilege of
friendship, and never told her grief: – No intellectual and accomplished
mother, who has surrendered early affluence, and accustomed comforts,
the pleasures of society, the indulgence of refined taste, and become a
menial as well as a mother to her children, and entered into all the harass-
ing details of minute daily economy, not with mere dogged submission, but
with active cheerful interest! Does he not know some daughter, who has
secluded herself from youthful companions and youthful pleasures, that
she may employ her health and spirits, her days and nights, in soothing a
parent to whom 'the grasshopper is become a burden', and existence a
pain, but who can, nevertheless, depart quietly to his long home, because
his last steps thither are supported by a beloved and affectionate child?
Does he not know a sister, whose mild influence has controlled the follies,
and whose tenderness, though at the risk of personal blame, has shielded
the faults of a brother? Or has he never seen an instance of female friendship; – not often, I grant, between young ladies, but between the young
and the old, – the matron who has safely trodden the ways of life, and the
young blooming girl, who is just entering upon them. It is a beautiful, ay,
and it is a frequent sight, to behold the calm gravity of age, tempering the
enthusiasm of youth; and the bright influence of youth shedding, as it
were, a sunset radiance over the sombre sky of age. But to come rather
closer to the feelings of our sceptic; – to touch upon his personal experience. If he ever lay upon a bed of sickness, what eyes became dim with
weeping, what cheeks pale with watching, over him? – What hand administered the medicine and smoothed the pillow? – Whose form glided
round his bed with the quiet care of a mortal, and yet ministering
spirit? – Whose tear soothed his dejection? – Whose smile calmed his
temper? – Whose patience bore with his many infirmities? – Unless he
live on a desert island, he will reply – Woman's! Woman's!

But to know to the full extent of such knowledge, how noble, how
sacred a thing is Woman's Love, it must be contemplated when strengthened by the bonds of duty, when called forth by the ties of nature. Some
may think it needless to lay such strong and repeated stress upon this
condition; but for my own part I do not believe that over the hearts of true
women, and such alone are worthy of mention, Love, the passion of Love,
has before marriage by any means the power generally supposed. I verily
think that many a most exemplary wife, has been the mistress –

Uncertain, coy, and hard to please.

No true woman will either do or suffer for the fondest and most faithful lover, a thousandth part of what she will do and suffer for a husband who is only moderately kind. No. – Love must with woman become a duty, a habit, a part of existence, a condition of life, before we can know how completely it unites and exemplifies the natures of the Lion and the Dove, the courage which no danger can dismay, with the constancy no suffering can diminish.

It has been much the fashion, of late, to write and talk about women's minds, and to make comparative estimates of the power of female and masculine intellect: Some, with pleasant malice, have made the scale preponderate on the gentleman's side; others, with pleasant gallantry, have made it preponderate on the side of the lady. Women of genius, never argue for the recognised equality of female intellect; and men of genius, never argue for its recognised inferiority; but, as in political questions, those dispute loudest who have least at stake. 'Master and mistress minds', move in their separate spheres, like the rulers of distinct and different kingdoms, seldom wishing, and scarcely ever tempted, to disturb each other's sovereignty. It is amongst those who reside in the nooks and corners of Parnassus, that disputes and litigations arise. We can fancy such small occupiers of intellectual territory, as Hayley, and Miss Seward, extremely agitated about the mutual recognition of rights, and claims, and divisions. We can only fancy Shakespeare, and Madame de Stael, regarding them with contempt and indifference. But by all means let the dispute go forwards, and if women are stimulated to give proof by their exertions, that there is such a thing as female genius, – and men are stimulated to give proof by their surpassing productions, that there is no genius in the world but what is masculine, the public will be the gainer any way. We shall have more clever people to write; – more clever books to be read. Without hazarding an opinion on the subject, for the very reason of not understanding its merits, I return to my own, my favourite theme, that with which I begun, and with which I would close, – 'Woman's Love'.

Let man take his claimed supremacy, and take it as his hereditary, his inalienable right. Let him have for his dower, sovereignty in science, in philosophy, in learning, in arts, and in arms; let him wear, unenvied, the ermine, the lawn, and the helmet; and wield, unrivalled, the sword, the pen, and the pencil. Let him be supreme in the cabinet, the camp, and the study: and to woman will still remain a 'goodly heritage', of which neither force nor rivalry can deprive her. The heart is her domain; and there she is a queen. To acquire over the unruly wills and tempers of men, an influence which no man, however great, however gifted, can acquire; – to manifest a faith which never fails, a patience that never wears out, a devotedness which can sacrifice and a courage which can suffer; – to perform the same, unvarying, round of duties, without weariness, – and endure the same unvarying round of vexations, without murmuring; – to requite neglect with kindness, and injustice with fidelity; – to be true, when all are false, – and firm, when all is hopeless; – to watch over the few dear objects of regard, with an eye that never sleeps, and a care that cannot change; – to think, to act, to suffer, to sacrifice, to live, to die, for them, their happiness and safety, – These are Woman's true triumphs; – this, this is WOMAN'S LOVE.

—

1826

73. Anna Barbauld
from *On Female Studies*

Every woman should consider herself as sustaining the general character of a rational being, as well as the more confined one belonging to the female sex; and therefore the motives for acquiring general knowledge and cultivating the taste are nearly the same to both sexes. The line of separation between the studies of a young man and a young woman appears to me to be chiefly fixed by this, – that a woman is excused from all professional knowledge. Professional knowledge means all that is necessary to fit a man for a peculiar profession or business. Thus men study in order to qualify themselves for the law, for physic, for various departments in political life, for instructing others from the pulpit or the professor's chair. These all require a great deal of severe study and technical knowledge; much of which is nowise valuable in itself, but as a means to that particular profession. Now as a woman can never be called to any of these professions, it is evident you have nothing to do with such studies. A woman is not expected to understand the mysteries of politics, because she is not called to govern; she is not required to know anatomy, because she is not to perform surgical operations; she need not embarrass herself with theological disputes, because she will neither be called upon to make nor to explain creeds.

Men have various departments in active life; women have but one, and all women have the same, differently modified indeed by their rank in life and other incidental circumstances. It is, to be a mother, a mistress of a family. The knowledge belonging to these duties is your professional knowledge, the want of which nothing will excuse. Literary knowledge therefore, in men, is often an indispensable duty; in women it can be only a desirable accomplishment. In women it is more immediately applied to the purposes of adorning and improving the mind, of refining the sentiments, and supplying proper stores for conversation. For general knowledge women have in some respects more advantages than men. Their avocations often allow them more leisure; their sedentary way of life disposes them to the domestic quiet amusement of reading; the share they take in the education of their children throws them in the way of books. The uniform tenor and confined circle of their lives makes them eager to diversify the scene by descriptions which open to them a new world; and they are eager to gain an idea of scenes on the busy stage of life from which they are shut out by their sex. It is likewise particularly desirable for women to be able to give spirit and variety to conversation by topics drawn from the stores of literature, as the broader mirth and more boisterous gaiety of the other sex are to them prohibited. As their parties must be innocent, care should be taken that they do not stagnate into insipidity. I will venture to add, that the purity and simplicity of heart which a woman ought never, in her freest commerce with the world, to wear off; her very seclusion from the jarring interests and coarser amusements of society, – fit her in a peculiar manner for the worlds of fancy and sentiment, and dispose her to the quickest relish of what is pathetic, sublime, or tender. To you, therefore, the beauties of poetry, of moral painting, and all in general that is comprised under the term of polite literature, lie particularly open, and you cannot neglect them without neglecting a very copious source of enjoyment.

Languages are on some accounts particularly adapted to female study, as they may be learnt at home without experiments or apparatus, and without interfering with the habits of domestic life; as they form the style, and as they are the immediate inlet to works of taste. But the learned languages, the Greek especially, require a great deal more time than a young woman can conveniently spare. To the Latin there is not an equal objection – and if a young person has leisure, has an opportunity of learning it at home by being connected with literary people, and is placed in a circle of society sufficiently liberal to allow her such an accomplishment, I do not see, if she has a strong inclination, why she should not make herself mistress of so rich a store of original entertainment: it will not in the present state of things excite either a smile or a stare in fashionable company. To those who do not intend to learn the language, I would strongly recommend the learning so much of the grammar of it as will explain the name and nature of cases, genders, inflexion of verbs, &c.; of which, having only the imperfect rudiments in our own language, a mere English scholar can with difficulty form a clear idea. This is the more necessary, as all our grammars, being written by men whose early studies had given them a partiality for the learned languages, are formed more upon those than the real genius of our own tongue.

—

74. Ann Radcliffe
from *On the Supernatural in Poetry*

'In nothing has Shakespeare been more successful than in . . . selecting circumstances of manners and appearance for his supernatural beings, which, though wild and remote, in the highest degree, from common apprehension, never shock the understanding by incompatibility with themselves – never compel us, for an instant, to recollect that he has a licence for extravagance. Above every ideal being is the ghost of Hamlet, with all its attendant accidents of time and place. The dark watch upon the remote platform, the dreary aspects of the night, the very expression of the officer on guard, 'the air bites shrewdly; it is very cold'; the recollection of a star, an unknown world, are all circumstances which excite forlorn, melancholy, and solemn feelings, and dispose us to welcome, with trembling curiosity, the awful being that draws near; and to indulge in that mixture of horror, pity, and indignation, produced by the tale it reveals. Every minute circumstance of the scene between those watching on the platform, and of that between them and Horatio, preceding the entrance of the apparition, contributes to excite some feeling of dreariness, or melancholy, or solemnity, or expectation, in unison with, and leading on towards that high curiosity and thrilling awe with which we witness the conclusion of the scene'.

❋❋❋❋

'If it were possible for me to believe the appearance of ghosts at all' replied Mr S–, 'It would certainly be the ghost of Hamlet; but I never can suppose such things; they are out of all reason and probability'.

'You would believe the immortality of the soul' said W–, with solemnity, 'even without the aid of revelation; yet our confined faculties cannot comprehend how the soul may exist after separation from the body. I do not absolutely know that spirits are permitted to become visible to us on earth; yet that they may be permitted to appear for rare and important purposes, such as could scarcely have been accomplished without an equal suspension, or a momentary change, of the laws prescribed to what we call *Nature* – that is, without one more exercise of the same CREATIVE POWER of which we must acknowledge so many millions of existing instances, and by which we ourselves at this moment breathe, think, or disquisite at all, cannot be impossible, and is, I think, probable'.

'How happens it then', said Mr S–, 'that objects of terror strike us very forcibly when introduced into scenes of gaiety, as, for instance, in the banquet scene in Macbeth?'

'They strike us, then, chiefly by the force of contrast', replied W–; 'but the effect, though sudden and strong, is also transient; it is the thrill of horror and surprise, which they then communicate, rather than the deep and solemn feelings excited under more accordant circumstances, and left long upon the mind. Who ever suffered for the ghost of Banquo, the gloomy and sublime kind of terror, which that of Hamlet calls forth? though the appearance of Banquo, at the high festival of Macbeth, not only tells us that he is murdered, but recalls to our minds the fate of the gracious Duncan, laid in silence and death by those, who, in this very scene, are revelling in his spoils. There, though deep pity mingles with our surprise and horror, we experience a far less degree of interest, and that interest too of an inferior kind. The union of grandeur and obscurity, which Mr Burke describes as a sort of tranquillity mingled with terror, and which causes sublime, is to be found only on Hamlet; or in scenes where circumstances of the same kind prevail'.

'That may be,' said Mr. S–, 'and I perceive you are not one of those who contend that obscurity does not make any part of the sublime.' 'They must be men of very cold imaginations,' said W–, 'with whom certainty is more terrible than surmise. Terror and horror are so far opposite, that the first expands the soul, and awakens the faculties to a high degree of life; the other contracts, freezes, and nearly annihilates them. I apprehend, that neither Shakespeare nor Milton by their fictions, nor Mr. Burke by his reasoning, anywhere looked to positive horror as a source of the sublime, though they all agree that terror is a very high one; and where lies the difference between horror and terror, but in the uncertainty and obscurity that accompany the first, respecting the dreaded evil?'

'But what say you to Milton's image –

"On his brow sat horror plumed"?'

'As an image, it certainly is sublime; it fills the mind with an idea of power, but it does not follow that Milton intended to declare the feeling of horror to be sublime; and after all, his image imparts more of terror than of horror, for it is not distinctly pictured forth, but is seen in glimpses through obscuring shades, the great outlines only appearing, which excite the imagination to complete the rest; he only says, 'sat horror plumed'; you will observe, that the look of horror and the other characteristics are left to the imagination of the reader; and according to the strength of that, he will feel Milton's image to be either sublime or otherwise. Milton, when he sketched it, probably felt, that not even his art could fill up the outline, and present to other eyes the countenance which his 'mind's eye' gave to him. Now, if obscurity has so much effect on fiction, what must it have in real life, when to ascertain the object of our terror is frequently to acquire the means of escaping it. You will observe, that this image, though indistinct or obscure, is not confused.'

'How can any thing be indistinct and not confused?' said Mr S–.

'Ay, that question is from the new school,' replied W–; 'but recollect, that obscurity, or indistinctness, is only a negative which leaves the imagination to act upon the few hints that truth reveals to it; confusion is a thing as positive as distinctness, though not necessarily so palpable; and it may, by mingling and confounding one image with another, absolutely counteract the imagination, instead of exciting it. Obscurity leaves something for the imagination to exaggerate; confusion, by blurring one image into another, leaves only a chaos in which the mind can find nothing to be magnificent, nothing to nourish its fears or doubts, or to act upon in any way; yet confusion and obscurity are terms used indiscriminately by those who would prove, that Shakespeare and Milton were wrong when they employed obscurity as a cause of the sublime, that Mr. Burke was equally mistaken in his reasoning upon the subject, and that mankind have been equally in error, as to the nature of their own feelings, when they were acted upon by the illusions of those great masters of the imagination, at whose so potent bidding, the passions have been awakened from their sleep, and by whose magic a crowded theatre has been changed to a lonely shore, to a witch's cave, to an enchanted island, to a murderer's castle, to the ramparts of an usurper, to the battle, to the midnight carousal of the camp or the tavern, to every various scene of the living world.'

'Then you seem to think there may be great poets, without a full perception of the picturesque; I mean by picturesque, the beautiful and grand in nature and in art – and with little susceptibility to what you would call the accordant circumstances, the harmony of which is essential to any powerful effect upon your feelings.'

'No; I cannot allow that. Such men have high talents, wit, genius, judgement, but not the soul of poetry, which is the spirit of all these, and also something wonderfully higher – something too fine for definition. It certainly includes an instantaneous perception, and an exquisite love of whatever is graceful, grand, and sublime, with the power of seizing and combining such circumstances of them, as to strike and interest a reader by the representation, even more than a general view of the real scene itself could do. Whatever this may be called, which crowns the mind of a poet, and distinguishes it from every other mind, our whole heart instantly acknowledges it.'

1827

75. Claire Clairmont
from *Journals*

Monday, January 3rd

I got into my sledge and went to Pomikoffs. It was about five in the afternoon – the moon was up and shining with a white light upon the white snow – we went thro' narrow by-streets – the window-shutters of the houses were all shut, the yard-doors likewise, not a soul was to be seen, not even a dog baying the moon or seeking stray morsels among the heaps of rubbish – all seemed at this early hour buried in repose. We glided along this scene like ghosts at midnight with the utmost swiftness and silence. Our motion was noiseless. I amused myself very much at Pomikoffs. I thumped all the boys, which they bore with great patience. We jumped up and down on the sofa. – I jogged Johnny's arm as he was drinking his tea; it spilt all over him, and he was furious. The tall Nicola opened his mouth and said: 'Oh! My God, Miss Clairmont, how you are funny!'

* * * *

Friday January 28th

I read Medwin's book upon Lord Byron. – My God, what lies that book contains! Poor Shelley is made to play quite a secondary part, and I particularly admire the patronizing tone which L.B. assumed, the more so when I recalled how he sneered at his talents at Geneva and thought him quite a dabbler in verses. This death-bed scene as related by Fletcher is quite proper and edifying, but one does not know how to settle its extreme tenderness for the Guiccioli in the first half of the work with his utter forgetfulness of her when dying except at that awful moment nothing less legitimate than a wife and daughter born in lawful wedlock could enter the mind of a man who respected the world's prejudices as much as he did. What is very droll, is that Fletcher who declared publicly that he talked of nothing but his wife and child, declared to Mary privately that he talked of me and seemed uneasy at my fate and anxious if possible to repair it. But this I always thought was a lie, invented by the tenderness of Fletcher's heart. – I knew the man too well to suspect he was ever sorry for the mischief he had done me. He planned that mischief in cold blood, executed it in cold blood and rejoiced at it in cold blood. . . .

When I was in bed I wept a great deal because my reading of today had brought back Shelley vividly to my mind. – It is cruel to think how his merit was lost upon the world, how that impostor Byron was admired for his imposture, how tenderly they relate of him that he declared he could not leave his monkeys behind because strangers could not take care of them, whilst he left his daughter to the care of ignorant bigoted mercenaries and let her die for want of care. How mean and detestable is the world – even those who knew this licked his hand and soothed him with soft words of praise because he had the world's voice with him.

1828

76. Felicia Hemans
Properzia Rossi

One dream of passion and of beauty more!
And in its bright fulfilment let me pour
My soul away! Let earth retain a trace
Of that which lit my being, though its race
Might have been loftier far. Yet one more dream!
From my deep spirit one victorious gleam
Ere I depart! For thee alone, for thee !
May this last work, this farewell triumph be –
Thou, loved so vainly! I would leave enshrined
Something immortal of my heart and mind,
That yet may speak to thee when I am gone,
Shaking thine inmost bosom with a tone
Of lost affection, – something that may prove
What she hath been, whose melancholy love

On thee was lavished; silent pang and tear,
And fervent song that gushed when none were near,
And dream by night, and weary thought by day,
Stealing the brightness from her life away –
While thou – Awake! not yet within me die!
Under the burden and the agony
Of this vain tenderness – my spirit, wake!
Even for thy sorrowful affection's sake,
Live! in thy work breathe out! – that he may yet,
Feeling sad mastery there, perchance regret
Thine unrequited gift.

II

    It comes! the power
Within me born flows back – my fruitless dower
That could not win me love. Yet once again
I greet it proudly, with its rushing train
Of glorious images: they throng – they press –
A sudden joy lights up my loneliness –
I shall not perish all!
    The bright work grows
Beneath my hand, unfolding, as a rose,
Leaf after leaf, to beauty – line by line,
Through the pale marble's veins, It grows! and now
I fix my thought, heart, soul, to burn, to shine:
I give my own life's history to thy brow,
Forsaken Ariadne! – thou shalt wear
My form, my lineaments; but oh! more fair,
Touched into lovelier being by the glow
Which in me dwells, as by the summer light
All things are glorified. From thee my woe
Shall yet look beautiful to meet his sight,
When I am passed away. Thou art the mould,
Wherein I pour the fervent thoughts, th' untold,
The self-consuming! Speak to him of me,
Thou, the deserted by the lonely sea,
With the soft sadness of thine earnest eye –
Speak to him, lorn one! deeply, mournfully,
Of all my love and grief! Oh! could I throw
Into thy frame a voice – a sweet, and low,
And thrilling voice of song! when he came nigh,

To send the passion of its melody
Through his pierced bosom – on its tones to bear
My life's deep feeling, as the southern air
Wafts the faint myrtle's breath – to rise, to swell,
To sink away in accents of farewell,
Winning but one, *one* gush of tears, whose flow
Surely my parted spirit yet might know,
If love be strong as death!

III

   Now fair thou art,
Thou form, whose life is of my burning heart!
Yet all the vision that within me wrought,
I cannot make thee. Oh! I might have given
Birth to creations of far nobler thought;
I might have kindled, with the fire of heaven,
Things not of such as die! But I have been
Too much alone! A heart whereon to lean,
With all these deep affections that o'erflow
My aching soul, and find no shore below;
An eye to be my star; a voice to bring
Hope o'er my path like sounds that breathe of spring,
These are denied me – dreamt of still in vain.
Therefore my brief aspirings from the chain
Are ever but as some wild fitful song,
Rising triumphantly, to die ere long
In dirge-like echoes.

IV

   Yet the world will see
Little of this, my parting work! in thee.
Thou shalt have fame! Oh mockery! give the reed
From storms a shelter – give the drooping vine
Something round which its tendrils may entwine –
Give the parched flower a rain-drop, and the meed
Of love's kind words to woman! Worthless fame!
That in his bosom wins not for my name
Th'abiding place it asked! Yet how my heart,
In its own fairy world of song and art,
Once beat for praise! Are those high longings o'er?
That which I have been can I be no more?
Never! oh, never more! though still thy sky

Be blue as then, my glorious Italy!
And though the music, whose rich breathings fill
Thine air with soul, be wandering past me still;
And though the mantle of thy sunlight streams
Unchanged on forms, instinct with poet-dreams.
Never! oh, never more! Where'er I move,
The shadow of this broken-hearted love
Is on me and around! Too well they know
Whose life is all within, too soon and well,
When there the blight hath settled! But I go
Under the silent wings of peace to dwell;
From the slow wasting, from the lonely pain,
The inward burning of those words – '*in vain*',
Seared on the heart – I go. 'Twill soon be past
Sunshine and song, and bright Italian heaven,
And thou, oh! thou, on whom my spirit cast
Unvalued wealth – who know'st not what was given
In that devotedness – the sad, and deep,
And unrepaid – farewell! If I could weep
Once, only once, beloved one! on thy breast,
Pouring my heart forth ere I sink to rest!
But that were happiness! – and unto me
Earth's gift is *fame*. Yet I was formed to be
So richly blessed! With thee to watch the sky,
Speaking not, feeling but that thou wert nigh;
With thee to listen, while the tones of song
Swept even as part of our sweet air along –
To listen silently; with thee to gaze
On forms, the deified of olden days –
This had been joy enough; and hour by hour,
From its glad wellsprings drinking life and power,
How had my spirit soared, and made its fame
A glory for thy brow! Dreams, dreams! – The fire
Burns faint within me. Yet I leave my name –
As a deep thrill may linger on the lyre
When its full chords are hushed – awhile to live,
And one day haply in thy heart revive
Sad thoughts of me. I leave it, with a sound,
A spell o'er memory, mournfully profound;
I leave it, on my country's air to dwell –
Say proudly yet – '*Twas hers who loved me well!*'

1829

77. Laetitia Landon
from *A History of the Lyre*

Methinks we must have known some former state
More glorious than our present, and the heart
Is haunted by dim memories, shadows left
By past magnificence; and hence we pine
With vain aspirings, hopes that fill the eyes
With bitter tears for their own vanity.
Remembrance makes the poet; 'tis the past
Lingering within him, with a keener sense
Than is upon the thoughts of common men
Of what has been, that fills the actual world
With unreal likenesses of lovely shapes,
That were and are not; and the fairer they,
The more their contrast with existing things;
The more his power, the greater is his grief.
– Are we then fallen from some unknown star,
Whose consciousness is an unknown curse,
And we feel capable of happiness
Only to know it is not of our sphere?

78. Sydney Owenson, Lady Morgan
from *Mathematical Ladies*

I can perfectly understand Lord Byron's antipathy to mathematical ladies. There is nothing in the study of numbers analogous to female intellect, which is essentially imaginative. Female mathematicians are seldom what the French call *aimables*. In the middle of the last century, Newton's sublime discoveries rendered mathematics fashionable; and fashion will reconcile a French lady even to the mathematics. . . .

The exact sciences are not made for woman. Her feelings are too petulant for cool, temperate calculation, in which fancy and sensibility go for nothing at all. When Nature, in her caprice, produces a Bolognese doctoress, really learned in such matters, the woman is sure to suffer by it.

The cleverest women are accused (and with some reason) of inaccuracy in their thoughts; but the defect does not arise (as some have imagined) from the want of the discipline of a course of mathematics. Madame de Stael was sometimes inconsequential in her reasoning; but neither she, nor many other female and non-mathematical writers of less power, have fallen into such 'bald and disjointed' twaddle as is to be found in the pamphlets of some of our university polemics and politicians. 'The high men,' as I am told they are called at Cambridge and Oxford, do not usually become the most distinguished statesmen and philosophers.

I suspect, therefore, that the current admiration for the mathematics, as an instrument of mental discipline, arises much more from the *safety* of such pursuits, and their disconnection with moral and political interests, than from the rigor and exactness of their methods of argumentation. At the end of a five years' college course, the student is not more likely to question established abuses, than if he had spent the time in playing shuttle-cock. His moral faculties have been kept perfectly quiescent. Indignation at public and private wrong, contempt for falsehood and dis-honesty, the kindling glow of approbation at patriotic self-sacrifice, have remained unawakened and cold. The pursuit of abstractions has shut out all interest or feeling for realities; and the university whippers-in have trained the young hound quite away from the pursuit of forbidden truths.

A mere mathematician is the fittest raw material for manufacturing a passive-obedience parson, or an all-confiding country gentleman. Placed in the foreground of the world's great scene of action, the most accomplished of the class is but on a par with a mere land-surveyor: he can estimate quantities, and nothing more. With the sole exception of the inventors (who, as in the other branches of knowledge, must be superior persons) the greatest proficients in the mathematics are often the dullest and least apprehensive of men; and as they mistake the superiority of their scientific methods, for their own aptitude to discover truth they are the most pre-sumptuous. These are the persons who sneer at lady writers, and imagine that there is no road to common sense and common observation, but over the Ass's Bridge.

Of mathematics, as a means to an end, as the hand-maid to the natural sciences, it would be absurd to speak slightingly; but as a mere discipline, I fancy I am not singular in doubting their efficacy; and I am certain that, for the female mind in particular, they can do little beyond encouraging pedantry; while they blunt that rapid intuition which serves a woman better than reason, and gives to superior females the influence they have so often possessed on public affairs. In literature, more especially, it is this intuition, this promptitude to feel, rather than analyze the truth, that has given not only their charm, but, I will add, their utility, to female writers. If they were more exact, they would be less striking. Their especial service is to keep alive the fervour of enthusiasm, and to avert the besetting sin of advanced civilization. One day, when complaining to a celebrated Irish wit of the faults of my early works, he replied, 'Let them alone, child; it is to your faults that you owe your success'.

—

79. Felicia Hemans
Woman and Fame

Thou hast a charmed cup, O Fame!
    A draught that mantles high,
And seems to lift this earthly frame
    Above mortality.
Away! to me – a woman – bring
Sweet waters from affection's spring!

Thou hast green laurel leaves, that twine
    Into so proud a wreath,
For that resplendent gift of thine,
    Heroes have smiled in death:
Give me from some kind hand a flower,
The record of one happy hour!

Thou hast a voice, whose thrilling tone
    Can bid each life-pulse beat,
As when a trumpet's note hath blown,
    Calling the brave to meet:
But mine, let mine – a woman's breast,
By words of home-born love be blessed.

A hollow sound is in thy song,
    A mockery in thine eye,
To the sick heart that doth but long
    For aid, for sympathy –
For kindly looks to cheer it on,
For tender accents that are gone.

Fame! Fame! thou canst not be the stay
  Unto the drooping reed,
The cool, fresh fountain in the day
  Of the soul's feverish need:
Where must the lone one turn or flee! –
Not unto thee – oh! not to thee!

      ━━━━

1829

80. Anna Jameson
from *Heroines of Modern Poetry*

It will be allowed, I think, that women have reason to be satisfied with the rank they hold in modern poetry; and that the homage which has been addressed to them, either directly and individually, or paid indirectly and generally, in the beautiful characters and portraits drawn of them, ought to satisfy equally female sentiment and female vanity. From the half ethereal forms which float amid moonbeams and gems, and odours and flowers, along the dazzling pages of Lalla Rookh, down to Phoebe Dawson, in the Parish Register: from that loveliest gem of polished life, the young Aurora of Lord Byron, down to Wordsworth's poor Margaret weeping in her deserted cottage – all the various aspects between these wide extremes of character and situation, under which we have been exhibited, have been, with few exceptions, just and favourable to our sex.

  In the literature of the classical ages, we were debased into mere servants of pleasure, alternately the objects of loose incense or coarse invective. In the poetry of the Gothic ages, we all rank as queens. In the succeeding period, when the Platonic philosophy was oddly mixed up with the institutions of chivalry, we were exalted into divinities . . . Then followed the age of French gallantry, tinged with classical elegance, and tainted with classical licence, when we were caressed, complimented, wooed and satirised by coxcomb poets . . . There was much expenditure of wit and of talent, but in an ill cause; – for the feeling was, *au fond*, bad and false; – 'et il n'est guère plaisant d'être empoisoné, même par l'esprit de rose'.

  In the present time a better spirit prevails. We are not indeed sublimated into goddesses; but neither is it the fashion to degrade us into the playthings of fopling poets. We seem to have found, at length, our proper level in poetry, as in society; and take the place assigned to us as women –

> As creatures not too bright or good,
> For human nature's daily food;
> For transient sorrows, simple wiles,
> Praise, blame, love, kisses, tears and smiles!

We are represented as ruling by our feminine attractions, moral or exterior, the passions and imaginations of men; as claiming, by our weakness, our delicacy, our devotion, – their protection, their tenderness, and their gratitude: and, since the minds of women have been more generally and highly cultivated; since a Madame de Stael, a Joanna Baillie, a Maria Edgeworth, and a hundred other names, now shining aloft like stars, have shed a reflected glory on the whole sex they belong to, we possess through them, a claim to admiration and respect for our mental capabilities. We assume the right of passing judgement on the poetical homage addressed to us, and our smiles alone can consecrate what our smiles first inspired.

✳ ✳ ✳ ✳

The life Lord Byron led was not calculated to give him a good opinion of women, or to place before him the best virtues of our sex. Of all modern poets, he has been the most generally popular among female readers; and he owes this enthusiasm not certainly to our obligations to him; for, as far as women are concerned, we may designate his works by a line borrowed from himself

> With much to excite, there's little to exalt.

But who, like him, could administer to that '*besoin de sentir*', which I am afraid is an ingredient in the feminine character all over the world?

Lord Byron is really the Grand Turk of amatory poetry – ardent in his love – mean and merciless in his resentment: he could trace passion in characters of fire, but his caustic satire burns and blisters where it falls. Lovely as are some of his female portraits, and inimitably beautiful as are some of his lyrical effusions, it must be confessed there is something very Oriental in all his feelings and ideas about women; he seems to require nothing of us but beauty and submission. Please him – and he will crown you with the richest flowers of poetry, and heap the treasures of the universe at your feet, as trophies of his love; but once offend, and you are lost. –

✳ ✳ ✳ ✳

Sir Walter Scott ought to have lived in the age of chivalry, (if we could endure the thoughts of his living in any other age but our own!) so touched with the true antique spirit of generous devotion to our sex are all his poetical portraits of women. I do not find that he has, like most other writers of the present day, mixed up his personal feelings and history with his poetry; or that any fair and distinguished object will be so thrice fortunate as to share his laurelled immortality. We must therefore treat him like Shakespeare, whom alone he resembles – and claim him for us all.

... And there is Coleridge who approaches women with a sort of feeling half earthly, half heavenly, like that with which an Italian devotee bends before his Madonna. ... and Wordsworth, lost in the depth of his own tenderness!

---

81. Caroline Lamb
Thou Woulds't Not Do What I Have Done

If thou coulds't know what 'tis to weep,
   To weep unpitied and alone,
The live-long night, while others sleep,
Silent and mournful watch to keep,
   Thou woulds't not do what I have done.

If thou could'st know what 'tis to smile,
   To smile while scorned by every one,
To hide by many an artful wile,
A heart that knows more grief than guile,
   Thou wouldst not do what I have done.

And oh! if thou coulds't think how drear,
   When friends are changed, and health is gone,
The world would to thine eyes appear,
If thou, like me, to none wert dear,
   Thou woulds't not do what I have done.

---

82. Caroline Lamb
Lines to Harriette Wilson

Harriette Wilson, shall I tell thee where,
Beside my being *cleverer*,
We differ? – thou wert hired to hold thy tongue,
Thou hast no right to do thy lovers wrong:

But I, whom none could buy or gain,
Who am as proud, girl, as thyself art vain,
And like thyself, or sooner like the wind,
Blow raging ever, free and unconfined.
What should withhold my tongue with pen of steel,
The faults of those who have wronged me to reveal?
Why should I hide men's follies, while my own
Blaze like the gas along this talking town?
Is it being bitter to be too sincere?
Must we adulterate truth as they do beer?
I'll tell thee why, then! as each has his price,
I have been bought at last – I am not ice;
Kindness and gratitude have chained my tongue,
From henceforth I will do no mortal wrong.
Prate those who please – laugh – censure those that will,
My mouth is sealed – my thoughts – my pen – are still.
In the meantime – we Lambs are seldom civil,
I wish thy book – not thee – at the Devil.

1830

83. Sydney Owenson, Lady Morgan
from *Anglomania*

Expecting a very early nursery visit from a new little relation, who has conferred on me a brevet rank by no means flattering . . . I was led into the vulgar nursery ambition of paying my court to my infant visitor, through her gastronomic propensities, by the toady-ism of comfits and sugar-plums; so I walked out in search of a confectioner. My intention was to proceed to my old mart for bon-bons, the *Fidele Berger*, in the Rue Vivienne. But as topography is not my forte, I stopped short at the first shop that fell in my way. With my head full of the poetical pastries of De Bar, some of whose bright conceptions I once gave to a country lady in Ireland, who ornamented her dress with them for an assize ball, – I asked boldly for some *Diablotins en papillote*, *Pastilles de Nantes*, and other sugared prettinesses; but a demoiselle behind the counter, as neat as English muslin and French *tournure* could make her, replied, conceitedly, in broken English, 'we sell no such a ting'. A little surprised, I asked what she would recommend that would melt in the mouth, and not soil the fingers – something fit for a *marmotte*; 'Dere is every ting that you may have want,' she replied, pointing to shelves piled with biscuits, – 'de cracker, de bun, de plom-cake, de spice gingerbread, de mutton and de mince-pye, de crompet and de muffin, de gelee of de calves foot, and de apple-dumplin, as bespoke.'

I was struck dumb! One of the things worth a visit to Paris, if you had no other motive for the journey, is its exquisite confectionery; so light, and so perfumed, that it resembles congealed odours, or a crystallization of the essence of sweet flowers. Plum-cake and apple-dumplings! – sugar of lead and leaden bullets! I thought of the *Fidele Berger*, its fanciful idealities, its trifles light as air, and infinite deal of (sweet) nothings; its candied epics and eclogues in spun sugar. Then, too, its *garcons*, like feathered Mercuries new lighted on a sponge cake or a carmel, giving to the *magazin* the air of a store-room of the Muses. What a contrast! A chubby young man and a phlegmatic old woman, were busily at work. Batter was beating with wooden spoons; force-meat was chopping with Birmingham hatchets. Currants were drying, and suet was melting in the sun; beefsteak gravy steamed from the hot hearth, the oven was redolent of apple-pye: in a word, the pandemonium of an English country kitchen on a Christmas eve, was exhibited on an April morning, within view of the violet beds and hyacinth banks of the elysium of the Tuileries. I rubbed my eyes, and scarcely believed their evidence. I looked up, and perceived a large black board, intimating, in gilt letters, that 'Here is to be had all sorts of English pastry,' by Tom or Jack somebody, 'pastry-cook, from London'. Placards, too, were in every pane of the windows, with 'Hot mutton pies,' 'Oyster patties', 'Devonshire cider,' 'Spruce beer,' and 'London porter'. Odd's nausea and indigestion! I though I should never get out of the atmosphere of Cornhill or St. Paul's churchyard. So, paying for a bundle of crackers, hard enough to crack the teeth of an elephant, I consigned them to my servant, and was hurrying away from the shop, when I was shot on the left cheek, and covered with a shower of froth, by the explosion of a bottle of 'Whitbread's entire', the pride of the counter, and the boast of its owner.

Annoyed beyond measure, I was hastening home, to cleanse myself of the stain, and the odour of this essence of aloes, liquorice, and *cocculus indicus*, when passing along the arcade, a perfumer's shop caught the most acute of all my senses. I never in my life was more in want of something to 'sweeten my imagination' withall, so I turned in. One has always a long list of wants on a first arrival at Paris, that renders any and every shop a station, where a franc may be dropped, or a *petit ecu* offered with advantage. I therefore prepared to 'air my vocabulary' in my best Paris accent, with all the classic names of *eaux*, *essences*, and *extraits*: but before I could make known a single want, the master of the shop pushed forward divers pint bottles of evident English manufacture; interrupting me with '*Oui, oui, madame, j'entends! voila tout ce qu'il vous faut, de lavender-vatre de Monsieur Gattie, de honey-vatre premiere qualite, de essence of burgamot, de tief his vinaigre, and de Vindsor soap*'; and addressing a young woman, who was tossing over a box of English fans and silk handkerchiefs, with O'Connell's handsome Irish face glowing in the centre, – '*Ecoutez, chere amie*,' he said, 'shew madame the *Regent's vash-ball*, de Hunt's blacking, de fish sauce, and the pill *anti-bilieux*.'

I heard no more, but gathering up my purse and reticule, quitted the shop in a fever of disappointment, which all the patches and pills it contained could not cure. On reaching home, I found a little basket lying on the table of the ante-room, labelled with a card; and an English livery-servant waiting for a receipt. The card ran thus: 'Mr. –'s best compliments to Sir C. M., with a flask of – genuine *poteen*!' This was too much! – Was it for this we left the snugness and economical comfort of our Irish home, and encountered the expensive inconveniences of a foreign journey, in the hope of seeing nothing British, 'till the threshold of that home should be passed by our feet': – to meet at every step with all that taste, health, and civilization we cry down at home, as cheap and as abundant abroad; – from the raw tough fibre of a hard *rosbif de mutton*, to genuine potteen, or, '*by your leave, Georgy*,' with all its original borrachio of still and bog?

1831

84. Maria Jane Jewsbury
Review of Joanna Baillie, 'The Nature and Dignity of Christ'

Joanna Baillie holds that rank amongst our elder modern authors, and her poetry is so connected with that re-awakening of our literature which took place about the commencement of the present century, that whatever she writes, however slight, or however unequal to the works which made her fame, has a peculiar claim to respectful attention. Of Joanna Baillie's intellectual strength, of her profound knowledge of the workings of passion, rendered more extraordinary by the placidity with which she herself delineates them – of Joanna Baillie's genius and language, which are both so essentially old-English, deep, sound, vigorous, unfeigned and unadulterate – we are proud to express our admiration. It would afford a subject for a long and not uninteresting article to point out the striking difference in the mind and writings of the literary women of thirty and forty years ago, and the literary women of the present time; those who have not perused their writings in connection, will hardly believe how great is the difference; – what a commentary the perusal affords on the entire change that has obtained in habits, manners, feelings, education, tastes, and life. Amongst the elders – with Joanna Baillie at their head, as regards mind – the distinguishing features are nerve, simplicity, vigour, continuity, unambitious earnestness, and good English. We also find elaborate and skilfully-developed plots. Amongst our distinguished women of later date, we find accomplishment, grace, brilliancy, sentiment, scenery poetically sketched, and character acutely handled; talent in all shapes and ways, but not so much that can claim the name of genius. There is nothing of what we have called continuity. Writing little but detached tales or novels, which, however clever, are only volumes of episodes, separate scenes, and striking characters, most of them unconnected with the main business of the book – it is as *sketchers*, whether for vivacity or pathos, nature or art; as *sketchers*, whether of the country, the town, or the heart, of life or of manners, that our gifted women are now chiefly distinguished. In the female poetry too of the present day, fascinating tenderness, brilliancy of fancy, and beauty of feeling, stand in the place of sustained loftiness of imagination, and compact artist-like diction. Our elder literary women were, in the spirit of their intellect, more essentially masculine; our younger ones are integrally feminine – women of fashionable as well as studious life, women generally, who not only write books but abound in elegant accomplishments.

We have not, and are not likely to have at present, another Mary Wollstonecraft (we merely speak of her as having exhibited grasp of mind), another Mrs Inchbald, another Mrs Radcliffe – Joanna Baillie is their only representative; adding, to the power of mind which they possessed, that dignified play of fancy, that amplitude of calm, bold thought, and that 'accomplishment of verse' which they possessed not. Modern imaginative literature in England owes much to her *Plays of the Passions*; perhaps more than to any other publication except Percy's *Reliques*; at all events, our greatest poets, who were young when her plays appeared, have nearly all borne testimony to the advantage and delight with which they perused them. With all this, the name of Joanna Baillie is not buzzed and blazoned about as very inferior names are; her works do not attain the honour of calf and gold in libraries where inferior works shine; poetical readers of strong sensibility and uncultivated taste do not dote upon *Basil*, or quote from

Ethwald; and we never, by any chance, saw a line of hers inscribed in an album! One or two of her Shakespearean snatches of song have been set to music; but, (to quote the words of an able critic) 'The celebrity of Joanna Baillie has been of a peculiar nature; her fame has about it a peculiar purity. It has been the unparticipated treasure of the world of taste and intellect'. We know that with this illustrious authoress there is a noble carelessness of praise, partly consequent on her years, her standing in society, and her having simply written at the instigation of her own genius; obeying the voice from the shrine, and not the command of the outer-court worshippers; but still, *we* feel vexed to see women of later date, and, however gifted, every way inferior to Joanna Baillie, written about, and likenessed, and lithographed, before HER – the senior and superior of all.

These casual remarks will prove that we appreciate Joanna Baillie; we can, therefore, with better grace express our regret that she has just published the little work, the name of which heads this notice. It is controversial, and controversy is best left to learned divines – certainly better left alone by ladies.

---

85. Maria Jane Jewsbury
from *Review of Shelley, 'The Wandering Jew'*

To make an article that has appeared in one journal the groundwork of an article in another, may be considered somewhat out of order; a proceeding, that, if the original article were good, is analogous to painting the lily and gilding refined gold. Nevertheless, *The Wandering Jew*, published in *Fraser's Magazine* for July, is to all intents and purposes, as important, in point of length, as Lord Byron's early poems; and we do not see why the accidental form of publication should militate against its lying equally open to criticism. Added to this, whilst, in the way of scorn, calumny, and unkindness, brimming measure has been dealt out to Shelley, few connected with periodical literature have taken the trouble to understand and appreciate his poetry, or to draw, for the benefit of the public, a line between his metaphysical subtleties and moral mistakes, and the remaining mass of his true, pure, beautiful poetry, – poetry instinct with intellectual life – radiant, harmonious, and strong.

* * * *

Lord Byron was sceptical, selfish, dissipated, and eccentric, and was believed to have taken higher degrees in evil than he really had; but he wrote impassioned and brilliant poetry that revolutionized the public taste, spell-bound the public heart; and though much of this poetry contained scepticism, selfishness, profligacy, and eccentricity, yet, by some strange anomaly, grave and good people, after protesting against these elements, spoke of and quoted the remainder with enthusiasm, – nay, very often felt an enthusiasm for the man. Let us see how Shelley was treated. He too was sceptical, and with more sincerity, with a conviction, perhaps, that disbelief of Christianity was a duty; he also was eccentric, but he was gentle-hearted, self-denying, a lover of his species, a yearner after its improvement. He too wrote poetry, some of it embodying his anti-Christian views – a paradise, in which the Tree of Life had been cut down, but certainly containing less to pollute the imagination, poison the spring of action, and sear virtuous emotions, than many of the writings of his noble friend and contemporary. But he was weighed in a different balance (we advert only to literary treatment), and it became suspicious to quote, and dangerous to admire him. Till latterly, he was a poet,

> Whom there were none to praise
> And very few to love.

Feeling, as we do, the very gravest disagreement with many of the political and religious opinions of Shelley; grieving, as we do, that he died when his genius was beginning to work clear, – we are yet indignant at the treatment he received. Could he have entertained the public with wit and satire, as Lord Byron entertained it, or had his poetry been palpable and impassioned, like Lord Byron's poetry, his scepticism would have been passed over like Lord Byron's scepticism. The public did not admire his poetry, and for that, more than for any other reason, expressed a horror of his principles. The public always looks after its own entertainment. Two circumstances combine to render the reprehensible parts of Shelley's poetry more innoxious than parts of several other poets who are never reprehended. In the first place, his theories are so out of the common track – they are so subtile, aerial, and attenuate – so abstracted from any connection with the ways of the world, that they cease to be dangerous by becoming unintelligible. There is no parallelism between his speculations and worldly licence; in Lord Byron's there is. Shelley was a visionary, desiring, and believing it possible, to build a palace upon a cloud – namely, human happiness – without super-human assistance. His poetry exhibits the contradiction of inculcating Christian ethics whilst spurning Christian doctrines, and of representing effects without ascribing them to adequate causes.

The other reason why Shelley's erroneous sentiments are comparatively

innoxious is, that by altering the names of his metaphysical agents, the
cipher finds a key, becomes intelligible, and is found, when interpreted, to
speak the truth. Let the spiritual nonentity, which the author calls Universal
Love, Harmony, Wisdom, Liberty, be called GOD, and the mist clears off,
and the poetry reads religiously, in the true meaning of the term. His most
magnificent production, (Greek sculpture in poetry) the *Prometheus
Unbound*, supplies an illustration: Shelley's own meaning with respect to
Jupiter, Demagorgon, and the like, matters nothing; most readers will, in
Prometheus himself, feel and see but a shadow of ONE, whose name, to be
suggested, needs not to be mentioned:

> Know ye not me,
> The Titan? he who made his agony
> The barrier to your else all-conquering foe?

With regard to Shelley as a poet, he is not likely, in our day, to dispute
the palm of popularity with many far inferior to him in intellect, feeling,
harmony, and knowledge. . . . The tone of his mind is antique, but its bias
is towards the future – his Elysium of perfection: the present being a
Tartarus that engulfs all good. He does not deal with things, but thoughts,
and thoughts that are often sublimated into phantoms. The very cadence
of his verse, the structure of his language, seems the struggle of spirit with
sound and form, manifests a yearning after immateriality – a desire to
make mere words ethereal essences, impersonations of beauty – melody
woke by the wind, drank by the dew, heard by the heart, and giving birth
to dreams of things not earthly –

> Low, sweet, faint sounds like the farewell of ghosts.

With the exception of Coleridge, the English language has not such a
consummate master of harmony – nor, with the same exception and the
addition of Wordsworth, a poet possessing such an exquisite knowledge of
external nature, from its grander aspects amongst seas and mountains, to
its fine and silent pencilling amongst moss and flowers. He could delineate
a storm and describe a sensitive plant; but when he treated of human life,
he wanted force, compression, and tangibility: his men and women are
'such stuff as dreams are made of' – his narratives perplexed – his incidents obscure; in short, all his worldly realities are unreal. But, send him
to the garden where grows the sensitive plant; or place him upon the
mountainous ruins of the Baths of Caracalla; or amidst the Euganean hills;
or in any spot where nature keeps court; and not only does he describe
exquisitely and accurately the real appearances before him; but he also

portrays that second and independent aspect, which, according to his mood, the scene would wear to the spectator.

Shelley's love of nature differs from that of any other poet: he seems to love it like a living thing – as if it possessed human attributes – were capable, like man, of feeling joy and sorrow. His sympathy has something strange in it, something sad; for he robs the soul of its birthright, to bestow it on matter. Gloomy, yet melodious, he is the fallen angel of song!

****

Shelley was only thirty when his mysterious and beautiful genius was quenched in death. He can scarcely be called a great poet; but had he lived, he would probably have become one, for all the powers were germinating in his mind. . . . More than this, we cannot help believing that, in matters of infinitely more importance, he would have come to his right mind: and after passing through the burning desert of Infidelity, striving in vain to cure its brackish water, and plant its sands with flowers, he would at last have emerged into 'Eden, the garden of God'. Shelley would then have been written amongst poets as 'full of wisdom and perfect in beauty'.

1832

86. Frances Trollope
from *Domestic Manners of the Americans*

The effect produced upon English people by the sight of slavery in every direction is very new, and not very agreeable, and it is not the less painfully felt from hearing upon every breeze the mocking words 'All men are born free and equal.'

****

The condition of domestic slaves, however, does not generally appear to be bad; but the ugly feature is, that should it be so, they have no power to change it. I have seen much kind attention bestowed upon the health of slaves; but it is on these occasions impossible to forget, that did this attention fail, a valuable piece of property would be endangered. Unhappily, slaves, too, know this; and the consequence is, that real kindly feeling very rarely can exist between the parties.

✳ ✳ ✳ ✳

The same man who his beards his wealthier and more educated neighbour with the bullying boast 'I'm as good as you,' turns to his slave, and
knocks him down, if the furrow he has ploughed or the log he has felled,
please not this stickler for equality. This is a glaring falsehood on the very
surface of such a man's principles that is revolting. It is not among the
higher classes that the possession of slaves produces the worst effects.
Among the poorer class of landholders, who are often as profoundly ignorant as the negroes they own, the effect of this plenary power over males
and females is most demoralising; and the kind of coarse, not to say
brutal, authority which is exercised, furnishes the most disgusting moral
spectacle I ever witnessed. In all ranks, however, it appeared to me that the
greatest and best feelings of the human heart were paralysed by the relative
positions of slave and owner. The characters, the hearts of children, are
irretrievably injured by it. In Virginia we boarded for some time in a family
consisting of a widow and her four daughters and I there witnessed a scene
strongly indicative of the effect I have mentioned. A young female slave,
about eight years of age, had found on the shelf of a cupboard a biscuit,
temptingly buttered, of which she had eaten a considerable portion before
she was observed. The butter had been copiously sprinkled with arsenic
for the destruction of rats, and had been thus most incautiously placed by
one of the young ladies of the family. As soon as the circumstance was
known, the lady of the house came to consult me as to what had best be
done for the poor child; I immediately mixed a large cup of mustard and
water (the most rapid of all emetics), and got the little girl to swallow it.
The desired effect was instantly produced, but the poor child, partly from
nausea and partly from the terror of hearing her death proclaimed by half-
a-dozen voices round her, trembled so violently that I thought she would
fall. I sat down in the court where we were standing, and, as a matter of
course, took the little sufferer in my lap. I observed a general titter among
the white members of the family, while the black stood aloof and looked
stupefied. The youngest of the family, a little girl about the age of the
young slave, after gazing at me for a few moments in utter astonishment,
exclaimed: 'Why! if Mrs Trollope has not taken her in her lap and wiped
her nasty mouth! Why, I would not have touched her mouth for two
hundred dollars!'

The little slave was laid on a bed, and I returned to my own apartments;
some time afterwards I sent to inquire for her, and learnt that she was in
great pain. I immediately went myself to inquire farther, when another
young lady of the family, the one by whose imprudence the accident had

occurred, met my anxious inquiries with ill-suppressed mirth – told me they had sent for the doctor and then burst into uncontrollable laughter. The idea of really sympathizing in the sufferings of a slave appeared to them as absurd as weeping over a calf that had been slaughtered by the butcher. The daughters of my hostess were as lovely as features and complexion could make them; but the neutralizing effect of this total want of feeling upon youth and beauty must be witnessed to be conceived.

There seems in general a strong feeling throughout America that none of the negro race can be trusted; and as fear, according to their notions, is the only principle by which a slave can be actuated, it is not wonderful if the imputation be just. But I am persuaded that, were a different mode of moral treatment pursued, most important and beneficial consequences would result from it. Negroes are very sensible to kindness and might, I think, be rendered more profitably obedient by the practice of it towards them, than by any other mode of discipline whatever. To emancipate them entirely throughout the Union cannot, I conceive, be thought of, consistently with the safety of the country; but, were the possibility of amelioration taken into the consideration of the legislature, with all the wisdom, justice, and mercy that could be brought to bear upon it, the negro population of the Union might cease to be a terror, and their situation no longer be a subject either of indignation or of pity.

I observed every where throughout the slave states that all articles which can be taken and consumed are constantly locked up, and in large families, where the extent of the establishment multiplies the number of keys, these are deposited in a basket, and consigned to the care of a little negress, who is constantly seen following her mistress's steps with this basket on her arm, and this, not only that the keys may be always at hand, but because, should they be out of sight one moment, that moment would infallibly be employed for purposes of plunder. It seemed to me in this instance, as in many others, that the close personal attendance of these sable shadows must be very annoying; but whenever I mentioned it, I was assured that no such feeling existed, and that use rendered them almost unconscious of their presence.

I had, indeed, frequent opportunities of observing this habitual indifference to the presence of their slaves. They talk of them, of their condition, of their faculties, of their conduct, exactly as if they were incapable of hearing. I once saw a young lady who, when seated at table between a male and a female, was induced by her modesty to intrude on the chair of her female neighbour to avoid the indelicacy of touching the elbow of a *man*. I once saw this very young lady lacing her stays with the most perfect composure before a negro footman. A Virginian gentleman told me that, ever since he had married, he had been accustomed to have a negro girl sleep in the same chamber with himself and his wife. I asked for what purpose this nocturnal attendance was necessary? 'Good heaven!' was the reply. 'If I wanted a glass of water during the night, what would become of me?'

1833

87. Sarah Flower Adams
from *A National Gallery*

'Write a chapter on the pictures,' says one; 'call it a lounge in the Louvre,' says another; the alliteration is good, no doubt, but he who could lounge in the Louvre, assuredly deserves to be kicked out of it. We prefer infinitely the sort of person who came to Paris within a week of the Cowes' Regatta, determined to see all the one, and return in time for the other. He entered the National Gallery, and while his party were lost 'in wonder, love, and praise' at one end, he was found returning from the other, exclaiming, 'I have seen it!' Oh, wonderful feat! – *foot*, rather, for he had a wooden leg, – oh harmonious combination of nature and art, to create such sympathy for a man in his extremities! but he was better than your lounger; as a brisk insect is better than a lazy slug. Lounge in the Louvre? No; the first sight of it is a sensation which you take, at least, that day and the next to recover–that is, if you have any consciousness of a nervous system about you. You do not attempt to look at a picture – you stand in a bewilderment of admiration, gazing down that arched street of paintings, letting your eyes wander in slow measurement along the walls, which seem elastic, and then walk gently forward in faith, that at some period of your life you will arrive at the other end. Do you want a moment's relief from all this? Turn to one of the many windows: – there is the Palace of the Tuilleries and the Place du Carrousel, with the triumphal arch in the centre, looking like a truant from Rome – surprised to find itself alone. Look at the people, carriages, soldiers, moving hither and thither, all brisk, busy, stirring, as bees in the sunshine; and they are even more like those happy creatures could you step beneath yonder entrance and see and hear them, humming and buzzing amongst the flowers, and fountains, and orange trees, and groves, of the Tuilleries' Gardens – and where do they come from? And you turn to an opposite window for answer – and there is the Seine, with its bridges covered with statues, or people, or shops, just as the Genius of the bridges may choose – and there are the quays, all living with happy humanity – and there are the buildings beyond, old, and stately, and colourful – the Institute; (why have not we an Institute?) and the Mint; (why have we a Mint? so it must be till better days come;) – and that tri-color flag (look at it – say, do we know any thing about colours in England?) above the statue of Henri Quatre, on the Pont Neuf. What would he say, could he rise from his grave and see it floating so proudly and gallantly in the sunshine? Peace to his manes, and that of his horse! for we question if he would be so good an instrument in the hands of Freedom, as he is now with her banner in his own. The houses opposite seem like a deputation, advancing from the isle Saint Louis, deprecating the mischief worked under the impolicy of its namesake, and about to do homage to the bravely-earned standard, floating on the breezy bridge. Behind them, is old Notre Dame, black and stately, like a cathedral in mourning, and the lofty light dome of the Pantheon, like a bride – (men of France become great and die, for the gratitude of the nation is waiting to bury you there –) – and the towers of St. Sulpice, and innumerable domes and towers in all directions, that keep the eye all a continued maze; and again you return to the Gallery with a sort of 'ah! whither shall I fly?' and you ask support for your limbs from one of the crimson benches and shade for your eyes from one of your hands, and you shut it all out for a while, and wait till you are fitted for a fresh encounter. If you are wise you will consider all this sufficient, and leave the poetry on the walls, and the exquisite forms and bright colours it chooses for its script, to be read, or be begun to be read, another day; and another day you come – and 'another, and another still succeeds;' and there is no one to stay your entrance, no money to give, no check to take or return, no written order from some man in office – not even your passport, which is equal to an order almost every where. Open all days except one – Monday, and that not one of aristocratic difference, but devoted to artists. No staring at a shabby hat, no rejection of a homely gown – free to be enjoyed by all as the light of heaven (that is to say, where there is no window-tax.) It is all that a National Gallery ought to be. Watch the people clustered round and being educated by their favourite pictures; look at their eager intelligent faces; listen to their doubly happy remarks, reading all they can from a picture, too poor to purchase a catalogue, and courteously asking the more fortunate to help them to its subject. Soldiers, too – but they are of the National Guard, not your mere legalized cut-throats; generals, colonels, and captains, would do well, if true to their profession, to keep all such from picture galleries. The arts are meant to refine – their system to brutalize. One fancies that soldiers would choose battle pieces, (of which be it said there are vastly too many taken as subjects by the French artists – more of that anon.) Not so; there is one with his eyes fixed on a picture of Annibal Carracci – the quietest, gentlest, most exquisitely touched! It is called 'Le Silence', and you hold your breath and do not speak as you look at it. The catalogue says, 'La Vierge recommande le silence a Saint Jean pour ne pas troubler le repos de Jesus'. That 'recommande' sounds strangely; but what other word could be found? The sweet earnest face of the mother, whose arm tenderly cradles the sleeping child – sleeping so placidly, that you hear in fancy the gentle breathing through its parted lips; her upraised hushing finger; her slight bending forward, as if to check the little disciple, who is making his whole body minister to one tiny finger, that it may fall like down upon the foot of the sleeper: Oh, it is all so beautiful! The soldier is still gazing, and if you asked him – why? he would perhaps answer, because the woman was so 'douce' and the children so 'jolis.' We would make answer for him, that he has a human heart – that he is enjoying, perhaps unconsciously, the expression of brotherly affection and expansive benevolence. The mother's face is alike free from the harshness of rebuke or the weakness of entreaty. She is careful of the feelings of the child of another, as she is watchful over the repose of her own; she is not one to exact obedience through fear, but to change it into pleasure through affection – the face of that mother, the act of that child, are lovely lessons of kindness and gentleness from which all, whether men, women, or children, may learn equally.

Another pleasure peculiar to the Louvre is the sight of so many women artists, who may work in safety without being insulted by the suspicious glances of the mischievous and ignorant, and who, by their judicious selection of subjects, and the truth and spirit with which they master them, show that they need but equal advantages to give them equal ability. They paint freely, easily, and have sufficient command over their pencils, or, rather, devotedness to their subject, to be perfectly indifferent to the looks or remarks of the people around them. They lose all consciousness of self in their love for the art – one of the distinguishing marks of true genius. 'What an intelligent face! What a beautifully organized hand! What is she copying?' The loves of Paris and Helen, by David; – one moment of them, but still sufficient to tell their whole history. Alone, away from all pursuit, secured even against the intrusion of the airs of heaven, by the full, soft, folded drapery that curtains the entrance; all around glowing with bright hues and exquisite forms, they, the centre of all, richly adorned, in the full pride of matchless physical beauty – Perfect, you would say but look, the lovely head of Helen is slightly drooping; – again, there is abstraction in her eye; – again, there is an unsatisfied, remorseful expression on the crimson lips: and Paris, as he draws her nearer to him, grasps her arm more than presses it, and looks up in her face with eyes of uneasy passion, as if asking why they are not happy now that they have attained the end of their wishes. Did a blessing ever rest on pleasure earned at the price of pain to others?

———

1834

88. Marguerite, Countess of Blessington
from *Conversations with Byron*

Byron has remarkable penetration in discovering the characters of those around him, and he piques himself extremely on it; he also thinks he has fathomed the recesses of his own mind; but he is mistaken: with much that is *little* (which he suspects) in his character, there is much that is great, that he does not give himself credit for: his first impulses are always good, but his temper, which is impatient, prevents his acting on the cool dictates of reason; and it appears to me, that in judging himself, Byron mistakes temper for character, and takes the ebullitions of the first for the indications of the nature of the second. He declares that, in addition to his other failings, avarice is now established.

This new vice, like all the others he attributes to himself, he talks of as one would name those of an acquaintance, in a sort of deprecating, yet half-mocking tone; as much as to say, you see I know all my faults better than you do, though I don't choose to correct them: indeed, it has often occurred to me, that he brings forward his defects, as if in anticipation of some one else exposing them, which he would not like; as, though he affects the contrary, he is jealous of being found fault with, and shows it in a thousand ways.

He affects to dislike hearing his works praised or referred to; I say affects, because I am sure the dislike is not real or natural; as he who loves praise, as Byron evidently does, in other things, cannot dislike it for that in which he must be conscious it is deserved. He refers to his feats in horsemanship, shooting at a mark, and swimming, in a way that proves he likes to be complimented on them; and nothing appears to give him more satisfaction than being considered a man of fashion, who had great success in fashionable society in London, when he resided there. He is peculiarly compassionate to the poor, I remarked that he rarely, in our rides, passed a mendicant without giving him charity, which was invariably bestowed with gentleness and kindness; this was still more observable if the person was deformed, as if he sympathised with the object.

Byron is very fond of gossiping, and of hearing what is going on in the London fashionable world: his friends keep him *au courant*, and any little scandal amuses him very much. I observed this to him one day, and added, that I thought his mind had been too great to descend to such trifles! he laughed, and said with mock gravity, 'Don't you know that the trunk of an elephant, which can lift the most ponderous weights, disdains not to take up the most minute? This is the case with my *great* mind, (laughing anew,) and you must allow the simile is worthy the subject. Jesting apart, I do like a little scandal, I believe all English people do.'

I have observed in Byron a habit of attaching importance to trifles, and *vice versa*, turning serious events into ridicule; he is extremely superstitious, and seems offended with those who cannot, or will not, partake this weakness. He has frequently touched on this subject, and tauntingly observed to me, that I must believe myself wiser than him, because I was not superstitious. I answered, that the vividness of his imagination, which was proved by his works, furnished a sufficient excuse for his superstition, which was caused by an over-excitement of that faculty; but that *I*, not being blessed by the *camera lucida* of imagination, could have no excuse for the *camera obscura*, which I looked on superstition to be. This did not, however, content him, and I am sure he left me with a lower opinion of my faculties than before. To deprecate his anger, I observed, that Nature was so wise and good that she gave compensations to all her offspring: that as to him she had given the brightest gift, genius; so to those whom she had not so distinguished, she gave the less brilliant, but perhaps as useful, gift of plain and unsophisticated reason. This did not satisfy his *amour propre*, and he left me, evidently displeased at my want of superstition. Byron is, I believe, sincere in his belief in supernatural appearances; he assumes a grave and mysterious air when he talks on the subject, which he is fond of doing, and has told me some extraordinary stories relative to Mr. Shelley, who, he assures me, had an implicit belief in ghosts. He also told me that Mr. Shelley's spectre had appeared to a lady, walking in a garden, and he seemed to lay great stress on this. Though some of the wisest of mankind, as witness Johnson, shared this weakness in common with Byron, still there is something so unusual in our matter-of-fact days in giving way to it, that I was at first doubtful that Byron was serious in his belief. He is also superstitious about days, and other trifling things – believes in lucky and unlucky days – dislikes undertaking any thing on a Friday, helping or being helped to salt at table, spilling salt or oil, letting bread fall, and breaking mirrors; in short, he gives way to a thousand fantastical notions, that prove that even *l'esprit le plus fort* has its weak side.

****

Byron is a strange *melange* of good and evil, the predominancy of either depending wholly on the humour he may happen to be in. His is a character that Nature totally unfitted for domestic habits, or for rendering a woman of refinement or susceptibility happy. He confesses to me that he is not happy, but admits that it is his own fault, as the Contessa Guiccioli, the only object of his love, has all the qualities to render a reasonable being happy. I observed, *apropos* to some observation he had made, that I feared La Contessa Guiccioli had little reason to be satisfied with her lot. He answered, 'Perhaps you are right; yet she must know that I am sincerely attached to her; but the truth is, my habits are not those requisite to form the happiness of any woman: I am worn out in feelings; for, though only thirty-six, I feel sixty in mind, and am less capable than ever of those nameless attentions that all women, but, above all, Italian women, require. I like solitude, which has become absolutely necessary to me; am fond of shutting myself up for hours, and, when with the person I like, am often *distrait* and gloomy. There is something I am convinced (continued Byron) in the poetical temperament that precludes happiness, not only to the person who has it, but to those connected with him. Do not accuse me of vanity because I say this, as my belief is, that the worst poet may share this misfortune in common with the best. The way in which I account for it is, that our *imaginations* being warmer than our hearts, and much more given to wander, the latter have not the power to control the former; hence, soon after our passions are gratified, imagination again takes wing, and, finding the insufficiency of actual indulgence beyond the moment, abandons itself to all its wayward fancies, and during this abandonment becomes cold and insensitive to the demands of affection. This is our misfortune, but not our fault, and dearly do we expiate it; by it we are rendered incapable of sympathy, and cannot lighten, by sharing, the pain we inflict. Thus we witness, without the power of alleviating, the anxiety and dissatisfaction our conduct occasions. We are not so totally unfeeling as not to be grieved at the unhappiness we cause; but this same power of imagination transports our thoughts to other scenes, and we are always so much more occupied by the ideal than the present, that we forget all that is actual. It is as though the creatures of another sphere, not subject to the lot of mortality, formed a factitious alliance (as all alliances must be that are not in all respects

equal) with the creatures of this earth, and, being exempt from its sufferings, turned their thoughts to brighter regions, leaving the partners of their
earthly existence to suffer alone. But, let the object of affection be snatched
away by death, and how is all the pain ever inflicted on them avenged! The
same imagination that led us to slight, or overlook their sufferings, now
that they are for ever lost to us, magnifies their estimable qualities, and
increases tenfold the affection we ever felt for them. . . . How did I feel this
when Allegra, my daughter, died! While she lived, her existence never
seemed necessary to my happiness; but no sooner did I lose her, than it
appeared to me as if I could not live without her. Even now the recollection is most bitter; but how much more severely would the death of Teresa
afflict me with the dreadful consciousness that while I had been soaring
into the fields of romance and fancy, I had left her to weep over my coldness or infidelities of imagination. It is a dreadful proof of the weakness
of our natures, that we cannot control ourselves sufficiently to form the
happiness of those we love, or to bear their loss without agony.'

The whole of this conversation made a deep impression on my mind,
and the countenance of the speaker, full of earnestness and feeling,
impressed it still more strongly on my memory. Byron is right: a brilliant
imagination is rarely, if ever, accompanied by a warm heart; but on this
latter depends the happiness of life; the other renders us dissatisfied with
its ordinary enjoyments.

---

89. Mary Leman Grimstone
Acephala

An essay on female education is ever a sort of writ of *ad quod damnum* to
ascertain how much a woman may be all allowed to know, without tres-
passing on the mental preserves of man, and how little, consistently with
securing for him every possible advantage. Her education is never considered otherwise than with reference to him; though his education is never
considered with reference to her.

The aim of female education has been to make woman a kind of *acephala*,
that is, an animal without a distinct head. It is now about being felt, that
this system does not work so well as it was hoped it would; that *indistinct
heads* descend, by hereditary right, on to the shoulders of sons as well as
daughters, and that by aid of a few sympathetic unions, we run a chance of
having some with *no heads at all*. This is going a step beyond Lord
Monboddo, who bore testimony to the opposite excess. In this wonderful

age such an event were nothing to wonder at, hardly to lament; some method for supplying heads by means of a patent machine would, doubtless, be forthwith forthcoming; and heads of any degree of intellect, 'warranted to wear well in all climates,' would speedily divide public patronage with the highest polish for boots and newest cut for periwigs.

I once heard it suggested by a humorist, that if an abstract of the male sex could appear, like some of the fabled deities of old, and address a similar abstract of the *female* sex on the subject in question, he would say, 'Whatever you do, see that you make *us* comfortable: on that condition we will give you lodging, food, and clothing, and as much of our fascinating company as we think proper. There is some talk about the better development of your head, we are quite unprepared upon the subject; had it been any plan for the enlargement of your heart, even though it might threaten aneurism, it should have our instant patronage, for it is clear that you cannot love us too much.' I cannot trust my memory regarding the reply to this characteristic harangue, but as far as the idea goes, it suggested to me that the general character of man, as modified by present education and manners, is not very unlike that of

> Little Jack Horner
>   Who sat in the corner
> Eating a Christmas pie,
> He put in his thumbs
> And pulled out the plums
>   And cried 'What a *good* boy am I!!!'

From what source he derives this most amazing fund of complacency for pulling out the plums *for himself*, it would be very difficult, upon any modern principle of sociality or philanthropy, to define. However, if I may be allowed to compare knowledge to anything so homely as a plum-pie, Jack Horner's plan is precisely that on which man has acted with regard to knowledge. The practice is about as wise and as worthy as would be the domestic arrangements of a man who should let the physical sustainment of his family depend upon *seeing him eat*. Much greater advance must we make to an acquaintance with the doctrine of sympathy, ere even a Falstaff of a father would have, by such means, any other than a most lean lachrymal family.

It is, says the Journal of Education (No 15, p. 26) a principle which cannot be too often repeated, that the foundation for a well-ordered society is the moral and intellectual culture given to all the members who compose it. I must all my life have been under a mistake as to the meaning of the word '*all*.' It is impossible that it can designate 'the whole number'; 'every body', as the dictionary gives it; and while I have fondly imagined that it meant the total, it must in fact only mean a moiety; for in what plan of education, public, private, or national, is *female* education even glanced at as a national or universal interest? Oh no; feed the boys, and the girls will grow fat, is the principle upon which *mental* nourishment is purveyed; when it is brought to bear, as it is to be hoped it will, upon *physical* nourishment, what a delightful thing it will be, in this politico-economical age; for

> 'Very good meat is cent. per cent.
> Dearer than very good argument.'

A writer in the last number of the journal already quoted, says, 'The great end of education is to fit woman to be the companion of a man of sense and information.' In the same article, the judicious acquirement of the accomplishments is recommended as being 'another link in the chain which binds men to their hearths.'

The great end of education is to fit woman, as an individual, to create happiness for herself by means as purely self-dependent as the nature of things will admit; and to fit her, as a relative creature, to be a zealous and liberal labourer in the midst of the whole human family for the advancement of the whole human race. It might be imagined, were there no avenues to a knowledge of human nature but through books, that for the cement of the union of the sexes, attraction need exist on one side only. How is this? Is it that personal preference and attachment is essential to satisfy the heart of woman, while necessitated or enforced adhesion is enough for that of man? As long as the mind possesses a power which spurns arbitrary control; by which it springs, in spite of law, or prudence, or policy, from that which disgusts to that which delights; so long must the charm which attracts, the spell which binds, be equally necessary to man as to woman; – unless to hold the hand without the heart suffice for him. I nauseate at all I read, and hear, and see upon this subject, tending, as it does, to universal evil. Thank heaven, with all that is said, the practice is not so bad as the preaching, and though marriage be a market, there be some above purchase; though domestic life be perpetually a slavery or a sovereignty, there be some above the debasement of either state.

Education ought to aim at perfecting men and women; instead of which it aims at making ladies, gentlemen, professional people, commercial people, mechanical people, and so on; and with all this there is such an utter absence of general harmony, that it is as impossible for them to blend and associate as it is to make a circle out of a triangle. As for the companionship of the sexes, like paper money, it passes current for that which it is not. How is it possible that it should be otherwise? Are they not the antipodes of each other in habits of thinking, in principles of taste, and possession of knowledge? Actuated by some motive of interest, fashion, customs or preference, they conform to, or they endure, each other's society; but among the millions who meet, how many *enjoy* each other's society? Oh, if drawing-rooms could bear evidence against the moral capital often floating through them, and show an account of the dividends of pleasure! Why our bank dividends, reduced, as they have been of late years, would look glorious in comparison with such a percentage. What, it may be asked, are the grounds of companionship? Some equality of powers of thinking, some degree of common knowledge, and community of regard for general interests. Who among men do we observe to be the companions of each other? Are the temperate and the hard drinkers ever companions? No, they mutually shun each other. Are the profound mathematician and the mere dancing-master ever companions? No, they mutually condemn each other. Are the generality of men and women more calculated to be companions than these? I fear not. Before ten years of age they are separated entirely from each other in education; but long before that, distinct systems of discipline have been adopted with each. The bandage upon the feet of a Chinese woman does not more effectually restrain her from the bounding elastic step natural to a young vigorous being, than do the admonitions of the mother or the governess restrain the growth of natural beauty in the mind and form of European girls. Walking sometime since in Kensington Garden, I saw a band of young boarding-school ladies; they were proceeding in as regular order as a file of soldiers going to relieve guard. Each of these girls had an open book in her hand; alas, to a fairer book spread out before them they were probably blind, of a profounder book which each carried in her own breast they will probably ever remain ignorant! The author of *Godolphin* (whoever that be) observes that it is delightful to woman to feel her dependence. Whence was this fancy won? It is delightful to her, being dependent, to feel perfect confidence in that on which she depends, as the wretch afloat from a wreck will rather grasp a rock than a reed. But the sense of enjoyment consorts alone with independence: self-power is the most invigorating, enjoying consciousness of which the human mind is capable; they who are happy without it are so from unexercised or deficient intellect; theirs is the bliss of the blind who never knew light. Constraint, acting in the place of rational instruction, is one of the grand ills of civilized humanity, beginning as it does with birth, and ending only when the lifeless frame mixes its ashes with the earth. The left-handed escapes made from this constraint form the rare and brief holidays of social existence. How rapturous is the emotion which the young man, first entering on life, experiences when he feels or fancies that he has the power of originating his own actions! What luxury of civilization can keep the savage from the life of freedom, although of hardship, which he leads in the wild? How joyously burst forth the energies of young children when they escape from school! Were it possible to put the question to the whole world, and to let it be decided by a show of hands, whether freedom, to those who had it, was not the first blessing, and to those who had it not, the first desire, we should have the skies darkened by the shadow of assenting palms, and the miserable few who did not lift their hands would die of terror during the brief eclipse. For my own part, I wonder that the electric spark of genius has ever been elicited amid the *conglaciation* of civilized life; for, as a free frame is necessary to a fine attitude, so is a free mind to fine thought, and its daring and divine expression. Why is it that the best light of the world, that which lives in the human eye, so rarely lightens with flashes of mind and heart; that eloquence leaps so rarely from the lip? Because constraint, induced or adopted, is continually putting winkers upon eyes, and bits and bridles into mouths, and the whole social machine moves in harness, and, withal, often too with *brass* enough about it. But if the icy and infected moral atmosphere has not prevented the appearance of genius, it has continually destroyed or perverted its power, and refracted its light. Many there are who have earned the meed of fame by submitting to desecration, and who then, if they had written till doomsday, would never have benefited the world. But I will not say

> Who builds a church to *God* and not to fame
> Will never mark the marble with his name.

Posterity is generally more just; it comes up with those whom contemporaries did not understand, and therefore could not properly appreciate, and thus it is, and thus it will long be, that the man of genius wants a meal while living, and receives a monument when dead. The multitude, educated as they are, prefer paying for amusement and flattery rather than for instruction and plain truth; thus singers and dancers are enabled to build palaces, and philosophers and philanthropists have not where to lay their heads.

To hasten the change which must arrive, if humanity be ever to know an approach to happiness, education must be the grand mover; and let me not be deemed partial when I say the education of woman even more than man. Amid all the narrowness and selfishness exhibited regarding her, there are among men many and splendid exceptions; and these, as much as the injury and injustice done to woman, make me yearn for her due elevation. Difficult is it to such men to find fitting mates, and evil is the consequence to themselves and to society. The union which does not improve the parties, deteriorates them; if it does not aid them to advance, it compels them to retrograde. If any views of this kind induce celibacy, then is the world defrauded of offspring, whose inherited nature and parental education might have made them treasures to their species. There is another point which must not be lost sight of – the mixed nature of humanity; the petty and the profound perpetually meet in the same person; the man who in the morning was sovereign in a hall of science, may in the evening be flattered by a compliment to the curl of his whiskers. Man needs the safeguard of mental strength in woman, as much as woman needs the safeguard of physical strength in man. None can view the subject truly, without feeling how much it is the interest of each to be equal friends and mutual sustainers. Some part of every person's nature is derived from progenitors; the mother often endows the son, and the sire the daughter; and the differences so strongly insisted on, arising out of organization and education, exist almost as much between man and man, as between man and woman. Were man wise, he would throw open the field of knowledge to his sister; nay more, he would allure her reluctant steps into the unaccustomed path, and say unto her, 'Come, learn with me.' Ah, but there is much that *he* studies, exclaims the objector, that is 'unfit for her perusal'. Then is it unfit for his, and he may abandon it with advantage. Corruption is corruption, be the recipient who it may, and, like all putrescence, is infectious. If such seeds be sown in the mind of the youth, what may we expect from his manhood and his age? That which we so often find. . . .

The hope that the principle which recognises universal humanity, and its happiness, as the grand object and rallying point of all reform, is advancing, surely, if slowly, is a hope of which I drink as a cordial. Day by day men and women will feel that their power is in proportion to their perfectness individually, and to their justice and benevolence socially: when the practical hand, and the cultivated head, are combined – the magic lanterns of a thousand fallacies will be broken, and the shadows which they bring upon the scene will pass away for ever.

1835

90. Laetitia Landon
from *On the Character of Mrs Hemans' Writings*

Did we not know this world to be but a place of trial – our bitter probation for another and for a better – how strange in its severity would seem the lot of genius in a woman! The keen feeling – the generous enthusiasm – the lofty aspiration and the delicate perception – are given but to make the possessor unfitted for her actual position. It is well! – such gifts, in their very contrast to the selfishness and the evil with which they are surrounded, inform us of another world – they breathe of their home, which is heaven; the spiritual and the inspired in this life but fit us to believe in that which is to come. With what a sublime faith is this divine reliance expressed in all Mrs Hemans's later writings! As the clouds towards nightfall melt away on a fine summer evening into the clear amber of the west, leaving a soft and unbroken azure whereon the stars may shine; so the troubles of life, its vain regrets and vainer desires, vanished before the calm close of existence – the hopes of heaven rose steadfast at last – the light shone from the windows of her home, as she approached unto it.

> No tears for thee! – though light be from us gone
> With thy soul's radiance, bright and restless one!
> No tears for thee!
> They that have loved an exile must not mourn
> To see him parting from his native bourne,
> O'er the dark sea.

We have noticed this yearning for affection – unsatisfied, but still unsubdued – as one characteristic of Mrs Hemans' poetry: the rich picturesque was another. Highly accomplished, the varied stores that she possessed were all subservient to one master science. Mistress both of German and Spanish, the latter country appears to have peculiarly captivated her imagination. At that period when the fancy is peculiarly alive to impression – when girlhood is so new, that the eagerness of childhood is still in its delights – Spain was, of all others, the country on which public attention was fixed – victory after victory carried the British flag from the ocean to the Pyrenees; but, with that craving for the ideal which is so great a feature in her writings, the present was insufficient, and she went back upon the past; – the romantic history of the Moors was like a storehouse, with treasures gorgeous like those of its own Alhambra.

It is observable in her minor poems, that they turn upon an incident rather than a feeling. Feelings, true and deep, are developed; but one single emotion is never the original subject. Some graceful or touching anecdote or situation catches her attention, and its poetry is developed in a strain of mourning melody, and in a vein of gentle moralising. I always wish, in reading my favourite poets, to know what first suggested my favourite poem. Few things would be more interesting than to know under what circumstances they were composed – how much of individual sentiment there was in each, or how, on some incident seemingly even opposed, they had contrived to engraft their own associations. What a history of the heart would such annals reveal! Every poem is in itself an impulse.

Besides the ideal and the picturesque, Mrs Hemans is distinguished by her harmony. I use the word harmony advisedly, in contradistinction to melody. Melody implies something more careless, more simple, than belongs to her style; it is song by snatches; our English ballads are remarkable for it. To quote an instance or two: there is a verse in that of *Yarrow Water* –

> O wind that wandereth from the south;
> Seek where my love repaireth;
> And blow a kiss to his dear mouth,
> And tell me how he fareth.

Nothing can exceed the tender sweetness of these lines; but there is no skill. Again, in *Faire Rosamonde*, the verse that describes the cruelty of Eleanor –

> With that she struck her on the mouth,
> So dyed double red;
> Hard was the heart that gave the blow,
> Soft were the lips that bled.

How musical is the alliteration! but it is music which, like that of the singing brook, has sprung up of itself. Now, Mrs Hemans has the most perfect skill in her science; nothing can be more polished than her versification. Every poem is like a piece of music, with its eloquent pauses, its rich combinations, and its swelling chords. Who that has ever heard, can forget the exquisite flow of 'The Voice of Spring?'

> I come, I come! ye have called me long –
> I come o'er the mountains with light and song!
> Ye may trace my step o'er the wakening earth
> By the winds which tell of the violet's birth,
> By the primrose-stars in the shadowy grass,
> By the green leaves opening as I pass.

It is like the finest order of Italian singing – pure, high, and scientific.

I can never sufficiently regret that it was not my good fortune to know Mrs Hemans personally: it was an honour I should have estimated so highly – a happiness that I should have enjoyed so keenly. I never even met with an acquaintance of hers but once; that once, however, was much. I knew Miss Jewsbury, the late lamented Mrs Fletcher. She delighted in speaking of Mrs Hemans; she spoke of her with the appreciation of one fine mind comprehending another, and with the earnest affection of a woman and a friend. She described her conversation as singularly fascinating – full of poetry, very felicitous in illustration by anecdote – happy, too, in quotation, and very rich in imagery; 'in short, her own poem on "The Treasures of the Deep" would best describe it.' She mentioned a very striking simile to which a conversation on Mrs Hemans's own poem of 'The Sceptic' had led. – 'Like Sinbad the sailor, we are often shipwrecked on a strange shore. We despair; but hope comes when least expected. We pass through the gloomy caverns of doubt into the free air and blessed sunshine of conviction and belief.' I asked her if she thought Mrs Hemans a happy person, and she said, 'No; her enjoyment is feverish, and she desponds. She is like a lamp whose oil is consumed by the very light which it yields.' What a cruel thing is the weakness of memory! How little can its utmost efforts recall of conversation that was once an instruction and a delight!

To the three characteristics of Mrs Hemans's poetry which have already been mentioned – viz. the ideal, the picturesque, and the harmonious – a fourth must be added, – the moral. Nothing can be more pure, more feminine and exalted, than the spirit which pervades the whole; it is the intuitive sense of right, elevated and strengthened into a principle. It is a glorious and a beautiful memory to bequeath; but she who left it is little to be envied. Open the volumes which she has left, legacies from many various hours, and what a record of wasted feelings and disappointed hopes may be traced in their sad and sweet complainings! Yet Mrs Hemans was spared some of the keenest mortifications of a literary career. She knew nothing of it as a profession which has to make its way through poverty, neglect, and obstacles: she lived apart in a small, affectionate circle of friends. The high-road of life, with its crowds and contention – its heat, its noise, and its dust that rests on all – was for her happily at a distance; yet even in such green nest, the bird could not fold its wings, and sleep to its own music. There came the aspiring, the unrest, the aching sense of being misunderstood, the consciousness that those a thousand times inferior were yet more beloved.

Genius places a woman in an unnatural position; notoriety frightens away affection; and superiority has for its attendant fear, not love. Its pleasantest emotions are too vivid to be lasting: hope may sometimes,

> Raising its bright face,
> With a free gush of sunny tears, erase
> The characters of anguish:

but, like the azure glimpses between thunder-showers, the clouds gather more darkly around for the passing sunshine. The heart sinks back on its solitary desolation. In every page of Mrs Hemans' writings is this sentiment impressed. What is the conclusion of 'Corinne crowned at the Capitol'?

> Radiant daughter of the sun!
> Now thy living wreath is won.
> Crowned of Rome! – oh, art thou not
> Happy in that glorious lot?
> Happier, happier far than thou
> With the laurel on thy brow,
> She that makes the humblest hearth
> Lovely but to one on earth.

What is poetry, and what is a poetical career? The first is to have an organisation of extreme sensibility, which the second exposes bareheaded to the rudest weather. The original impulse is irresistible – all professions are engrossing when once begun; and, acting with perpetual stimulus, nothing takes more complete possession of its follower than literature. But never can success repay its cost. The work appears – it lives in the light of popular applause; but truly might the writer exclaim –

> It is my youth – it is my bloom – it is my glad free heart
> I cast away for thee – for thee – ill-fated as thou art.

If this be true even of one sex, how much more true of the other! Ah! Fame to a woman is indeed but a royal mourning in purple for happiness.

---

91. Laetitia Landon
The Factory

> There rests a shade above yon town,
>   A dark funereal shroud:
> 'Tis not the tempest hurrying down,
>   'Tis not a summer cloud.

The smoke that rises on the air
 Is as a type and sign;
A shadow flung by the despair
 Within those streets of thine.

That smoke shuts out the cheerful day,
 The sunset's purple hues,
The moonlight's pure and tranquil ray,
 The morning's pearly dews.

Such is the moral atmosphere
 Around thy daily life;
Heavy with care, and pale with fear,
 With future tumult rife.

There rises on the morning wind
 A low appealing cry,
A thousand children are resigned
 To sicken and to die!

We read of Moloch's sacrifice,
 We sicken at the name,
And seem to hear the infant cries –
 And yet we do the same; –

And worse – 'twas but a moment's pain
 The heathen altar gave,
But we give years, – our idol, Gain,
 Demands a living grave!

How precious is the little one,
 Before his mother's sight,
With bright hair dancing in the sun,
 And eyes of azure light!

He sleeps as rosy as the south,
 For summer days are long;
A prayer upon his little mouth,
 Lulled by his nurse's song.

Love is around him, and his hours
    Are innocent and free;
His mind essays its early powers
    Beside his mother's knee.

When after-years of trouble come,
    Such as await man's prime,
How will he think of that dear home,
    And childhood's lovely time!

And such should childhood ever be,
    The fairy well, to bring
To life's worn, weary memory
    The freshness of its spring.

But here the order is reversed,
    And infancy, like age,
Knows of existence but its worst,
    One dull and darkened page; –

Written with tears, and stamped with toil,
    Crushed from the earliest hour,
Weeds darkening on the bitter soil
    That never knew a flower.

Look on yon child, it droops the head,
    Its knees are bowed with pain;
It mutters from its wretched bed,
    'Oh, let me sleep again!'

Alas! 'tis time, the mother's eyes
    Turn mournfully away;
Alas! 'tis time, the child must rise,
    And yet it is not day.

The lantern's lit – she hurries forth,
    The spare cloak's scanty fold
Scarce screens her from the snowy north,
    The child is pale and cold.

And wearily the little hands
    Their task accustomed ply;
While daily, some mid those pale bands,
    Droop, sicken, pine, and die.

Good God! to think upon a child
    That has no childish days,
No careless play, no frolics wild,
    No words of prayer or praise!

Man from the cradle – 'tis too soon
    To earn their daily bread,
And heap the heat and toil of noon
    Upon an infant's head.

To labour ere their strength be come,
    Or starve, – is such the doom
That makes of many an English home,
    One long and living tomb?

Is there no pity from above, –
    No mercy in those skies;
Hath then the heart of man no love
    To spare such sacrifice?

Oh England! though thy tribute waves
    Proclaim thee great and free,
While those small children pine like slaves,
    There is a curse on thee!

———

1836

92. Caroline Bowles
from *The Birthday*

Say with a friend we contemplate some scene
Of natural loveliness, from which the heart
Drinks in its fill of deep admiring joy;

Some landscape scene, all glorious with the glow
Of summer evening, when the recent shower
(Transient and sudden) all the dry white road
Has moistened to red firmness; every leaf
(Washed from the dust) restored to glossy green;
In such an evening oft the setting sun,
Flaming in gold and purple clouds, comes forth
To take his farewell of our hemisphere;
Sudden the face of Nature brightens o'er
With such effulgence, as no painter's art
May imitate with faint similitude.
The rain-drops dripping fast from every spray
Are liquid topazes; bright emeralds those
Set on the green foil of the glistening leaves
And every little hollow, concave stone,
And pebbly wheel-track, holds its sparkling pool
Brimming with molten amber. Of those drops
The blackbird lights to drink; then scattering thick
A diamond shower among his dusty plumes,
Flies up rejoicing to some neighbouring elm,
And pours forth such a strain as wakens up
The music of unnumbered choristers.
Thus Nature to her great Creator hymns
An halleluiah of ecstatic praise.
And are our voices mute? Oh! no, we turn
(Perhaps with glistening eyes) and our full heart
Pour out in rapturous accents, broken words,
Such as require no answer, but by speech
As little measured, or that best reply,
Feeling's true eloquence, a speaking look.
But other answer waits us; for the *friend*
(Oh! heaven! that there are such) with a calm smile
Of sweet *no-meaning* gently answers – 'Yes,
Indeed it's very pretty – Don't you think
It's getting late though – time to go to tea?'

NOTES

Further information on names marked with an asterisk can be found under
Biographical Notes.

1. Text: *Elegaic Sonnets*, 5th edn (Cadell and Davies: London, 1789) p. 44
   Title] 'Middleton is a village on the margin of the sea, in Sussex, containing
   only two or three houses. There were formerly several acres of ground between
   its small church and the sea, which now, by its continual encroachments,
   approaches within a few feet of this half-ruined and humble edifice. The wall,
   which once surrounded the church-yard, is entirely swept away, many of the
   graves broken up, and the remains of bodies interred washed into the sea;
   whence human bones are found among the sand and shingles on the shore'
   (CS's note, pp. 101–2)
   life's long storm] see Biographical Note on CS
2. Text: *A Year with the Ladies of Llangollen*, ed. E. Mavor (Penguin Books:
   Harmondsworth, 1986)
   ***Tristram Shandy*]** novel (1759–67) by Laurence Sterne
3. Text: *The Death of Amnon. A Poem. With an Appendix containing Pastorals
   and Other Poetic Pieces* (Rollason: Coventry, 1789) pp. 115–16
   in her sleeve] privately
   The Duty of Man] *The Whole Duty of Man* (1658), a highly popular devotional
   text
   Betty] generic name for female servant
4. Text: *Observations and Reflections made in the Course of a Journey through
   France, Italy and Germany*, 2 vols (Strahan and Cadell: London, 1789) vol. i,
   pp. 102–5
   pin-money] small personal allowance
5. Text: *Gentleman's Magazine*, August 1789, p. 743
   which sprung . . . shores] American Revolution (1776)
6. Text: *A Vindication of the Rights of Men* (Johnson: London, 1790) pp. 109–15,
   116–17
   Context: written in response to Edmund Burke, *Reflections on the Revolution in
   France* (1790), and published anonymously. The second edition, with MW's
   name on the title page, appeared six weeks later. MW not only attacks Burke's

204

conservative, anti-Revolutionary politics, but also his sentimentality, his specious wit, and his sexual politics.

Dr Price's sermon] Burke's *Reflections* was written in response to a pro-Revolutionary sermon by Dr Richard Price, published as *A Discourse on the Love of Our Country* (1789). Price was a friend of MW

Enquiry ... weakness] *A Philosophical Enquiry into the Origin of our Ideas of the Sublime and Beautiful* (1757), III ix and III xvi.

'learn ... creatures'] Burke, Sublime and Beautiful III ix: 'they learn to lisp, to totter in their walk, to counterfeit weakness and even sickness', adapts *Hamlet* III i 146–8: 'You jig and amble, and you lisp, you nickname God's creatures and make your wantonness your ignorance'.

the musselman's creed] a widespread misconception at this period held that the Muslim religion denied that women had souls.

Plato and Milton] cf Plato, *Symposium*, 178–85; Milton, *Paradise Lost*, VIII, 589–92

Spartan regulations] the Spartans of ancient Greece were subjected to rigorous training from early childhood.

assembly of unlettered clowns] Burke had accused the newly formed French Assembly of 'coarseness and vulgarity' (*Reflections*, p. 118).

7. Text: as (2)

fire kindled by Lord George Gordon] the anti-papist Gordon riots, in 1780, led by Lord George Gordon (1751–93), subjected London to a week of fires, murder and destruction.

I tremble for France] the entry is written on the first anniversary of the fall of the Bastille.

8. Text: *Letters on Education, with Observations on Religious and Metaphysical Subjects* (Dilly: London, 1790) pp. 46–50, 203–9

Hortensia] CM's fictitious correspondent

a perfect woman's but a softer man] Misquoted from Pope, 'Moral Essays: Epistle to a Lady': 'Heav'n, when it strives to polish all it can/ Its last best work, but forms a softer Man'; (ll. 271–2)

Rousseau] Jean-Jaques Rousseau, *Emile* (1762, 1763), a work which is also subjected to heavy criticism by Wollstonecraft in *Vindication of the Rights of Woman* (1792)

the judicious Addison] See *The Spectator*, no. 66 (16 May 1711) (wrongly attributed by CM to Joseph Addison (1672–1719), but actually by his co-editor Richard Steele (1672–1729)): 'The general mistake among us in educating our children, is, that in our daughters we take care of their persons and neglect their minds. ... the management of a young lady's person is not to be overlooked, but the erudition of her mind is much more to be regarded'.

summum bonum] the highest, or supreme, good

desideratum] thing desired

the polite ... Chesterfield] Philip Dormer Stanhope, 4th Earl of Chesterfield (1694–1773). See *Letters to his Son* (1774), letter CLXI (5 Sept 1748).

9. Text: *Letters Written in France, in the Summer of 1790, to a Friend in England* (T. Cadell: London, 1790) pp. 22–5, 216–18

A . . . restons pas] To the Bastille – but we will not stay there

Man! proud man . . . the angels weep] *Measure for Measure*, II, ii, 114–22, adapted

Sterne says] Laurence Sterne, *A Sentimental Journey through France and Italy* (1767), 'The Passport: Versailles'

10. Text: *Epistle to William Wilberforce, Esq. on the Rejection of the Bill for Abolishing the Slave Trade* (Johnson: London,1791) pp. 5–8, 9–11, 13–14

    title] William Wilberforce (1759–1833), member of parliament and anti-slavery campaigner. His bill for abolishing the slave trade was rejected in 1791. It was finally passed in 1807, although slavery in British possessions was not abolished until 1833.

    Astrean] from Astrea, goddess of justice

    Lo! . . . inflicting wounds] cf. Wollstonecraft, *Rights of Man* (1790) (no. 6)

    Scythian . . . Sybarite] Natives of the ancient region of Scythia, in Russia, were known for barbarity and tortures; those of ancient Greek Sybaria were noted for sensuality.

11. Text: *Vindication of the Rights of Woman* (Johnson: London, 1792) pp. 1–2, 8–9, 37–8, 40–2, 337–40, 386–9

    plain-work, mantua-making] simple sewing, dressmaking

12. Text: *Plans of Education, with Remarks on the Systems of other Writers* (Hookham and Carpenter: London, 1792) pp. 79–82, 130–9

13. Text: *Village Politics. Addressed to all the Mechanics, Journeymen, and Day Labourers, in Great Britain. By Will Chip, A Country Carpenter* (Simmons, Kirkey and Jones: Canterbury, 1793) pp. 3–8, 13–15

    Rights of Man] pro-Revolutionary text by Thomas Paine, published in two parts, 1791 and 1792

    Whole Duty of Man] highly popular devotional text on the subject of man's duty to God, first published in 1658

    'Study . . . business'] *1 Thessalonians* 1.3

14. Text: *The Poems of Charlotte Smith*, ed. S. Curran (Oxford: Oxford University Press, 1993) Book II, ll. 1–61

    Context: dated April 1793, two months after the execution of Louis XVI, referred to in line 55

15. Text: *Letters on the Female Mind* (Hookham and Carpenter: London, 1793) pp. 6–14, 18–25

    prolated] expanded

    physic] medicine

16. Text: *Letters and Essays, Moral and Miscellaneous* (T. Knott: London, 1793) Essay III, pp. 19–30

    Plutus] god of riches

    the rights of woman . . . Wollstonecraft] see no. 11

17. Text: *British Synonymy; or, an Attempt at Regulating the Choice of Words in Familiar Conversation*, 2 vols (Robinson: London, 1794) vol. i, pp. 1–9, 220–1

18. Text: *Letters for Literary Ladies* (Johnson: London, 1795) pp. 23–32, 46, 52–4, 61–5, 73–4

    a poet, who was a friend to the fair sex] Pope, *The Rape of the Lock*, Canto IV

Turkish ignorance] the Turks were noted for their total neglect of female education.

19. Text: *The Royal Captives*, 4 vols (Robinson: London, 1795) vol. iv, pp. 68–9
    Title] Anarchy, a personification of the Terror in France, is the speaker of this sonnet.

20. Text: as 19, vol. iv, pp. 105–6, 109–10
    Title] Louis XVI, executed in 1793
    animalcula] minute animals
    elder sons of Gallia] the aristocracy of France
    Sapphic measures] sensual poems or songs, from Sappho, ancient Greek poetess (see no. 22)

21. Text: *Letters Written During a Short Residence in Sweden, Norway and Denmark* (Johnson: London, 1796) pp. 7–11, 14–16, 66, 73–4
    Context: MW undertook a business trip to Scandinavia, on behalf of Gibert Imlay, in 1795, accompanied by her daughter Fanny Imlay, aged 18 months, and her maid Marguerite. In *Letters . . .* she adapted her personal letters to Imlay, with whom her relations had become troubled, into a travel book.
    it was prohibited] Sweden's poor economy led to coffee prohibition from 1794–6.
    'maidens . . . idleness'] *Midsummer Night's Dream*, II, i, 168

22. Text: *Sappho and Phaon. In a Series of Legitimate Sonnets, with Thoughts on Poetical Subjects, and Anecdotes of the Grecian Poetess* (Gosnell: London, 1796) pp. 40, 48, 50, 60, 81
    Title] Sappho (c. 612–580 BC), Greek lyric poet and leader of a female literary coterie, was said to have committed suicide when she was abandoned by the boatman Phaon.
    sensate] endowed with sensibility
    tessellated] mosaic
    Lethean] causing oblivion or forgetfulness (from Lethe, river in Greek mythology, whose waters made their drinkers forget the past)

23. Text: *Monthly Magazine*, vol. iii, April 1797, pp. 279–82
    Dr Johnson . . . genius] 'The true genius is a mind of large general powers, accidentally determined to some particular direction', *Life of Cowley*, 1799–81.
    Thomson . . . poet] See *Life of Thomson*, 1799–81.
    camera] from *camera obscura*, a darkened box or room into which images could be projected through a lens: here used in a figurative sense for the eye.

24. Text: *Journals*, ed. E. de Selincourt, 2 vols (Macmillan: London, 1941) vol. i, pp. 3–5, 21–3
    Alfoxden] Alfoxden House, in Somerset, residence of William and DW from 16 July 1797–25 June 1798
    Poole's] Thomas Poole (1765–1837), friend and neighbour of Coleridge's in Nether Stowey
    a Hamburg inn] the Wordsworths travelled to Germany in November 1798, in the company of Coleridge and John Chester.

25. Text: *An Appeal to the Men of Great Britain in Behalf of Women* (Johnson: London, 1798) pp. 158–65

26.   Text: E. Betham, *A House of Letters* (Jarrold and Son: London, n.d. [1908]) pp. 55–6
      Context: Given in c.1798 to Lady Boughton as 'a little continuation of some verses I had met with'

27.   Text: *Reflections on the Present Condition of the Female Sex; with Suggestions for its Improvement* (Johnson: London, 1798) pp. 1–5, 63–7
      Dr Adam Smith] (1723–1790). The arguments are those of his *Wealth of Nations* (1776), which defined wealth in terms of labour.
      There is . . . object] cf. no. 31

28.   Text: 'Introductory Discourse', *A Series of Plays in which it is Attempted to Delineate the Stronger Passions of the Mind*, 3 vols (Cadell & Davies: London, 1798–1812) vol. i, pp. 23–5, 28–31, 37
      heroic ballad] epic poetry

29.   Text: 'Hints' no. 22–6, from *Posthumous Works of the Author of a Vindication of the Rights of Woman*, ed. William Godwin, 4 vols (Johnson: London, 1798) vol. iii, pp. 187–92
      Context: Published by Godwin as 'Hints [Chiefly designed to have been incorporated in the second part of the *Vindication of the Rights of Woman*]' (ibid., p. 175), these aphorisms, thirty-two in all, cover a wide range of subject matter, much of it clearly unrelated to MW's feminist polemics. 'Hints' 22–6 may be material rejected from the essay 'On Poetry' (no. 23).
      baseless fabric of a vision] *The Tempest*, IV, i, 151, slightly misquoted
      Genesis 1. 3] 'And God said, "Let there be light", and there was light'

30.   Text: *Original Sonnets on Various Subjects* (Sael: London, 1799) p. 73

31.   Text: *The Female Advocate; or an Attempt to Recover the Rights of Woman from Male Usurpation* (Vernor and Hood: London, 1799) pp. 29–33, 36–7
      Siddonian powers] the acting abilities of Sarah Siddons (1755–1831), the most celebrated actress of the day

32.   Text: *A Letter to the Women of England, on the Injustice of Mental Subordination* (Longman and Rees: London, 1799) pp. 90–5
      Messalinas . . . Portias and Arrias] ancient Roman women. Messalina was noted for immorality; Portia (wife to Brutus) and Arria for their virtues.
      petrifying torpedo] electric ray (cartilaginaceous fish) capable of delivering a powerful electric shock

33.   Text: *Strictures on the Modern System of Female Education, with a View of the Principles and Conduct Prevalent among Women of Rank and Fortune*, 2 vols (Cadell and Davis: London, 1799) vol. i, pp. ix, 135, 96–8, 163–9
      Sempronia] daughter of Scipio Africanus, celebrated for her virtues and accomplishments
      'one thing. . . needful'] *Luke* 10.42

34.   Text: *Poems* (Dilly: London, 1799) pp. 40–3
      Context: An anti-Revolutionary satire, in which the Head represents the monarchy and the other parts of the body the people

35.   Text: as 24, vol. i, pp. 37–8, 39, 40–1
      Context: the Wordsworths had moved into Dove Cottage, Grasmere, in December 1799.

John] John Wordsworth (1772–1805), sailor brother of William and DW
into Yorkshire] to visit Mary Hutchinson, William's future wife
Sir Michael's] Rydal Hall, owned by Sir Michael le Fleming

36. Text: *Letters to a Young Lady*, 3 vols (Longman, Hurst, Rees and Orme: London, 1800) vol. ii, pp. 449–52

37. Text: *Letters on the Elementary Principles of Education*, 2nd edn, 2 vols (Robinson: London, 1801) vol. i, pp. 254–7, 300–4; vol. ii, pp. 389–91

38. Text: *Memoirs; with some Posthumous Pieces*, 4 vols (R. Phillips: London, 1801) vol. ii, pp. 44–52
     Context: The Prince of Wales, later George IV (1762–1830), began his pursuit of MR following her appearance as Perdita in *A Winter's Tale* in 1780. He sent her a number of letters through his intermediary, Lord Malden, of which she doubted his authorship, and finally invited her to attend a concert at which he would be present. This extract is the last part of MR's narrative: her daughter wrote the continuation of her life after her death in 1800.
     Gazed . . . again] Dryden, *Alexander's Feast*, 110–13, adapted
     eclat] scandal
     Mr Meyer] Jeremiah Meyer (1735–89)
     'Je ne . . . mourant'] I will not change until I die
     Duke of Cumberland] Henry Frederick (1745–90), uncle of the Prince of Wales
     Buckingham House] now Buckingham Palace

39. Text: *Poems* (Longman and Rees: London, 1802) pp. 3–9

40. Text: *A Tour Made in Scotland, A.D. 1803*, as 24, vol. i, pp. 249–52, 286
     Context: widely circulated in manuscript, but not published until 1847. DW, William (Wm.) and Coleridge (C.) set off for Scotland on 15 August 1803. They parted from Coleridge two weeks later, and returned to Grasmere on 25 September.

41. Text: *Psyche; or The Legend of Love* (Carpenter and Whittingham: London, 1805) pp. 53–7

42. Text: *Poetical Works, including many pieces never before published*, 3 vols (Phillips: London, 1806) vol. iii, pp. 303–5

43. Text: Letter LI, *Letters from the Mountains; being the Real Correspondence of a Lady between the Years 1773 and 1807*, 2nd edn, 3 vols (Longman, Hurst, Rees and Orme: London, 1807) vol. ii, pp. 268–75
     Trinculo . . . for shelter] *The Tempest*, II, ii
     One foot . . . constant never] from the song 'Sigh no more, ladies', *Much Ado about Nothing*, II, iii, 59–60
     wool-sacks] in the House of Lords, the seat of the Lord High Chancellor, dating from the Middle-Ages when wool was the principal source of English wealth

44. Text: *The Artist*, vol. i, no. 14, 13 June 1807, pp. 9–11
     successful practice] EI's novel *A Simple Story* (1791) had become instantly popular.
     Mrs Radcliffe or Maria Edgeworth] the two most popular novelists of the day

45. Text: *Beachy Head, Fables, and Other Poems* (Johnson: London, 1807) ll. 346–89

46. Text: Felicia Dorothea Browne, *England and Spain; or Valour and Patriotism* (Cadell and Davies: London, 1808)

Context: Written when FH was fourteen. One of her two soldier elder brothers
was serving under Sir John Moore in the Peninsular War.
Albion] England
Spartans] ancient Greek race celebrated for valour
Hymettus] mountain near Athens
Hindostan] India
Ormuz and Golconda] ancient trading cities (in Iran and India respectively)
celebrated for wealth
Montezuma] Aztec emperor (1466–1520)
Parian] from Greek island of Paros, source of finest white marble
Sabaean] from island of Saba, in the West Indies
cassia] cinammon-like spice
savannas] open grasslands
Elysium] paradise
Promethean] creative

47. Text: *Patriotic Sketches of Ireland, written in Connaught*, 2 vols (Dobbin and
     Murphy, Callender and Wills: Baltimore, 1809) vol. i, pp. ix–x, 50–4
     The Wild Irish Girl] SO's first novel, published 1806

48. Text: *Epistles on the Character and Conditions of Women in Various Ages and
     Nations* (Johnson: London, 1810) pp. v–vi, 78–81
     its last best gift] See Alexander Pope, 'Moral Essays: Epistle to a Lady': 'Heav'n,
     when it strives to polish all it can/ Its last best work, but forms a softer Man'; (ll.
     271–2).
     Hesperian tree] in Gr. myth, bearing golden apples and growing in the
     Hesperides or Islands of the Blessed
     amaranthine] of everlasting, fadeless flowers

49. Text: *The British Novelists; with an Essay, and Prefaces Biographical and
     Critical*, 50 vols (Rivington *et al*.: London, 1810) vol. i, pp. 1–3, 42, 44–6, 56
     D'Arblay] married name of Fanny Burney

50. Text: *A Series of Popular Essays, Illustrative of Principles essentially connected
     with the Improvement of the Understanding, the Imagination, and the Heart*,
     2nd edn, 2 vols (Manners and Miller: Edinburgh/Longman, Hurst, Rees, Orme
     and Brown, and T. Cadell: London) vol. i, essay III, 'On the Effects Resulting
     from a Peculiar Direction of Attention on the Power of Imagination, and in
     Producing the Emotions of Taste', chapter I: 'Observations on the power of
     imagination as affording exercise to such of the intellectual faculties as have pre-
     viously been developed and cultivated. Correspondence between the degree in
     which any of these faculties habitually operate, and the nature of the combi-
     nations formed in the imagination, illustrated by various examples', pp. 157–77
     foil] metallic fabric

51. Text: *Psyche; with Other Poems*, 2nd edn (Longman, Hurst, Rees, Orme and
     Brown: London, 1811) p. 220

52. Text: *Eighteen Hundred and Eleven: A Poem* (Johnson: London, 1812) pp. 4–8,
     23–4
     Midas] King of Phrygia, granted by Dionysus the power of turning everything
     he touched to gold

Lockes ... Paleys] John Locke (1632–1704), whose *Two Treatises on Government* (1690) were the cornerstone of Whig democracy; William Paley (1743–1805), theological utilitarian and author of *Principles of Moral and Political Philosophy* (1785)

platan] plane tree

Hagley's woods] celebrated beauty spot in Worcestershire, seat of Lord Lyttleton

Thomson] James Thomson (1700–48), author of the important landscape poem *The Seasons* (1726–30)

53. Text: *A Narrative Concerning George and Sarah Green of the Parish of Grasmere: Addressed to a Friend*, ed. E. de Selincourt (Clarendon Press: Oxford, 1936) pp. 51–7

Context: A local couple of very poor cottagers, George and Sarah Green, had died on the snow-covered fells near Grasmere on the night of 19 March, leaving eight children under 16 to be looked after. The eldest daughter, Sally, was already working as a servant for the Wordsworths. DW's narrative was written in May, at the urging of William, but remained unpublished.

My sister Mary] Mary Wordsworth, William's wife

old man's up-grown daughters] children of George Green's first wife who had died twenty years earlier

our Molly] servant to the Wordsworth family

car] carriage

54. Text: *Poetical Effusions* (M. Braithwaite: Kendal, 1814) pp. 1–2

chaplets] wreaths

55. Text: *The Journals*, ed. M. K. Stocking with D. Stocking (Harvard University Press: Cambridge, Mass., 1968) pp. 31–4, 48–50

Context: CC had accompanied her half-sister Mary Godwin on her elopement with Shelley to France, and lived with the couple in London after their return. Cf. no. 57.

Letters from Norway] Mary Wollstonecraft, *Letters Written During a Short Residence* ... (1796). See no. 21.

Beyond ... water snakes] *Ancient Mariner*, ll. 272–3

Peacock] Thomas Love Peacock (1785–1866), novelist, satirist, essayist, poet

Political Justice] by William Godwin (1793)

56. Text: *The British Ladies' Magazine and Monthly Miscellany*, no. 4, April, 1815, pp. 257–60

plain-worker] one who does plain sewing, as distinguished from embroidery or fancy-work

57. Text: *History of a Six Weeks' Tour through a Part of France, Switzerland, Germany and Holland* (Hookham and Ollier: London, 1817) pp. 5–7, 13–17, 40–5

Context: cf. no. 55. S*** and C*** are Shelley and Claire.

les Dames...enlevees] the ladies will certainly be abducted

58. Text: *Essays in Rhyme on Morals and Manners* (Taylor and Hessey: London, 1816) pp. 1–5

twelves ... rush] kinds of candles and rush lights

warm, fore-handed] affluent, well provided for the future

lappet] fold or flap of fabric

own theory . . . Sir Isaac] theory of gravity, developed by Isaac Newton (1643–1727)

59. Text: *I Know My Own Heart: The Diaries of Anne Lister, 1791–1840*, ed. Helena Whitbread (Virago Press: London, 1988) pp. 6, 14, 15

Euclid] *Elements*, in thirteen books, by Greek mathematician Euclid (c. 330–c. 260 BC), of which nine deal with geometry

Walkingham] *The Tutor's Assistant* (1751), popular school arithmetic by Francis Walkingame

Miss Browne] local girl to whom AL is attracted

stays] corsets

Marianne] Marianne or Mary Lawton, *née* Belcome, with whom AL had been in love for five years.

married a blackguard] Marianne had married Charles Lawton, of Lawton Hall, Cheshire, to satisfy conventions and in hope that he would soon die and she would inherit his considerable wealth.

60. Text: *Memoirs of Mrs E.H. with Selections from her Correspondence and Unpublished Writings*, ed. E. O. Benger, 2 vols (Longman, Hurst, Rees and Orme: London, 1818) vol. i, pp. 131–6, 139, 155–61

Dr Bell . . . National School] Andrew Bell (1753–1832), founder of the Madras system of (mutual) education, which he put into practice as superintendent of the National Society for Promoting Education of the Poor in Principles of the Established Church (founded 1811)

an English party] as a Scot, EH is visiting England as a tourist

Goths] invaders

Hagley oaks] Hagley woods, in Worcestershire, seat of Lord Lyttleton, was a famous beauty spot

Thomason's manufactory] Factory owned by Sir Edward Thomason (1769–1849)

Shem and Japhet] sons of Noah

61. Text: as 59, p. 56

1819

62. Text: as 2.
     Context: EB was 90 years old in 1819.

63. Text: as 59, pp. 78–9, 119–20, 145, 159, 160

to   **Miss Browne]** see note to 59

65. **Mr Kelly]** Miss Browne's suitor
     M–] Marianne (see note to 59)
     Mr Montagu] an earlier suitor of AL's
     a good kiss] AL's euphemism for sexual satisfaction
     C–] Charles Lawton, Marianne's husband (see note to 59)

66. Text: *Memoirs of Queens, Illustrious and Celebrated* (Allman: London, 1821) pp. 125–33
     Context: Caroline of Brunswick (1768–1821), daughter of Karl Wilhelm, Duke

of Brunswick, married her first cousin the Prince of Wales in 1795, but separated from her husband after the birth of their daughter Princess Charlotte Augusta in 1796. She was offered an annuity of £50,000 on her husband's ascension to the throne in 1820 on condition that she stay abroad and renounce her claim to the title of queen. She returned, however, and fought her case successfully. Her initial popularity as a result waned dramatically when she tried to force her way into her husband's coronation, but rose again after her sudden death the following month. MH presents her as a victim of court culture, led into error by a system she did not understand.

Burke ... away] See Edmund Burke (eulogising Marie Antoinette), *Reflections on the Revolution in France* (1790), p. 113.

the man in question] Caroline had been accused of adultery with Bartolomeo Bergami.

67. Text: *Italy*, 2 vols (Gagliani: Paris, 1821) vol. i, pp. 31–3, 367–70

    'horrible imaginings'] *Macbeth*, I, iii, 138

    'that ... eternity'] *Paradise Lost*, II, 147

    In 1814 ... liberation] In April 1814, William Cavendish Bentinck (1774–1839, English statesman, later first governor general of India) granted independence to the Genoese Republic against the orders of the British government. He was recalled, and Britain handed Genoa over to the King of Sardinia.

    Jerome Serra] Count Juliemo Serra

68. Text: *The Monthly Repository of Theology and General Literature*, vol. xviii, February 1823, pp. 79–81

    the female converts ... friends] see *Romans* 16. 1–2, 6, 12–13, 15

    'great thoughts ... minds'] unidentified

    blue-stockings] descriptive of a circle of learned women at the end of the eighteenth century, which included Carter, Talbot and Chapone (see note below); this term had become perjorative.

    More ... Cappe] *Hannah More, *Anna Barbauld, *Maria Edgeworth, *Elizabeth Hamilton, Elizabeth Carter (1717–1806), poet and translator from French, Italian and Greek (*Epictetus*, 1758); Catherine Talbot (1721–70), essayist, poet and letter-writer; Elizabeth Smith (1776–1806), oriental scholar; Hester Chapone (1727–1801), poet and prose writer; *Anne Grant; *Lucy Aikin; Louisa Capper (1776–1840), author of an abridgement of Locke's *Essay on Human Understanding* (1811)

    in ours] HM adopts a male persona

69. Text: *New Monthly Magazine, n.s.*, vol. 7, 1823, pp. 439–40

70. Text: *London Magazine*, 9, March 1824, pp. 253–6

    Epigraph] Wordsworth, *The Affliction of Margaret*, 57–60

    New Holland] Australia, especially Western Australia

    mare incognitum] unknown sea

    Mungo Park] (1771–1806), African explorer

    Thetis] sea nymph

    Characterless ... nothing] *Troilus and Cressida*, III, ii, 195–6

    Brutus's dream] *Julius Caesar*, IV, iii, 273–84

    Lord Lyttleton's vision] Thomas Lyttleton, 2nd Baron Lyttleton (1744–79) was warned in a dream that he would die in three days, and did so.

dead majesty of Denmark] the ghost of Hamlet's father

Every ... light] Shelley, *The Cenci*, II, i, 179–80

the former] Thomas Jefferson Hogg (1792–1862)

Ponsi ... manca] put itself on the left side of the bed

The Italian] Angelo Mengaldo

M. G. Lewis] Matthew Gregory ('Monk') Lewis (1775–1818), Gothic novelist

71. Text: *Memoirs of Harriette Wilson*, 2nd edn, 4 vols (Stockdale: London, 1825) vol. i, pp. 5–9; vol. ii, pp. 310–16

Lord Craven] William Craven, 2nd Earl of Craven (1770–1825)

cocoa trees ... fellows] Craven owned West Indian plantations, manned by slaves

Honorable Frederick Lamb] (1782–1853), later 3rd Viscount Melbourne

Lord Melbourne] 1st Viscount Melbourne

Prince of Wales] later George IV

Lady Caroline Lamb] married to Henry William Lamb (1779–1848), 2nd Viscount Melbourne, and brother to Frederick (see note above). See no. 81 for CL's response.

Her ladyship's only son] see Biographical Note on CL

to *dedommager* herself] to cheer herself up

Glenarvon ... Lord Byron] *Glenarvon* (1816), CL's first novel, was closely based on her relationship with Byron.

72. Text: *Phantasmagorea; or, Sketches of Life and Literature*, 2 vols (Hurst, Robinson & Co: London, 1825) vol. i, pp. 107–15

Uncertain ... please] Scott, *Marmion*, xxx

Hayley and Miss Seward] William Hayley (1745–1820) and *Anna Seward, both, in MJJ's view, minor poets

Madame de Stael] Anne Louise Germaine de Stael (1766–1817)

73. Text: *A Legacy for Young Ladies, consisting of Miscellaneous Pieces in Prose and Verse*, ed. Lucy Aikin (Longman, Reed, Hurst, Orme and Brown: London, 1826) pp. 42–7

74. Text: *New Monthly Magazine n.s.*, vol. 16, 1826, pp. 147–51

Title] 'Having been permitted to extract the above eloquent passages from the manuscripts of the author of the *Mysteries of Udolpho*, we have given this title to them, though certainly they were not intended by the writer to be offered as a formal or deliberate essay, under this, or any other denomination. They were, originally, part of an INTRODUCTION, to the Romance, or Phantasie, which is about to appear [*Gaston de Blonville* (1826)]. The discussion is supposed to be carried on by two travellers in Shakespeare's native country, Warwickshire' [editor's note].

'the air ... cold'] *Hamlet*, I, iv, 1

the scene ... Horatio] *Hamlet*, I, i

banquet scene] *Macbeth*, III, iv

Mr Burke ... terror] Edmund Burke, *A Philosophical Enquiry into the Sublime and Beautiful* (1757), I, iii ('a sort of tranquillity shadowed with horror')

'On his brow ... plumed'] *Paradise Lost*, IV, 988–9

1827

75. Text: as 55, pp. 405-6, 408-10
    Medwin's book upon Lord Byron] Thomas Medwin, *Journal of the Conversations of Lord Byron* (London, 1824)
    at Geneva] in 1816, when Byron and the Shelley entourage were neighbours
    Fletcher] Byron's manservant, who gave Medwin an account of his death at Missolonghi, in Greece
    the Guiccioli] Countess Teresa Guiccioli, with whom Byron lived for the last three years of his life
    this ... a lie] the story is, however, confirmed by Mary Shelley (see MS, *Letters*, vol. i, p. 298)
    the mischief he had done me] probably less Byron's abandonment of CC, than his neglect of their daughter Allegra and her subsequent death (see Biographical Note on CC)
76. Text: *Records of Woman: with Other Poems* (Blackwood: Edinburgh/Cadell: London, 1828) pp. 45-54
    Title] FH probably derived her information from Giorgio Vasari, *Lives of the Most Eminent Painters, Sculptors and Architects* (1568)
    Forsaken Ariadne] in Greek mythology, daughter of King Minos of Crete; she married Theseus, whom she had rescued from the Minotaur, only to be abandoned by him on the island of Naxos.
77. Text: *The Venetian Bracelet and other Poems* (Longman, Reed, Orme, Brown and Green: London, 1829) pp. 263-5
78. Text: *The Book of the Boudoir*, 2 vols (Henry Colburn: London, 1829) vol. i, pp. 208-12
    Lord Byron's antipathy] *Don Juan*, I, xii
    a Bolognese doctoress] the University of Bologna, in Northern Italy, admitted women in the Middle Ages.
    Madame de Stael] Anne Louise Germaine de Stael (1766-1817)
    the Ass's Bridge] *Pons asinorum*, a humorous name given to the fifth proposition of the first book of Euclid's *Elements*
79. Text: *The Amulet* (1829) p. 89
80. Text: *Loves of the Poets*, 2 vols (Henry Colburn: London,1829) vol. i, pp. 342-5, 349-51
    Lalla Rookh] (1817), a series of oriental tales in verse by Thomas Moore (1779-1852)
    Parish Register] (1807), poem by George Crabbe (1754-1832)
    young Aurora] Byron, *Don Juan*, Cantos XV and XVI
    poor Margaret] Wordsworth, *Excursion*, I
    the Gothic ages] the medieval period
    the succeeding period] the Renaissance
    the age of French gallantry] the Restoration
    au fond] fundamentally
    'et il ... de rose'] and it is never pleasant to be poisoned, even by the spirit of the rose
    As ... smiles] unidentified

Madame de Stael] Anne Louise Germaine de Stael (1766–1817)
With . . . exalt] *Don Juan*, XIV, xvi, 1.
'besoin de sentir'] need to feel

81.   Text: *Fugitive Pieces and Reminiscences of Lord Byron . . . also some Original Poetry, Letters and Recollections of Lady Caroline Lamb*, ed. I Nathan (Whittaker, Treacher and Co: London, 1829) p. 159
      Context: see Biographical Note on CL

82.   Text: as 81, pp. 195–6
      Context: see 71

83.   Text: *France in 1829–30*, 2 vols (Saunders and Otley: London, 1830) vol. i, pp. 102–8
      brevet rank] promotion (normally military, but in this case to that of great-aunt)
      bon-bons] sweetmeats
      Diablotins . . . Nantes] imps in pastry, Nantes pastilles
      tournure] figure
      marmotte] child
      epics and eclogues] kinds of poems
      garcons] waiters
      magazin] shop
      'Whitbread's entire'] bottled beer
      cocculus indicus] dried berries of the plant *annamirta cocculus*, a powerful poison used to increase the intoxicating power of English beer
      'sweeten my imagination'] *King Lear*, IV, vi, 133
      petit ecu] small coin
      eaux, essences . . . extraits] waters, essences and extracts
      'Oui . . . soap'] Yes, yes, madam, I understand! here is everything you need, Gattie's Lavender Water, prime quality honey-water, essence of bergamot, de Tief's vinegar, and Windsor soap [i.e. all English-made cosmetics].
      O'Connell] Daniel O'Connell (1775–1847), Irish politician, and first Roman Catholic to be elected to Parliament (1828), thus forcing the government to grant Catholic emancipation
      'Ecoutez, chere amie'] Listen, my dear friend
      Regent's vash-ball] kind of soap
      anti-bilieux] anti-bilious
      poteen] illicit Irish liquor, usually made from potatoes
      'till . . . feet'] unidentified
      rosbif de mutton] roast mutton
      'by your leave, Georgy'] poteen (Georgy being George III, by whose dispensation illicit liquor-making was encouraged)
      borrachio of still and bog] flavour of the illicit distillery and of bog-water

84.   Text: 'Review of Joanna Baillie, *The Nature and Dignity of Christ*', *The Athenaeum*, 28 May 1831, p. 337.
      Percy's *Reliques*] *Reliques of Ancient Poetry* (3 vols, 1765), a collection of ballads and other ancient poems collected by Bishop Thomas Percy
      Basil . . . Ethwald] two of Baillie's *Plays of the Passions*

85. Text: 'Review of Shelley, "The Wandering Jew"', *The Athenaeum*, 16 July 1831,
     pp. 456-7
     Whom ... to love] Wordsworth, 'She dwelt among untrodden ways', ll. 3-4
     Know ye ... foe?] *Prometheus Unbound*, I, 116-19
     Elysium] in Gr. myth, the place of dwelling after death
     Tartarus] in Gr. myth, a gulf beneath the underworld
     Low ... ghosts] unidentified
     'such stuff ... made of'] *The Tempest*, IV, i, 156-7

86. Text: *Domestic Manners of the Americans*, 2 vols (Whittaker, Treacher & Co:
     London, 1832) vol. ii, pp. 20-5
     but ... conceived] 'Perhaps the most disgusting part of the spectacle (except
     the often recurring infliction of personal punishment) is that in which all that is
     most hateful in our nature is displayed in the infant tyranny of white children
     towards their slaves. I cannot even at this distance of time recall the puny bully-
     ing and well-taught ingenious insult of almost baby children towards stalwart
     slaves, who raised their heads towards heaven like men, but seemed to have lost
     the right of being so classed, without a feeling of indignation that makes my heart
     beat painfully' [FT's note].

87. *The Monthly Repository of Theology and General Literature*, vol. vii, 1833, pp.
     840-5
     Louvre] formerly the palace of the French kings in Paris, it was converted by
     Napoleon to an art gallery in 1793.
     Henri Quatre] Henry IV (1553-1610), king of France from 1589
     window-tax] duty levied on windows, imposed in 1695 and not abolished
     until 1851
     Annibal Carracci] Italian painter (1560-1609)
     David] Jean Louis David (1748-1825), court painter to Napoleon

88. Text: *Conversations with Lord Byron* (Colburn: London, 1834) pp. 35-7, 40-2,
     69-73
     camera lucida] light room
     camera obscura] dark room
     amour propre] self-love
     l'esprit le plus fort] the strongest spirit
     melange] mixture
     Contessa Guiccioli] Teresa Guiccioli, with whom Byron lived for the last three
     years of his life
     when Allegra ... died] Allegra, B.'s daughter by *Claire Clairmont. Cf Bio-
     graphical Note on CC and no. 75.

89. Text: *The Monthly Repository of Theology and General Literature*, vol. viii,
     1834, pp. 771-7
     Title] (supposed) headless animal
     ad quod damnum] damned with respect to this
     Lord Monboddo] James Burnett (1714-99), Scottish judge
     Very ... argument] unidentified
     The author of *Godolphin*] Edward George Earle Lytton, 1st Baron Lytton

(1803–73), novelist publishing either anonymously (as in the case of *Godolphin* (1833)), or under the name of Bulwer Lytton
conglaciation] freezing
winkers] blinkers
brass] money (with a pun on horse-brass)
Who . . . name] unidentified

1835

90.   Text: *New Monthly Magazine, n.s.*, vol. 44, 1835, pp. 265–8
      Context: One of many tributes paid to FH following her death in 1835
      No tears . . . sea] FH, *The Requiem of Genius*, 1–6
      Raising . . . anguish] FH, *Arabella Stuart*, 37–9
      Radiant . . . earth] FH, *Corrine at the Capitol*, 37–44
      It is . . . art] FH, *The Chamois Hunter's Love*, 17–18
91.   Text: *The Vow of the Peacock and other Poems* (Longman, Reed, Orme, Brown and Green: London, 1835) pp. 231–7
      Context: One of several poems written in support of factory reform following the Factory Act of 1833, which, although it outlawed the employment of children under 9, still allowed 9- to 13-year-olds to work eight hours a day, and 14- to 18-year-olds twelve hours
      Moloch] god of the Ammonites, who demanded child sacrifices (2 Kings 23:10)
92.   Text: *The Birth-Day, a Poem in 3 Parts; to which are added Occasional Verses* (Blackwood: Edinburgh, 1836) pp. 98–100

BIOGRAPHICAL NOTES

Items marked with an asterisk can be found in this anthology.

Adams, Sarah Flower, later Fuller (1805-48)
Daughter of radical Unitarian journalist Benjamin Flower, she lived after her father's death in the household of William J. Fox, editor of *The Monthly Repository*, to which she contributed regularly. Her other works were mainly hymns (of which the best known is 'Nearer my God to Thee') and a five-act verse drama, *Vivia Perpetua* (1841), based on the life of an early Christian woman convert. Her early death, at the age of 43, was due to tuberculosis.
    See: Mineka (1944)

Aikin, Lucy (1781-1864)
Daughter of Dr John Aikin, physician and author, and niece of *Anna Barbauld, she began her writing career with contributions to her brother Arthur Aikin's *Annual Review* (1803-8). Her *Poetry for Children* (1803) was republished many times. In 1810 she published a long poem, *Epistles on Women* (1810), and her only fiction, *Lorimer*, in 1814. She then established herself as a historical writer, producing *Memoirs of the Court of Queen Elizabeth* in 1818, followed by *Memoirs of the Court of James I* (1822) and *Memoirs of the Court of Charles I* (1833). She also published a memoir of her father in 1823, and in 1826 an edition of Anna Barbauld's *Works* with a memoir. Her last major work was her *Life of Addison* (1843).
    See: Le Breton (1864)

Alcock, Mary, *née* Cumberland (c. 1742-98)
Born in Northamptonshire, she moved to Ireland with her parents when her father became Bishop of Clonfert. She was married to 'Archdeacon Alcock', possibly John Alcock, Archdeacon of Raphoe. After his death she settled in Bath where, despite extremely weak health, she brought up a family of orphan nieces. Her poem *The Air-Balloon* was published in 1784. Her niece Joanna Hughes edited her posthumous *Poems* in 1799.
    See: Cumberland (1807); Lonsdale (1989); Ashfield (1995)

Baillie, Joanna (1762-1851)
Born in Bothwell, Scotland, where her father was minister, she moved to London in her early twenties. Her first publication was *Poems* (1790), which received little

219

notice. She was much more successful when she turned to drama, and the first volume of her *Series of Plays, in which it is Attempted to Delineate the Stronger Passions of the Mind* (3 vols, 1798–1812) brought her instant celebrity. Her successful tragedy *De Monfort* (1800) was produced at Drury Lane. She had even greater success with *A Family Legend* (1810). She also published *Metrical Legends* (1823) and *Fugitive Verses* (1840) which included many of the poems from her 1790 volume. She entertained many important literary figures at her house in Hampstead, where she died at the age of 88.

See: Carhart (1923, repr. 1970); Schofield and Macheski (1991); Catherine B. Burroughs in Feldman and Kelley (1995); Lonsdale (1989); Ashfield (1995)

Barbauld, Anna Laetitia, *née* Aikin (1743–1825)

Daughter of Dr John Aikin, she was precociously talented, apparently reading before she was 3. Her father and his colleagues at the Warrington Dissenting Academy encouraged her education and she became fluent in Latin and Greek as well as in modern languages. With her brother John, she published *Miscellaneous Pieces in Prose and Verse* in 1773, and the same year her own *Poems*. She married in 1774 a dissenting minister, Rochemont Barbauld (who suffered from mental problems, which worsened with age), and the couple opened a school in Sussex. Here she published *Lessons for Children* (1778) and *Hymns in Prose for Children* (1781). The school closed in 1785 and after some time travelling abroad the Barbaulds settled in London. She wrote a number of political pamphlets, published poems in her brother's *Monthly Magazine*, edited the poems of Akenside (1794) and Collins (1797) and the letters of Richardson (1804). Her husband was institutionalised, and found drowned in 1808. In 1810, she published a fifty-volume edition of *The British Novelists*, with biographical introductions and a prefatory essay, *'On the Origin and Progress of Novel Writing'. Her educational anthology *The Female Speaker* appeared in 1811, and her anti-war poem, *Eighteen Hundred and Eleven*, in 1812. The poem was heavily criticised, and she never published again.

See: Rodgers (1958); Curran (1988); Lonsdale (1989); McCarthy and Kraft (1994); Ashfield (1995); William McCarthy in Feldman and Kelley (1995)

Betham, Matilda (1776–1852)

Born in Suffolk and educated at home, she published her *Biographical Dictionary of Celebrated Women* in 1804. She moved to London, where she gave readings from Shakespeare, and moved in literary circles. Her two volumes of poetry appeared in 1797 and 1808, and a longer poem, *The Lay of Marie*, in 1816.

See: Edwards (1880)

Blessington, Marguerite, Countess of, *née* Power (1789–1849)

Born in Ireland, she was forced into marriage with Maurice St Leger Farmer at the age of 14. She returned to her parents' home three months later, but remained officially married until her husband died in a drunken brawl in 1817. Her second husband was the Earl of Blessington. The Blessingtons established a friendship with Byron in 1823. Following her husband's death in 1829 she found her income much diminished and began to write in consequence. Her most successful work was *Conversations with Lord Byron*, which appeared in 1834. She also published a number of 'silver fork' novels of contemporary society, and edited two literary annuals,

Heath's Book of Beauty and *The Keepsake*, to both of which she contributed prolifically. Declared bankrupt following the Irish famine of 1849, she fled to Paris with her
companion of twenty years, Alfred, Count d'Orsay (her daughter's estranged husband), where she died a few months later.
   See: Madden (1855)

Bowles, Caroline Anne, later Southey (1786-1854)
Born in Hampshire, she began writing and publishing after her parents' deaths, when
a dishonest guardian cheated her out of her inheritance. She sent the manuscript of
Ellen Fitzarthur, a long narrative poem (1820), to Robert Southey, whom she met
shortly afterwards. Her *The Widow's Tale and other Poems* (1822) was followed by
Solitary Hours (1826) and *Chapters from Churchyards* in 1829. She published *Tales
of the Factories* (verse, 1833), and a long autobiographical poem, *The Birthday* (evidently influenced by Wordsworth's then unpublished *Prelude*) in 1836. She married
Southey in 1839, after his first wife's death, but he became senile three months later,
and the years before his death in 1843 were a severe trial. She gave up writing, and
retired to her native Hampshire, receiving a crown pension of £200 two years before
her death in 1854.
   See: Ashfield (1995)

Butler, Lady Eleanor (?1739-1829)
Daughter of the Anglo-Irish Earl of Ormonde, she and her devoted friend Sarah
Ponsonby (?1735-1831) fled the homes of their parents in 1778, Butler under threat
of a convent and Ponsonby to evade the advances of her guardian. Despite fierce
familial opposition, they set up house together at Plas Newydd, near Llangollen in
North Wales, where they remained until their deaths. Much celebrated as the 'Ladies
of Llangollen', their Gothic retreat was visited by many of the intelligensia of the day.
Wordsworth and Southey addressed poems to them, and *Anna Seward paid tribute
to them in her *Llangollen Vale* (1795). Her journals have been published as *Life with
the Ladies of Lllangollen* and *A Year with the Ladies of Llangollen* (both ed. E. Mavor).
   See: Mavor (1971)

Clairmont, Claire (formerly Jane) (1798-1879)
Daughter of Mary Jane Clairmont, the second wife of William Godwin, she was step-
sister to *Mary Shelley. The children of the household were comprehensively educated at home. Claire was fluent in French and had a marked talent for music and
singing. When Mary eloped with Shelley in 1814, Claire accompanied them, and
continued to live with them, despite intermittent disharmony between herself and
Mary. In 1816 she pursued Byron, who became her lover. Their child Allegra was
born in 1817, by which time the relationship had ended. She was deeply attached to
Allegra, but Byron persuaded her to send the child to live with him. He later placed
her in a convent, where she died in 1822, aged 4. Claire became a governess, and lived
abroad for most of her long life. She never married.
   See: Gittings and Manton (1995)

Edgeworth, Maria (1767-1849)
Eldest daughter of wealthy Anglo-Irish landowner Richard Lovell Edgeworth, who
remarried twice after her mother's death and fathered twenty-two children, she was

educated at school in England, but returned to Ireland at the age of 15 to help her father run his estate and remained there, unmarried, for the rest of her life. She published *Letters for Literary Ladies* in 1795, and *The Parent's Assistant* in the same year. She collaborated with her father on *Practical Education* (1798). Her successful career as a novelist began with an Irish novel, *Castle Rackrent* (1800). She published further Irish novels, including *The Absentee* (1812) and *Ormond* (1817), and several contemporary English novels, among them *Belinda* (1801), *Patronage* (1814) and *Helen* (1834), as well as several collections of moral tales.

See: Hare (1894); Butler (1972); Mellor (1993); Mitzi Myers in Feldman and Kelley (1995)

Grant, Anne, née McVicar (1755-1838)

Born in Glasgow, she spent her youth in New York, returning to Scotland in 1768. She married the Reverend James Grant in 1779, and the couple moved to Laggan in Inverness-shire where she remained until her husband's death in 1801. To support her eight surviving children she turned to writing, publishing *Poems* in 1803 and the highly acclaimed *Letters from the Mountains* in 1807. *Memoirs of an American Lady* followed in 1808, giving her even greater celebrity. She was less successful with her last two ventures, *Essay on the Superstitions of the Highlanders of Scotland* (1811) and *Eighteen Hundred and Thirteen: A Poem* (1814). She spent her final years in Edinburgh.

See: Grant (1844)

Grimstone, Mary Leman, later Gilles (c. 1800-?50)

Born in Hamburg, where her father was an expatriate. In 1826-9 she lived in Tasmania. An ardent social reformer and feminist, she began contributing to the *Monthly Repository* in 1833. Her contributions, which included poetry, fiction and essays, continued until 1837. She also wrote a number of novels: *The Beauty of the British Alps; or, Love at First Sight* (1825); *Louisa Egerton, or Castle Herbert* (1830); *Woman's Love* (1832); *Character; or Jew and Gentile* (1833); and *Cleone: A Tale of Married Life* (1834).

See: Murphy (1988); Mineka (1944)

Hamilton, Elizabeth (1758-1816)

Brought up in Scotland, she began to write for publication in 1792, and published her satire on contemporary society, *Letters of a Hindoo Rajah* (1796). A second novel, *Memoirs of Modern Philosophers* (1800), satirised *Mary Hays and other members of London radical circles. Her *Letters on Education*, first published in 1801, was a successful and moderately radical work, and was republished several times. It was followed by a number of other moral works.

See: Benger (1818); Butler (1975); Kelly (1993)

Hands, Elizabeth (fl. 1789)

Originally a servant, she married a blacksmith at Bourton, near Rugby. Her earliest published poetry appeared in the *Coventry Mercury*. Her poem *The Death of Amnon* was seen by Philip Bracebridge Homer, a master at Rugby School and minor poet, who enlisted the help of other Rugby masters and his vicar father in raising subscriptions for its publication. *The Death of Amnon. A Poem. With an Appendix; Containing Pastorals and other Poetical Pieces* was published in Coventry in 1789.

See: *Gentleman's Magazine*, June 1790; *Monthly Review*, 3, 1790; Bedford (1889); Lonsdale (1989)

Hawkins, Laetitia Matilda (1759–1835)
Born in London, daughter of biographical writer Sir John Hawkins, who brought up his children to consider themselves valueless. Her writing career began with a novel published while still in her teens, which was anonymous, as was her *Letters on the Female Mind* (1793), addressed to *Helen Maria Williams. Later novels included *The Countess and Gertrude, or Modes of Discipline* (1811), *Roseanne, or A Father's Labour Lost* (1814), *Heraline, or Opposite Proceedings* (1821) and *Annaline, or Motive-Hunting* (1824). She also collaborated with her brother on *Sermonets* (1814), and wrote two volumes of *Memoirs* (1823, 1824).
See: Jones (1990)

Hays, Mary (1760–1843)
Brought up in Southwark by her widowed mother, her first publication was *Cursory Remarks* (1792), a defence of public worship. As a result, she became a member of the London radical circle which included *Mary Wollstonecraft, of whom she became an ardent follower and who advised her over the publication of her *Letters and Essays, Moral and Miscellaneous* (1793). Her first novel, *Memoirs of Emma Courtney* (1796), caused a scandal for its heroine's offer to live unmarried with her lover, and her second, *The Victim of Prejudice* (1799), was equally radical. She is generally assumed to be the author of the anonymous *An Appeal to the Men of Great Britain on behalf of Women* (1798). Her six-volume *Female Biography* (1803) does not, however, include Wollstonecraft. She continued to support herself by writing, supplemented by school-teaching, until her death in London at the age of 83.
See: Wedd (1925); Spencer (1986); Todd (1989); Jones (1990); Kelly (1993)

Hemans, Felicia Dorothea, *née* Browne (1793–1835)
Born in Liverpool, and educated at home by her mother, she published her first volume, *Poems* (1808), at the age of 15. Two years later she followed this with *The Domestic Affections and Other Poems* (1812), and the same year she married Captain Alfred Hemans. Six years later, while she was pregnant with her fifth son, Hemans departed permanently for Italy, after which she moved back to live with her mother. She wrote and published prolifically, producing a new collection of poems almost every year until her early death, from tuberculosis and heart disease, at the age of 41. One of the most popular and successful poets of her day, her earnings from poetry and contributions to annuals were substantial. Her best known mature volumes include *The Forest Sanctuary; Lays of Many Lands* (1825); *Records of Woman and Other Poems* (1828); and *Songs of the Affections* (1830).
See: Hughes, (1839); Chorley (1836); Trinder (1984); Clarke (1990); Leighton (1992); A. J. Harding in Feldman and Kelley (1995); Ashfield (1995)

Inchbald, Elizabeth, *née* Simpson (1753–1821)
Daughter of a Catholic farmer in Suffolk, she had no formal education. She ran away from home at 18 to become an actress, and in 1772 married fellow Catholic actor Joseph Inchbald, many years her senior, to escape other unwelcome advances. She worked mainly in the provincial theatre until she was widowed in 1779. She began

writing plays in the 1780s, mainly comedies and farces. Her novel *A Simple Story* was published in 1791. Her second novel, *Nature and Art* (1796), was more radical and less successful. She edited and wrote introductions to several collected editions of plays. She died in a home for Roman Catholic women in Kensington, after burning the four volumes of memoirs she had compiled.

See: Boaden (1833); McKee (1935); Spencer (1986); Schofield and Macheski (1991)

Jameson, Anna Brownell, *née* Murphy (1794-1860)

Born in Dublin, she published a fictionalised version of her journal describing travels through France and Italy as a governess, as *A Lady's Diary* (1826). She married Robert Jameson, a barrister, in 1825, but separated after four years. She wrote prolifically, producing *Loves of the Poets* (2 vols, 1829), *Memoirs of Celebrated Female Sovereigns* (1831); *Characteristics of Women*, a study of Shakespeare's heroines (2 vols, 1832), *Visits and Sketches at Home and Abroad* (1834), and *Winter Sketches and Summer Rambles in Canada* (1838). The publications of the later part of her life were mostly on the subject of art or on feminist issues.

See: Erskine (1915); Thomas (1967)

Jewsbury, Maria Jane, later Fletcher (1800-33)

Born and educated in Derbyshire, she moved with her family to Manchester in 1818. Her *Phantasmagoria; or, Sketches of Life and Literature*, a collection of prose and verse, was published in two volumes in 1825. The dedication to Wordsworth brought her into contact with the poet and his family, whom she visited on numerous occasions. Her collection of poems, *Lays of Leisure Hours* (1829) was dedicated to *Felicia Hemans, and she also published a popular advice manual, *Letters to the Young* (1828). Her *Three Histories* (1830) went into three editions. She contributed to numerous annuals and periodicals, including reviews and articles for *The Athenaeum* in 1831. She married the Reverend William Fletcher, a chaplain of the East India Company, in 1832, travelled with him to India, and died of cholera in Poona fourteen months later at the age of 33.

See: Gillet (1932); Clarke (1990); Ashfield (1995)

Lamb, Lady Caroline, née Ponsonby (1785-1828)

Only daughter of Frederick Ponsonby, 3rd Earl of Bessborough, she was married at 20 to William Lamb (later to become Prime Minister Lord Melbourne). Her only child was born mentally retarded, and died at the age of 29. Her meeting with Byron in 1812 led to a brief and passionate affair lasting for about a year. When Byron ended the relationship, she reacted with such violence that her husband sought a legal separation, although the couple were finally reconciled. She published *Glenarvon*, a fictionalised account of Byron and his circle, in 1816. In 1819, following the publication of Byron's *Don Juan*, she parodied his work in *A New Canto* (1819). Two more novels followed, *Graham Hamilton* (1822) and *Ada Reis* (1823). Her precarious mental balance was finally overturned by a chance meeting with Byron's funeral procession in 1824, and this led to her husband's final separation from her. She died from dropsy at the age of 42.

See: Jenkins (1932); Blyth (1972)

Lamb, Mary Ann (1764–1847)
Born in London, the elder sister of Charles Lamb, she stabbed her mother to death in a fit of madness in 1796. The court brought in a verdict of temporary insanity and she was given into the care of her brother Charles where she remained throughout her life, spending short periods in mental institutions whenever her mental condition deteriorated, which happened with increasing frequency as she grew older. In 1807 they jointly prepared and published the hugely successful *Tales from Shakespeare*, although Mary's name did not appear on the title page despite the fact that she had written most of the tales based on the comedies. She published a collection of educational tales, *Mrs Leicester's School*, in 1809, and, together with Charles, *Poetry for Children* in the same year. Her essay *'On Needlework' appeared in the *British Ladies' Magazine* in April 1815. She survived her brother by thirteen years.
    See: T. Hutchinson (1924); Marrs (1975–8); Gilchrist (1883); Aaron (1991)

Landon, Laetitia Elizabeth ('L.E.L.'), later Maclean (1802–38)
Born and educated in London, she began publishing in the *Literary Gazette* in 1820, and her first volume, *The Fate of Adelaide*, appeared the following year. She was a prolific writer, going on to publish six more volumes of poetry. She also wrote a number of novels, including the historical *Ethel Churchill* (1837), edited and contributed to *Fisher's Drawing Room Scrapbook* (1832–8), *Heath's Book of Beauty* (1833) and the *New Juvenile Keepsake* (1838). Her earnings at the peak of her career were estimated at over £2500, enough to support her mother and brother in separate households and to buy her brother a clerical living. Her personal life was surrounded by gossip and scandal, and a rumoured affair put an end to her engagement to Dickens's future biographer John Forster. Shortly afterwards she married George Maclean, Governor of Cape Coast Castle (now Ghana). She travelled to Africa after her marriage in July 1838, and in October of the same year was found dead in her room, a bottle of prussic acid in her hand. Accidental death, suicide and murder have all been put forward as possible causes. Her popularity remained high throughout the nineteenth century, with many collections of her work appearing posthumously.
    See: Blanchard (1841); Ashton (1936); Leighton (1992); Ashfield (1995)

Lickbarrow, Isabella (*fl.* 1814)
Born in Kendal in humble circumstances, early orphaned and self-educated, she began writing poetry at an early age. Her *Poetical Effusions* (Kendal, 1814) was published with subscribers including Wordsworth and Southey. Her only other recorded work, apart from poems in magazines and anthologies, was *Lament* (Liverpool, 1818).
    See: Jonathan Wordsworth (ed.) *Poetical Effusions* (Woodstock, 1994)

Lister, Anne (1791–1840)
Born at Shibden Hall, near Halifax, which she inherited in 1826, she determinedly educated herself in a number of subjects including classical literature. Her *diaries, kept from 1817, run to over two million words and are partly in code. They record her day-to-day life, including her successful management of her estate, her views on politics and social change, but also her lesbian fantasies and love affairs. She travelled widely in later life, spent a considerable time in Paris, visited the Ladies of Llangollen, went pot-holing and mountaineering, and died of plague in Georgia. Her selected letters have been edited by M. Green (1992).

See: MSS in Halifax Central Library; *Transactions of Halifax Antiquarian Society*; Whitbread (1992)

Macaulay, Catharine, *née* Sawbridge, later Graham (1731–91)
She came of wealthy and well-established Whig stock, and became an important and influential figure in the field of radical politics in the second half of the eighteenth century. Her eight-volume *History of England from the Accession of James I to that of the Brunswick Line* (1763–83) played a part in forming the basis of the political ideology of the American Revolution. She was much denigrated when, at the age of 41, she married William Graham, who was twenty years her junior, but the marriage, like her first, seems to have been a happy one. Her last major work was *Letters on Education* (1790), a work which influenced *Mary Wollstonecraft's *Rights of Woman* (1792).
See: Hill (1992)

Martineau, Harriet (1802–76)
Born in Norwich, into a leading Unitarian family, she suffered from chronic ill-health and deafness for most of her life. Her first publication was the essay *'On Female Education', published in the *Monthly Repository* in 1822. This was followed by a collection of moral tales, *Illustrations of Political Economy* (1832–4). Her *Society in America* (1837) and *A Retrospect of Western Travel* (1838) criticised American society, which she had experienced during a tour a few years earlier. She began writing fiction with *Deerbrook* (1839), and subsequently published *The Hour and the Man* (1841), *The Playfellow* (1841) and *Forest and Game-Law Tales* (1845–6). She settled in Ambleside, where she became a friend of Wordsworth's, in 1844. She published the radical *History of England 1816–1846* in 1848–50 and, having lost her religious faith, the anti-theological *Laws of Man's Nature* in 1851. She was a prolific writer for periodicals, and some of her articles were published as *Biographical Sketches* in 1867. Her *Autobiography*, written in 1855, was published posthumously in 1877.
See: Sanders (1990); Mineka (1944); Webb (1960); Pichanick (1980); Sanders (1986)

More, Hannah (1745–1833)
Born in Bristol, she learned Latin and mathematics from her schoolmaster father and modern languages at a school run by her sisters. She began her literary career with various dramatic works, but turned increasingly to moral and religious subjects. The first of her many educational and moral works was *Slavery: A Poem* (1788). Her concern with the poor and the lower classes led to her writing of a number of anti-Revolutionary tracts in the 1790s, collected as *Cheap Repository Tracts* in 1795–6, which sold two million copies in its first year of publication. She opposed all forms of radicalism, including *Mary Wollstonecraft's *Rights of Woman* (1792), although her own *Strictures on the Modern System of Education* (1799) made a moderate plea for educational reform where women were concerned. Her only novel was the moralistic, but popular, *Coelebs in Search of a Wife* (1808). Her poem on the abolition of slavery, *The Feast of Freedom* (1819) was set to music by Charles Wesley. Her last prose work was *Moral Sketches* (1819).
See: Roberts (1834); Mitzi Myers in Schofield and Macheski (eds) (1986); Lonsdale (1989); Kathryn Sutherland in Everest (1991); Ashfield (1995)

Opie, Amelia, *née* Alderson (1769-1853)
Born in Norwich, daughter of a radical Unitarian physician, she began publishing poetry in newspapers and magazines in her teens, and her first novel, *The Dangers of Coquetry*, in 1790. On a visit to London in 1794 she was introduced to the radical circle including *Mary Wollstonecraft, for whom she developed a profound admiration. In 1798 she married the divorced portrait painter John Opie. Her second novel, *The Father and Daughter*, appeared in 1801, and her popular and often reprinted *Poems* in 1802. Her best remembered novel is *Adeline Mowbray* (1805), which is loosely based on the life of Wollstonecraft but concludes that her anti-matrimonial views were flawed. She became a Quaker in 1825, after which she published only improving works. She died at the age of 84.
    See: Spencer (1986); Ashfield (1995)

Owenson, Sydney, later Lady Morgan (1776-1859)
The daughter of an Irish actor, she was born and educated in Dublin. Her first publication was *Poems* (1801), followed by *Twelve Original Hibernian Melodies* (1805). She also wrote fiction, and her third novel, *The Wild Irish Girl* (1806), brought her considerable success. She continued to write on Irish themes, publishing *The Lay of an Irish Harp* (1807), and several Irish novels, including *O'Donnel: A National Tale* (1814), *Florence McCarthy* (1818) and *The O'Briens and the O'Flahertys* (1827), all of which were attacked by Tory reviewers for their strong Irish nationalist views. She published several travel books on France, Italy and Belgium, collected her articles from the *New Monthly Magazine* as *Absenteeism* (1827), and a series of essays and sketches as *The Book of the Boudoir* (2 vols, 1829). An important late work, arguing for the equality (or superiority) of women, was *Woman and her Master* (1840). She married Sir Charles Morgan in 1812, and died in London at the age of 76. Her *Memoirs*, ed. H. Dixon, appeared in 1862.
    See: Fitzpatrick (1860); Stevenson (1936); Campbell (1988); Newcomer (1990); Jeanne Moskal in Feldman and Kelley (1995); Richard C. Sha in Feldman and Kelley (1995)

Piozzi, Hester Lynch, *née* Salusbury (1741-1821)
Born in Wales, she was brought up by her father's brother Sir Thomas Salusbury in Herefordshire. She learned Latin and modern languages, and was publishing articles in *St James's Chronicle* at the age of 15. Married against her wishes to Henry Thrale in 1763, she bore twelve children of whom only four survived to adulthood. The Thrales became close friends with Samuel Johnson. Henry Thrale died in 1781, leaving his wife financially independent. Three years later she caused a scandal by marrying an Italian Roman Catholic musician, Gabriel Piozzi. The Piozzis moved to Italy, where she wrote and published her well-known *Anecdotes of the Late Samuel Johnson* (1786) and began work on her edition of Johnson's letters (1788). The couple returned to England in 1788. She published *Observations and Reflections made in the Course of a Journey through France, Italy and Germany* in 1789, and *British Synonymy* in 1794. Her last published work was a world history, *Retrospection* (1801). Piozzi died in 1809. *Thraliana*, her journals and poetry from 1776 to 1809, was edited by K. C. Balderson and published in 1942.

See: Edward and L. Bloom (1989–); Clifford (1941; 2nd edn 1968); Mc Carthy (1985)

Radcliffe, Ann, née Ward (1764–1823)
Brought up in Bath, she married lawyer and journalist William Radcliffe in 1787. She published two early novels, *The Castles of Athlin and Dunbayne* (1789) and *A Sicilian Romance* (1790), but is celebrated for her three hugely successful Gothic novels, *The Romance of the Forest* (1791), *The Mysteries of Udolpho* (1794) and *The Italian* (1797), for the last two of which she received the remarkably high payments of £500 and £800. Her last novel, *Gaston de Blonville*, written in 1802, was not published until after her death in 1826. She also published a travel book, *A Journey Made . . . through Holland and . . . Germany*, in 1794. She also wrote poetry, some of it contained in her novels, much of which appeared in her *Posthumous Works* (4 vols, 1833) and *Poetical Works* (1834). Her essay *'On the Supernatural in Poetry' appeared after her death in the *New Monthly Magazine*.
  See: Lonsdale (1989); Mellor (1993); Ashfield (1995)

Radcliffe, Mary Ann (c. 1746–post 1810)
Born in Scotland, she secretly married (at 14) the Catholic Joseph Radcliffe, whose alcoholism and business failures rapidly depleted her inherited fortune. Eventually, in order to support her eight children, she worked as a housekeeper and companion, a governess, a shopkeeper and a schoolmistress. Her *The Female Advocate* (1799) was a bitter response to her personal difficulties. She republished it as part of her *Memoirs . . . in Familiar Letters to her Female Friend* (1810). She also wrote at least three novels, *The Fate of Velinda* (1790), *Radzivil* (1790) and the Gothic *Manfrone; or the One-Handed Monk* (1810), which was initially declined by the publishers Minerva Press, as too violent and sexually explicit. She also edited a publication specialising in Gothic tales, *Radcliffe's New Novelist's Pocket Magazine*, for a short period in 1802.
  See: Howells (1978); Ferguson (1985); Jones (1990); Mellor (1993)

Reeve, Clara (1729–1807)
Rigorously educated by her father, a Suffolk vicar, she started publishing relatively late in life with *Original Poems on Several Occasions* (1769). She translated John Barclay's Latin novel *Argenis* (1621) and published it as *The Phoenix* (1772). Her best known work is her Gothic novel *The Old English Baron*, first published in 1777 as *The Champion of Virtue: A Gothic Story*. This was followed by two epistolary novels, *The Two Mentors* (1783) and *The Exiles* (1788), and another Gothic novel, *Memoirs of Sir Roger de Clarendon* (1793). Her non-fictional prose included a critique of the novel, *The Progress of Romance* (1785), and the didactic educational conduct books, *The School for Widows* (1791) and *Plans of Education* (1792).
  See Jones (1990); Ferguson (1985)

Robinson, Mary, née Darby (1758–1800)
Born in Bristol, she was initially educated at the school run by *Hannah More's sisters. At 16 she married Thomas Robinson. In 1775 her husband was imprisoned for debt, and she spent ten months in prison with her infant daughter, during which she wrote and published *Poems* (1775). She became an actress at Drury Lane the follow-

ing year. In 1780, her performance as Perdita attracted the attention of the Prince of Wales (later George IV), who offered her £20,000 to become his mistress. He failed to pay the bond after the relationship failed a year later, and the ensuing scandal ended her acting career. She formed a relationship with Colonel Banestre Tarleton the following year, which lasted until 1798 when he married an heiress. Her health never recovered fully from a miscarriage suffered some time in the 1780s, which left her partially crippled. Her very large number of publications included, in poetry, *Poems* (1791), *Modern Manners* (1793), **Sappho and Phaon* (1796), and *Lyrical Tales* (1800). She also wrote a number of successful novels, including *Vancenza* (1792), *The Widow* (1794), *Herbert de Sevrac* (1796), *Walsingham* (1797) and *The Natural Daughter* (1799). A friend of *Mary Wollstonecraft, whose radical views she shared, she published **A Letter to the Women of England, on the Injustice of Mental Subordination* in 1799 under the name Anne Frances Randall. She died at the age of 42.

See: Mackower (1908); Bass (1957); Curran (1988); Lonsdale (1989); Ashfield (1994); Judith Pascoe in Feldman and Kelley (1995)

Seward, Anna (1742–1809)

Her father, with whom she lived for most of her life, was a Canon of Lichfield Cathedral. She began publishing poetry in the *Gentleman's Magazine*, and became well known as a poet following her elegy on Captain Cook (1780), her *Monody on the unfortunate Major Andre* (1781) and *Louisa: A Poetical Novel* (1782). Celebrated as 'the Swan of Lichfield', she became prominent in literary circles, both in the Midlands and in London, but she disliked and disapproved of the writings and politics of her female contemporaries. Her *Llangollen Vale* (1796) was written after a visit to *Lady Eleanor Butler and Sarah Ponsonby. She also published **Original Sonnets* (1799), and *Memoirs on the Life of Dr Darwin* (1804). Her posthumous *Poetical Works* (3 vols, Edinburgh, 1810) were edited by Sir Walter Scott.

See: Pearson (1936); Lonsdale (1989); Ashfield (1995)

Shelley, Mary, *née* Godwin (1797–1851)

Daughter of William Godwin and of *Mary Wollstonecraft, who died ten days after her birth. She eloped to the continent with the poet Shelley in 1814, accompanied by her step-sister *Claire Clairmont, and published an account of their journey as **History of a Six Weeks Tour* in 1817. She married Shelley after his first wife committed suicide in 1816, by whom she had four children, only one of whom, Percy, survived. Her most famous work is *Frankenstein; or The Modern Prometheus*, begun when she was 18 and published in 1818. After Shelley's death in 1822 she largely supported herself and her son, managing to send him to Harrow and Cambridge, by writing. She wrote several other novels, including *Valperga* (1823), *The Last Man* (1826), *Lodore* (1835) and *Falkner* (1837), contributed a number of stories to annuals and periodicals, and contributed to Lardner's *Cabinet Cyclopedia*. Her important editions of Shelley's *Poetical Works* (1839) and of his *Essays, Letters from Abroad, Translations and Fragments* (1840) remain standard today. Her last major work was *Rambles in Germany and Italy* (1844). She never remarried, and died in London at the age of 53.

See: Bennett (1980–8); Feldman and Kilvert (1987), Crook (1995–); Moers (1977); Poovey (1984); Mellor (1988); Alexander (1989); Blumberg (1993); Stephen Behrendt in Feldman and Kelley (1995)

Smith, Charlotte, *née* Turner (1749–1806)

Born in London, she was married at 15 to Benjamin Smith who proved to be a feckless and extravagant husband. She gave birth to twelve children, to whom her father-in-law left his estate on his death in 1776, but the complications of his will led to a lifetime of legal tussles in an attempt to gain access to the money. Her husband was imprisoned for debt in 1783 and, forced into the position of breadwinner for the family, she put to use an early talent for poetry. Her *Elegaic Sonnets and Other Essays* (1784) was an immediate success, going through eight editions by the end of the century, and Smith won an enduring reputation as a poet. Her long blank-verse poem *The Emigrants* (1792) indicates the change which her early Revolutionary sympathies underwent as a result of the excesses of the French Revolution. She also published a number of successful novels, among them *Emmeline* (1788), *Ethelinde* (1789); *Celestina* (1791); *Desmond* (1792); and *The Old Manor House* (1793). Her collection of tales, *Letters of a Solitary Wanderer*, appeared in 1799, and she wrote several children's books. Her *Beachy Head* was published posthumously in 1807.

See: Curran (1988); *Poems of Charlotte Smith*, ed Stuart Curran (1993)

Taylor, Jane (1783–1824)

Born in Ongar, Essex, she and her sister Ann jointly produced the highly successful *Original Poems for Infant Minds* (2 vols, 1804–6), *Rhymes for the Nursery* (1806) (which included her best-known poem, 'Twinkle twinkle little star') and *Hymns for Infant Minds* (1810), as well as other collections of children's tales and verse. After her sister's marriage in 1813, she continued to write and publish on her own, publishing *Display: A Tale for Young People* in 1815 and her most important work, *Essays in Rhyme on Morals and Manners* in 1816. She contributed essays to *Youth's Magazine* from 1816 to 1822, collected and published as *Contributions of QQ* in 1824. Her *Memoirs and Correspondence* were published posthumously in 1825, following her death from cancer at the age of 40.

See: Knight (1880); Armitage (1975); Curran (1988)

Tighe, Mary, *née* Blachford (1772–1810)

Born in Dublin, the daughter of a wealthy Irish clergyman who died soon after her birth, she was comprehensively educated by her well-connected mother. She married her cousin, Henry Tighe, who was a historian and poet as well as Member of the Irish Parliament, when she was 20, but the marriage was not a happy one. She began writing poetry after developing tuberculosis, and her *Psyche; or the Legend of Love* was printed privately in 1805. It appeared as *Psyche; with other Poems* in 1811, following her early death at the age of 38. The poem was much admired and probably influenced Keats.

See: Weller (1928); Henchy (1957)

Trollope, Frances (Fanny), *née* Milton (1780–1863)

The daughter of a West Country vicar, she married the unsuccessful barrister Thomas Anthony Trollope in 1809. Her husband's financial mismanagement led her to attempt to support herself and her seven children (among them the future novelist Anthony Trollope) by opening a department store in Cincinnati, Ohio. When this venture failed she turned to writing, and her *Domestic Manners of the Americans (1832) brought her instant literary fame. She wrote three more travel books, none as successful as her first, and contributed stories to annuals and periodicals. Following her husband's death in 1835 she began writing fiction and produced a total of thirty-five novels, the best known of which are The Vicar of Wrexhill (1837), The Widow Barnaby (1839) and Life and Adventures of Michael Armstrong, the Factory Boy, an early industrial novel (1840), before her death in Florence at the age of 83.

See: A. Trollope (1883); F. E. Trollope (1895); Heineman (1979); Johnston (1979)

Wakefield, Priscilla, née Bell (1751-1832)

Born into an eminent Quaker family, married to a London merchant, the mother of three children, she spent her early married life engaged in various philanthropic endeavours. She turned to writing in the 1790s, producing a number of educational books on natural history and travel for children. Many were highly successful: Juvenile Anecdotes (2 vols, 1795-8) appeared in eight editions; The Juvenile Travellers (1801) in nineteen editions; and An Introduction to Botany in eleven. Her only work for adults was *Reflections on the Present Condition of the Female Sex (1798), which argued in favour of training women in professions such as science, teaching, portrait-painting, and farming.

See: Jones (1990); Ferguson (1985)

West, Jane, née Iliffe (1758-1852)

Born in Northamptonshire, she was entirely self-educated. She married a farmer, Thomas West, and was the mother of three sons. Her first publication was Miscellaneous Poetry (1786), followed by Miscellaneous Poems and a Tragedy (1791). Her conservative politics are evident in her novels, which include The Advantages of Education (1793), A Gossip's Story (1796), and A Tale of the Times (1799). She also wrote educational works, including Letters to a Young Man (1801) and *Letters to a Young Lady (3 vols, 1806). Her Poems and Plays were published in four volumes between 1799 and 1805. She survived her husband for nearly thirty years, and died, aged 96, in the village she had lived in for her entire adult life.

See: Butler (1975); P. M. Spacks in Schofield and Macheski (1986); Lonsdale (1989); Ashfield (1995)

Williams, Helen Maria (?1761-1827)

Brought up and educated in Scotland, she moved to London in 1781. Her first poem, Edwin and Eltrude, published the following year, brought her immediate success. It was followed by An Ode on the Peace (1783), Peru (1784), Collected Poems (1786), Poems (1791) and Poem on the Slave Bill (1788). Her radical opinions were evident in this last work, and also in her novel Julia (1790). Her enthusiasm for the Revolution led her to visit France in the summer of 1790 and to her hugely successful *Letters Written in France in the Summer of 1790 (1790), which was expanded to four volumes as Letters from France (1792-6). She settled in Paris, where she entertained English sympathisers including *Mary Wollstonecraft, and was imprisoned briefly in

1793. Her reputation was badly damaged by her liaison with John Hurford Stone. She published many books about France, including *Sketches of the State of Manners . . . in the French Republic* (1801), *Narrative of Events . . . in France* (1815) and *Letters on Events . . . since the Restoration* (1819). She also continued to publish poetry, producing *Poems on Various Subjects* in 1823. After Stone's death in 1818 she moved to Amsterdam, and died in Paris in 1827.

See: Woodward (1930); Mellor (1993); Kelly (1993); Richard C. Sha in Feldman and Kelley (1995)

Wilson, Harriette (1788–1846)
Daughter of John James Dubouchet, a Mayfair shopkeeper, she supported herself for many years as a courtesan. She moved to Paris in c. 1820, but returned to London to publish her *Memoirs*, which went through numerous 'editions', in 1825. The last years of her life were lived in obscurity, probably in France.

See: Laver (1927); Blanch (1955)

Wollstonecraft, Mary, later Godwin (1759–97)
Born in London, and largely self-educated. Her father dissipated his inheritance and she was forced to support herself from the age of 18, working at various times as a lady's companion, needleworker and governess before setting up a school with her two sisters in Newington Green. Her *Thoughts on the Education of Daughters* (1787) brought her into contact with the radical publisher Joseph Johnson, who later published her novel *Mary: A Fiction* (1788) and *Original Stories from Real Life* (1789). Johnson employed her as a translator, and as a reviewer on his newly established *Analytical Review*. Her first major work was *A Vindication of the Rights of Men* (1790), a radical response to Burke's *Reflections on the Revolution in France*. Two years later she published her celebrated *Vindication of the Rights of Woman* (1792), after which she travelled to France and took up residence in Paris. While there she wrote *An Historical and Moral View of the . . . French Revolution* (1794), and also lived unmarried with an American, Gilbert Imlay, by whom she gave birth to a daughter, Fanny, in 1794. Imlay became increasingly distant and she followed him back to London to find he had entered into another relationship, after which she made two suicide attempts. She also made a business trip to Scandinavia on Imlay's behalf, after which she published her *Letters Written . . . in Sweden* (1796). After she finally acknowledged that her relationship with Imlay was over, she renewed an acquaintance with the philosopher and novelist William Godwin. When their liaison resulted in her pregnancy, they married, in March 1797, although keeping separate houses in the same street. She died of a puerperal fever as a result of the birth of their daughter *Mary Wollstonecraft Godwin (later Shelley) in September 1797. Godwin published her *Posthumous Works* and his *Memoir* in 1798. Her reputation suffered badly from his well-meaning revelations of her private life, and her importance to feminism and the history of ideas of her period was not fully recognised until the twentieth century.

See: Wardle (1979); Todd and Butler (1989); Tomalin (1974); Poovey (1984); Alexander (1989); Kelly (1992); Jump (1994)

Wordsworth, Dorothy (1771–1855)
Born in Cockermouth, Cumbria, she was the younger sister of the poet William Wordsworth, from whom she was separated at an early age owing to the deaths of

both their parents. She was brought up by relatives before being reunited with her brother in 1794. They set up house together in Dorset in 1795 and moved to Somerset in 1797, where she began writing her *journal in 1798. They travelled to Germany at the end of that year, and in 1799 set up house in Dove Cottage, Grasmere. She never married, remaining in her brother's household after his marriage and helping with the care of the children. She continued to write journals, accounts of various journeys in Scotland and abroad, and occasional poems, though she had a 'horror of appearing in public as an author'. Her health deteriorated in 1829 and the final years of her life were spent suffering from Alzheimer's disease, with occasional periods of lucidity, under the care of her brother and his family.

See: Poovey (1984); Levin (1987); Alexander (1989); Mellor (1993)

Yearsley, Ann, *née* Cromartie (1752–1806)
Her father was a farm labourer, and her mother had a milk-round which she later took over. Her brother taught her to read and write. She married John Yearsley, an illiterate farm labourer, in 1774, and had six children, one of whom died. In the little time she had after work, housework and child-care duties were finished, she read, and wrote poetry. *Hannah More arranged for the publication of her *Poems on Several Occasions* (1785) with more than 1000 subscribers. More invested the proceeds, believing financial gain rendered the working classes unfit for their traditional role in society. After much acrimony, Yearsley obtained the money. She later published *Poems on Various Subjects* (1787), *Poem on the Inhumanity of the Slave Trade* (1788), *Stanzas of Woe* (1790). Her *Earl Goodwin; A Tragedy* was produced in both Bath and Bristol in 1791. She published a historical novel, *The Royal Captives*, in 1796, and her final volume of poetry, *The Rural Lyre*, in 1796. She enjoyed considerable popularity in her heyday, but after a brief period running a circulating library her health failed and her final years were spent reclusively in Wiltshire.

See: Landry (1990); Lonsdale (1989); Ashfield (1995)

BIBLIOGRAPHY

References

Aaron, Jane (1991), *A Double Singleness: Gender and the Writings of Charles and Mary Lamb*, Oxford: Clarendon Press.

Alexander, Meena (1989), *Women in Romanticism: Mary Wollstonecraft, Dorothy Wordsworth, and Mary Shelley*, Towota, N.J.: Barnes & Noble.

Armitage, D. M. (1975), *The Taylors of Ongar*, London: W. Heffer & Sons Ltd.

Ashfield, Anthony (ed.) (1995), *Romantic Women Poets 1770–1838: An Anthology*, Manchester and New York: Manchester University Press.

Ashton, H. (1951), *Letty Landon*, London: Collins.

Bass. R. D. (1957), *The Green Dragoon*, New York: Holt.

Bedford, W. K. R. (1889), *Three Hundred Years of a Family Living: Being the History of the Rilands of Sutton Coldfield*, Birmingham: Cornish Brothers.

Benger, E. O. (ed.) (1818), *Memoirs of Mrs Elizabeth Hamilton with Selections from her Correspondence and Unpublished Writings*, London: Longman, Hurst, Rees, Orme & Brown.

Bennett, Betty T. (ed.) (1980–8), *Letters of Mary Wollstonecraft Shelley*, 3 vols, Baltimore: Johns Hopkins University Press.

Blanch, Lesley (1955), *The Game of Hearts: Harriette Wilson and her Memoirs*, London: Century.

Blanchard, S. L. (1841), *Life and Literary Remains of L.E.L*, 2 vols, London: Colburn.

Blumberg, J. (1993), *Mary Shelley's Early Novels*, Basingstoke: Macmillan.

Blyth, H. (1972), *Caro: The Fatal Passion*, London: Hart-Davis.

Boaden, James (1833), *Memoirs of Mrs Inchbald*, London: Bentley.

Breen, Jennifer (1992), *Women Romantic Poets*, London: Everyman.

Butler, M. (1972), *Maria Edgeworth*, Oxford: Clarendon Press.

Butler, M. (1975; repr. 1987), *Jane Austen and the War of Ideas*, Oxford: Oxford University Press.

Campbell, M. (1988), *Lady Morgan*, London: Pandora.

Carhart, S. M. (1923, repr. 1970), *Life and Work of Joanna Baillie*, London: Oxford University Press.

Chorley, H. F. (1836), *Memorials of Mrs Hemans*, London: Saunders & Otley.

Clarke, Norma (1990), *Ambitious Heights: Writing, Friendship, Love: The Jewsbury Sisters, Felicia Hemans, and Jane Welsh Carlyle*, London & New York: Routledge.

Clifford, J. L. (1941; 2nd edn 1968; repr. 1987), *Hester Lynch Piozzi*, Oxford: Clarendon Press.

Crook, N. (ed.) (1995–), *Works of Mary Wollstonecraft Shelley*, London: Pickering and Chatto.
Cumberland, R. (1807), *Memoirs*, London: Lackington, Allen & Co.
Curran, Stuart (1988), 'Romantic Poetry: The I Altered', in Anne K. Mellor (ed.), *Romanticism and Feminism*, Bloomington, Indiana: Indiana University Press.
Curran, Stuart (ed.) (1993), *Poems of Charlotte Smith*, Oxford: Oxford University Press.
Edward, A. and Lillian D. Bloom (1989–), *The Piozzi Letters: Correspondence of Hester Lynch Piozzi, 1784–1821*, London: Associated University Presses.
Edwards, M. Betham (1880), *Six Life Studies of Famous Women*, London: Griffith & Farran.
Erskine, Mrs S. (1915), *Anna Jameson: Letters and Friendships 1812–60*, London: Unwin.
Everest, Kelvin (ed.) (1991), *Revolution in Writing: British Literary Responses to the French Revolution*, Milton Keynes: Open University Press.
Feldman, P. R. and D. Scott Kilvert (eds) (1987), *Journals of Mary Wollstonecraft Shelley*, 2 vols, Oxford: Clarendon Press.
Feldman, Paula R. and Theresa M. Kelley (eds) (1995), *Romantic Women Writers: Voices and Countervoices*, Hanover, N.H. and London: University Press of New England.
Ferguson, Moira (ed.) (1985), *The First Feminists: British Women Writers 1578–1799*, Bloomington, Indiana: Indiana University Press.
Fitzpatrick, W. J. (1860), *Lady Morgan*, London: Skeet.
Gilchrist, A. (1883), *Mary Lamb: A Biography*, London: Allen & Co.
Gillett, E. (ed.) (1932), *Maria Jane Jewsbury: Occasional Papers*, Oxford: Oxford University Press.
Gittings, Robert and Jo Manton (1995), *Claire Clairmont and the Shelleys*, Oxford: Oxford University Press.
Grant, J. P. (ed.) (1844), *Memoirs and Correspondence of Mrs Grant of Laggan*, London: Longman, Brown, Green & Longman.
Hare, A. J. C. (1894), *Life and Letters of Maria Edgeworth*, London: Arnold.
Heineman, H. (1979), *Mrs Trollope: The Triumphant Feminine in the 19th Century*, Athens, O.: Ohio University Press.
Henchy, P. (1957), *The Works of Mary Tighe*, Dublin: Bibliographic Society of Ireland.
Hill, Bridget (1992), *The Republican Virago: The Life and Times of Catharine Macaulay, Historian*, Oxford: Clarendon Press.
Homans, Margaret (1980), *Women Writers and Poetic Identity*, Princeton, N.J.: Princeton University Press.
Howells, C. A. (1978), *Love, Mystery and Misery: Feeling in Gothic Fiction*, London: Athlone Press.
Hughes, Harriet (ed.) (1839), *Works of Mrs Hemans*.
Hutchinson, T. (ed.) (1924), *The Works of Charles and Mary Lamb*, London: Oxford University Press.
Jenkins, E. (1932 repr. 1972, 1974), *Lady Caroline Lamb*, London: Gollancz.
Johnston, J. (1979), *Fanny Trollope*, London: Alan Sutton.
Jones, Vivien (1990), *Women in the Eighteenth Century: Constructions of Femininity*, London and New York: Routledge.
Jump, H. D. (1994), *Mary Wollstonecraft: Writer*, Hemel Hempstead: Harvester.
Kelly, Gary (1992), *Revolutionary Feminism: The Mind and Career of Mary Wollstonecraft*, Basingstoke: Macmillan.

Kelly, Gary (1993), *Women, Writing, and Revolution 1790–1827*, Oxford: Clarendon Press.

Knight, H. C. (1880), *Jane Taylor: Her Life and Letters*, London: Nelson.

Kowaleski-Wallace, Elizabeth (1991), *Their Fathers' Daughters: Hannah More, Maria Edgeworth and Patriarchal Complicity*, New York: Oxford University Press.

Landry, Donna (1990), *Muses of Resistance: Labouring Class Women's Poetry in Britain 1739–1796*, Cambridge: Cambridge University Press.

Laver, James (ed.) (1927), *Harriette Wilson's Memoirs*, London: P. Davies.

Le Breton, P. H. (1864), *Memoirs, Miscellanies, Letters of Lucy Aikin*, London: Longman, Green, Longman, Roberts & Green.

Leighton, Angela (1992), *Victorian Women Poets: Writing Against the Heart*, Hemel Hempstead: Harvester Wheatsheaf Press.

Levin, Susan (1987), *Dorothy Wordsworth*, New Brunswick, N.J.: Rutgers University Press.

Linkin, Harriet (1991), 'The Current Canon in British Romantic Studies', *College English*, 53.

Lonsdale, Roger (ed.) (1989), *Eighteenth Century Women Poets: An Oxford Anthology*, Oxford: Oxford University Press.

McCarthy, W. (1985), *Hester Thrale Piozzi*, Chapel Hill, N.C.: University of North Carolina Press.

McCarthy, W. and Elizabeth Kraft (eds) (1994), *Anna Laetitia Barbauld: Poems*, Athens, Ga.: University of Georgia Press.

McGann, Jerome (1993), *Romantic Period Poetry*, Oxford: Oxford University Press.

McKee, W. (1935), *Elizabeth Inchbald: Novelist*, Washington, D.C.: Catholic University of America.

Mackower, S. V. (1908), *Perdita*, London: Hutchinson.

Madden, R. R. (1855), *Literary Life and Correspondence of the Countess of Blessington* London: Newby.

Marrs, E. W. (ed.) (1975–8), *The Letters of Charles and Mary Lamb*, Ithaca, N.Y. and London: Cornell University Press.

Mavor, Elizabeth (1971), *The Ladies of Llangollen: A Study in Romantic Friendship*, London: Michael Joseph.

Mellor, A. K. (1988), *Mary Shelley: Her Life, Her Fiction and Her Monsters*, London: Methuen.

Mellor, Anne K. (ed.) (1988), *Romanticism and Feminism*, Bloomington, Indiana: Indiana University Press.

Mellor, Anne K. (1993), *Romanticism and Gender*, New York and London: Routledge.

Mineka, F. E. (1944), *The Dissidence of Dissent: The Monthly Repository 1806–1838*, Chapel Hill, N.C.: University of North Carolina Press.

Moers, Ellen (1977), *Literary Women*, Garden City, N.Y.: Anchor Books.

More, Hannah (1799), *Strictures on the Modern System of Female Education*, 2 vols, London: Cadell and Davis.

Murphy, M. M. (1988), *Women Writers and Australia*, Melbourne: University of Melbourne Library.

Newcomer, J. (1990), *Lady Morgan the Novelist*, London: Associated University Presses.

Pearson, H. (1936), *The Swan of Lichfield*, London: Hamish Hamilton.

Pichanik, V. K. (1980), *Harriet Martineau: The Woman and her Work*, Ann Arbor, Mich.: University of Michigan Press/London: Heinemann.

Polwhele, Richard (1798), *The Unsexed Females*, London: Cadell & Davies.

Poovey, Mary (1984), *The Proper Lady and the Woman Writer: Ideology as Style in the Works of Mary Wollstonecraft, Jane Austen and Dorothy Wordsworth*, Chicago and London: University of Chicago Press.

Roberts, W. (1834), *Memoirs of the Life and Correspondence of Hannah More*, London: Seeley.

Rodgers, B. (1958), *Georgian Chronicle: Mrs Barbauld and her Family*, London: Methuen.

Ross, Marlon (1989), *The Contours of Masculine Desire: Romanticism and the Rise of Women's Poetry*, Oxford and New York: Oxford University Press.

Sanders, V. (1986), *Reason over Passion: Harriet Martineau and the Victorian Novel*, Brighton: Harvester.

Sanders, V. (ed.) (1990), *Harriet Martineau: Selected Letters*, Oxford: Clarendon Press.

Schofield, M. A. and C. Macheski (eds) (1988), *Fetter'd or Free? British Women Novelists 1670–1815*, Athens, O.: Ohio University Press.

Schofield, M. A. and C. Macheski (eds) (1991), *Curtain Calls: British and American Women in the Theatre 1660–1820*, Athens, O.: Ohio University Press.

Spencer, Jane (1986), *The Rise of the Woman Novelist*, Oxford: Blackwell.

Stevenson, L. (1936), *The Wild Irish Girl*, London: Chapman & Hall.

Thomas, C. (1967), *Love and Work Enough: The Life of Anna Jameson*, London: Macdonald.

Todd, J. M. (1989), *The Sign of Angelica*, London: Virago.

Todd, J. M. and M. Butler (eds) (1989), *Works of Mary Wollstonecraft*, 7 vols, London: Pickering and Chatto.

Tomalin, Claire (1974), *Life and Death of Mary Wollstonecraft*, Harmondsworth: Penguin.

Trinder, Peter (1984), *Mrs Hemans*, Cardiff: University of Wales Press.

Trollope, A. (1883), *Autobiography*, Edinburgh: Blackwood.

Trollope, F. E. (1895), *Frances Trollope*, London: Bentley.

Wardle, R. M. (ed.) (1979), *Letters of Mary Wollstonecraft*, Ithaca, N.Y.: Cornell University Press.

Webb, R. K. (1960), *Harriet Martineau: A Radical Victorian*, London: Heinemann.

Wedd, Annie (1925), *The Love Letters of Mary Hays*, London: Methuen.

Weller, E. V. (1928), *Keats and Mary Tighe*, New York: Century.

Whitbread, H. (ed.) (1992), *No Priest But Love: Excerpts from the Diaries of Anne Lister 1824–6*, Otley: Smith-Settle.

Woodward, L. D. (1930), *Une Anglaise, amie de la Revolution Française*, Paris: Bibliotheque de la Revue de Litterature Comparée.

Wu, Duncan (1994), *Romanticism: An Anthology*, Oxford: Blackwell.

Further Reading

Alston, Robin (1990), *A Checklist of Women Writers 1801–1900*, London: British Library.

Barker-Benfield, G. J. (1992), *The Culture of Sensibility*, Chicago: Chicago University Press.

Benstock, Shari (ed.) (1988), *The Private Self – Theory and Practice of Women's Auto-biographical Writings*, Chapel Hill, N.C.: University of North Carolina Press.

Butler, Marilyn (1989), 'Repossessing the Past: The Case for an Open Literary

History', in M. Levinson (ed.), *Rethinking Historicism: Critical Readings in Romantic History*, Oxford: Blackwell.

Cline, Cheryl (1989), *Women's Diaries, Journals and Letters: An Annotated Bibliography*, New York: Garland.

Conger, Sydny McMillen (1990), *Sensibility in Transformation: Creative Resistance to Sentiment from the Augustans to the Romantics*, Rutherford, N.J.: Fairleigh Dickenson.

Davis, G. and B. A. Joyce (1989), *Personal Writings by Women to 1900: A Bibliography of American and British Writers*, London: Mansell.

Fergus, Jan and Janice Farrar (1987), 'Women, Publishers and Money', in *Studies in Eighteenth-Century Culture*, vol. 17, Wisconsin: University of Wisconsin Press.

Ferguson, Moira (1992), *Subject to Others: British Women Writers and Colonial Slavery 1670–1834*, New York and London: Routledge.

Gallagher, Catherine (1994), *Vanishing Acts of Women Writers in the Market Place 1670–1820*, Oxford: Clarendon Press.

Homans, Margaret (1986), *Bearing the Word: Language and Female Experience in Nineteenth-Century Women's Writing*, Chicago: Chicago University Press.

Jackson, J. R. de J. (1993), *Romantic Poetry by Women: A Bibliography 1770–1835*, Oxford: Clarendon Press.

Landes, Joan B. (1988), *Women and the Public Sphere in the Age of the French Revolution*, Ithaca, N.Y.: Columbia University Press.

Lerenbaum, Miriam (1977), '"Mistresses of Orthodoxy": Education in the Lives and Writings of Late Eighteenth-Century Women Writers', *Proceedings of the American Philosophical Society*, 121, 4.

Mellor, Anne K. (1990), 'Why Women Didn't Like Romanticism: The Views of Jane Austen and Mary Shelley', in Gene Ruoff (ed.), *The Romantics and Us: Essays on Literature and Culture*, New Brunswick, N.J.: Rutgers University Press.

Nussbaum, Felicity (1989), *The Autobiographical Subject: Gender and Ideology in Eighteenth-Century England* , Baltimore: Johns Hopkins University Press.

Poovey, M. (1988), *Uneven Developments: The Ideological Work of Gender in Mid-Victorian England*, Chicago: University of Chicago Press.

Rendell, Jane (1985), *The Origins of Modern Feminism: Women in Britain, France and the United States, 1780–1860*, Basingstoke and London: Macmillan.

Ross, Marlon B. (1989), *The Contours of Masculine Desire: Romanticism and the Rise of Women's Poetry*, London and New York: Oxford University Press.

Shattock, Joanne (1994), *The Oxford Guide to British Women Writers*, Oxford and New York: Oxford University Press.

Shevelov, Kathryn (1989), *Women and Print Culture*, London: Routledge.

Shiner, Carol (ed.) (1994), *Revisioning Romanticism: British Women Writers 1776–1837*, Philadelphia, PA.: University of Pennsylvania Press.

Taylor, Irene, and Gina Luria (1977), 'Gender and Genre: Women in British Romantic Literature' in M. Springer (ed.), *What Manner of Woman: Essays on English and American Life and Literature*, New York: New York University Press.

Todd, Janet M. (1986), *Sensibility: An Introduction*, London and New York: Methuen.

Turner, Cheryl (1992), *Living by the Pen: Women Writers in the Eighteenth Century*, London and New York: Routledge.

Watkins, Donald P. (1993), *A Materialist Critique of English Romantic Drama*, Gainsville, Florida: University of Florida Press.

INDEX OF AUTHORS

Numbers refer to individual items, not pages.

Adams, Sarah Flower, 87
Aikin, Lucy, 48
Alcock, Mary, 34

Baillie, Joanna, 28
Barbauld, Anna, 10, 49, 52, 73
Betham, Matilda, 26
Blessington, Marguerite, Countess of, 88
Butler, Lady Eleanor, 2, 7, 63

Clairmont, Claire, 55, 75

Edgeworth, Maria, 18

Grant, Anne, 43
Grimstone, Mary Leman, 89

Hamilton, Elizabeth, 37, 50, 60
Hands, Elizabeth, 3
Hawkins, Laetitia, 15
Hays, Mary, 16, 25, 66
Hemans, Felicia, 46, 69, 76, 79

Inchbald, Elizabeth, 44

Jameson, Anna, 80
Jewsbury, Maria Jane, 72, 84, 85

Lamb, Lady Caroline, 81, 82
Lamb, Mary Ann, 56
Landon, Laetitia, 90, 91
Lickbarrow, Isabella, 54
Lister, Anne, 59, 61, 62, 64, 65

Macaulay, Catharine, 8
Martineau, Harriet, 68
More, Hannah, 13, 33

Opie, Amelia, 39
Owenson, Sydney, Lady Morgan, 47, 67, 78, 83

Piozzi, Hester Lynch, 4, 17

Radcliffe, Ann, 74
Radcliffe, Mary Ann, 31
Reeve, Clara, 12
Robinson, Mary, 22, 32, 38, 42

Seward, Anna, 5, 30
Shelley, Mary, 57, 70
Smith, Charlotte, 1, 14, 45

Taylor, Jane, 58
Tighe, Mary, 41, 51
Trollope, Frances, 86

Wakefield, Priscilla, 27
West, Jane, 36
Williams, Helen Maria, 9
Wilson, Harriette, 71
Wollstonecraft, Mary, 6, 11, 21, 23, 29
Wordsworth, Dorothy, 24, 35, 40, 53

Yearsley, Ann, 19, 20

INDEX OF THEMES

Numbers refer to individual items, not pages

condition of England, social criticism, 31, 39, 46, 52, 56, 91
diaries, journals, 2, 7, 24, 35, 55, 59, 60, 61, 62, 63, 64, 65, 75
education, female capacities, 6, 8, 11, 12, 15, 16, 18, 26, 27, 32, 33, 36, 37, 59, 60, 68, 73, 78, 89
English abroad, the, 4, 9, 21, 24, 40, 55, 57, 67, 75, 83, 86, 87
Factories Act, 91
feminisms and anti-feminisms, 8, 11, 12, 15, 16, 18, 25, 26, 27, 31, 32, 33, 36, 37, 43, 49, 56, 68, 72, 73, 76, 78, 79, 89
French Revolution, 5, 6, 9, 13, 14, 19, 20, 34
friendship, love, sexuality, marriage, 2, 7, 22, 38, 39, 41, 59, 61, 62, 63, 64, 71, 72, 75, 76, 80, 81
history, biography, memoirs, 66, 88, 90
imagination, aesthetics, literary criticism, 23, 28, 29, 44, 49, 50, 74, 79, 84, 85, 87, 90
male poets, 55, 57, 70, 75, 80, 85, 88
nature and the Sublime, 1, 7, 21, 23, 24, 29, 30, 35, 45, 51, 54, 67, 69, 92
religion, 13, 43, 50
self-portraits, autobiography, 1, 14, 20, 38, 42, 45, 54, 57, 71, 81
slavery, 6, 10, 12, 86
supernatural, ghosts, 55, 70, 74
travel writing, foreigners, 4, 21, 24, 40, 55, 57, 67, 75, 83, 86, 87
women as writers, 3, 18, 20, 22, 45, 48, 54, 79, 84, 90